SWORD AND BLOSSOM

Peter Pagnamenta is a writer and television documentary maker, with a special interest in Japan. He conceived and wrote the eight-part BBC series *Nippon*, an archival and testimonial history of Japan's recovery after 1945, as well as *Bubble Trouble*, about Japan in the 1990s. Other series for the BBC include the twentieth-century industrial history *All Our Working Lives*, for which he wrote the book with Richard Overy, and the twenty-six-part *People's Century*. He is a former editor of the weekly current-affairs television program *Panorama*.

Momoko Williams was born and brought up in Japan and went to Britain in 1966 after graduating from Meiji University, Tokyo. She has coordinated and produced programs for Japanese broadcasters in Britain and Japan. She worked on the major NHK series *The Twentieth Century* and *Pacific War*. Interested in Anglo-Japanese cultural connections, the initiated and produced the photographic exhibition *Japanese in Britain, 1863–2001*. She is married to an Englishman and lives in London.

SWORD AND BLOSSOM

A BRITISH OFFICER'S ENDURING
LOVE FOR A JAPANESE WOMAN

PETER PAGNAMENTA
AND MOMOKO WILLIAMS

PENGUIN BOOKS

PENGUIN BOOKS

Published by the Penguin Group

Penguin Group (USA) Inc., 375 Hudson Street, New York, New York 10014, U.S.A.
Penguin Group (Canada), 90 Eglinton Avenue East, Suite 700, Toronto,
Ontario, Canada M4P 2Y3 (a division of Pearson Penguin Canada Inc.)
Penguin Books Ltd, 80 Strand, London WC2R 0RL, England
Penguin Ireland, 25 St Stephen's Green, Dublin 2, Ireland (a division of Penguin Books Ltd)
Penguin Group (Australia), 250 Camberwell Road, Camberwell,
Victoria 3124, Australia (a division of Pearson Australia Group Pty Ltd)
Penguin Books India Pvt Ltd, 11 Community Centre,
Panchsheel Park, New Delhi–110 017, India
Penguin Group (NZ), 67 Apollo Drive, Rosedale, North Shore 0745, Auckland,
New Zealand (a division of Pearson New Zealand Ltd)
Penguin Books (South Africa) (Pty) Ltd, 24 Sturdee Avenue,
Rosebank, Johannesburg 2196, South Africa

Penguin Books Ltd, Registered Offices: 80 Strand, London WC2R 0RL, England

First published in the United States of America by The Penguin Press,
a member of Penguin Group (USA) Inc. 2006
Published in Penguin Books 2007

1 3 5 7 9 10 8 6 4 2

Published in Great Britain as *Falling Blossom* by Century, an imprint of Random House (UK).

Acknowledgments for permission to use letters and diaries appear on pages xi and 325–28.

Photograph credits appear on page 329.

Kanji characters on page 35 by Momoko Williams
Line drawings and other calligraphic writings courtesy of Takako Inoue
Map illustrations by ML Design, London

THE LIBRARY OF CONGRESS HAS CATALOGED THE HARDCOVER EDITION AS FOLLOWS:
Pagnamenta, Peter.
Sword and blossom : a British officer's enduring love for
a Japanese woman / Peter Pagnamenta and Momoko Williams.
p. cm.
Includes bibliographical references and index.
ISBN 1-59420-089-0 (hc.)
ISBN 978-0-14-311214-3 (pbk.)
1. Hart-Synnot, Arthur Henry Seton, 1870–1942. 2. Suzuki, Masako, 1878–1965.
3. Armed Forces—Officers—Biography. 4. Love. 5. Interracial dating.
6. Great Britain—Biography. 7. Japan—Biography. I. Williams, Momoko. II. Title.
CT788.H325P37 2006
941.081092—dc22   2005058180

Printed in the United States of America
Designed by Stephanie Huntwork

CONTENTS

PREFACE

L ong before the advent of the tin trunk or the fiber suitcase, the most useful storage container in traditional Japanese houses was the *nagamochi*—a long wooden box, made from thin planks of paulownia or cedar wood. An older generation of Japanese would use the chests to keep everything from kimonos to family documents. In 1982 Tetsuko Suzuki, a retired Tokyo school-teacher, was going through furniture and possessions that had belonged to her mother-in-law and had been left undisturbed in a storeroom for twenty years after her death. When she lifted the lid of a *nagamochi* she saw bundle after bundle of old letters packed tightly together. Tied with ribbon, they were still in their original envelopes, encrusted with wax seals and carrying foreign stamps and postmarks dating back to 1904.

Tetsuko began to open a few of the letters, trying to decide whether she could throw them out, but they were hard to read. Running from right to left, the vertical columns of Japanese characters, sometimes made with ink brushstrokes and sometimes in pencil, were in the *hentai kana* style of writing, no longer used today. Many of the expressions were in a feminine and colloquial style. Small mistakes in vocabulary and syntax suggested they were the work of a foreigner, not a native Japanese, though the written characters were elegantly formed. The letters themselves were fragile and difficult to handle. When withdrawn from their narrow envelopes they were tight wads of folded paper, which had to be unrolled and flattened as they were read. The featherweight handmade paper was in continuous lengths rather than separate sheets, so a single letter could unroll to a length of several feet. Out of many of the envelopes fell pressed leaves and flowers, poppies, primroses, and forget-me-nots, so desiccated after eighty years that several crumbled immediately. Tetsuko knew who they were from, but had no idea of the full story they would reveal.

From these eight hundred letters, written by an English officer, a clear narrative gradually emerged, though the clues and pieces of the jigsaw puzzle were widely dispersed through the batches of letters and over the years. They showed how two people, first brought together by a now forgotten alliance between their two countries, tried to overcome differences in background and culture, and how their lives became entwined in the conflicts of the first half of the twentieth century. Though the letters from the *nagamochi* provide the genesis for this book, they are not the only source. Taking references in the letters as a starting point, we have consulted the papers and diaries of Westerners who were in Japan in the same era, and sought out family and land records in Tokyo, London, Belfast, and Dublin. We have correlated accounts in the letters with Russo-Japanese and Great War operations and battles, and looked at British Army documents at the National Archives in London, as well as Japanese school, university, and military records.

This book would not have been possible were it not for the work that had already been done by others in Tokyo. Tetsuko Suzuki soon saw the historic interest of the correspondence, and for several years she planned to write a book about them herself, working with Takako Inoue, a Tokyo writer who took over the project entirely when Tetsuko's health started to fail. Miss Inoue carried on, and completed her own book, *Peachblossom e* (To Peachblossom), under the nom de plume Natsu Hazuki, published by the Fujiwara Shoten company in Tokyo in 1998. Her book was written for readers in Japan, with a Japanese focus, and she was unable to discover much about Arthur Hart-Synnot's own background or his family in Britain. When we approached her, she was keen that the Anglo-Japanese encounter that had so moved her should be explored further, five years after her own book was completed. She guided us back to the original letters, and we translated them and cross-checked them with British sources and family members. She told us about her own conversations with Tetsuko Suzuki, who had lived with her mother-in-law, Masa Suzuki, for many years, and whose account helps to fill the gaps and suggests how Masa responded at pivotal moments. We did more research in Japan itself, as well as in Hong Kong, France, Britain, and Ireland, and interviewed members of the Hart, Hart-Synnot, Drower, and Suzuki families. A full list of the many people who helped us appears separately, but we want to acknowledge our particular thanks to Takako Inoue and her publisher, Yoshio Fujiwara, who have been generous with their time, patient, and collaborative.

To avoid confusion, the names of Japanese individuals are written in the Western order, with given name first and family name second. A certain bewilderment is almost unavoidable with East Asian place names during this period. Before 1914, Japanese words were still being romanized in several ways, which expatriates tended to use in a carefree manner. In 1905, "Tokio" and "Tokyo" were almost interchangeable, as were "Shinjiku" and "Shinjuku," "Yedo" and "Edo." But names are hardest to keep track of in Manchuria, which was itself briefly renamed Manchukuo, in the years when the region of North China was a Japanese puppet state. Port Arthur became Ryojun under Japanese control after 1905 and is now Lushun. The Chinese port of Ta-lien became Dalny under the Russians, then changed to Dairen under the Japanese, before it became today's Dalian. The old capital that had been Mukden is the city we now know as Shenyang. Tsingtao is now Qingdao.

Though the landscape, the place names, and even the language and writing style may have altered, the underlying themes of this story are eternal. The gulf of physical distance may have shrunk today, and barriers of social class and race take a different form, but individuals can still find themselves trapped by forces and events beyond their control, and their personal lives torn away from them and redirected in ways they never expected or wanted.

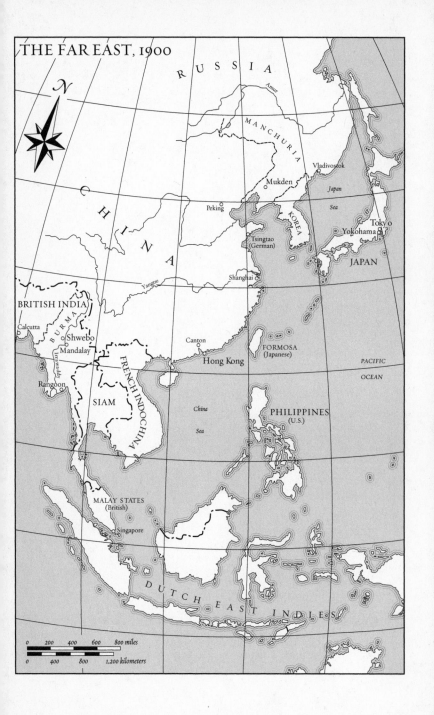

THE FAR EAST, 1900

RUSSIA

Amur

MANCHURIA

Vladivostok

Mukden

Japan
Sea

CHINA

Peking

KOREA

Tokyo
Yokohama

Tsingtao
(German)

JAPAN

Yangtse

Shanghai

BRITISH INDIA

Calcutta

BURMA

Shwebo
Mandalay

Irrawaddy

Canton

FORMOSA
(Japanese)

PACIFIC

Rangoon

Hong Kong

OCEAN

SIAM

FRENCH INDOCHINA

China

Sea

PHILIPPINES
(U.S.)

MALAY STATES
(British)

Singapore

DUTCH EAST INDIES

0   200   400   600   800 miles

0   400   800   1,200 kilometers

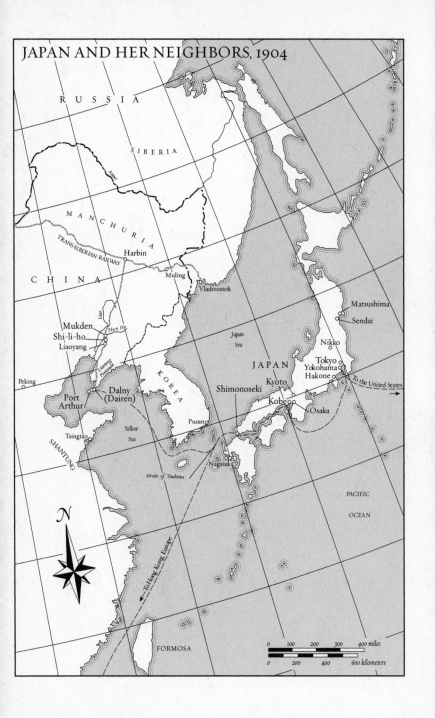

JAPAN AND HER NEIGHBORS, 1904

RUSSIA

SIBERIA

Amur

MANCHURIA

TRANS-SIBERIAN RAILWAY

Harbin

Muling

CHINA

Vladivostok

Liao

Japan
Sea

Mukden

Hun Ho

Shi-li-ho

Liaoyang

JAPAN

Matsushima

Sendai

Nikko

Tokyo

Yokohama

Peking

Liaotung Peninsula

KOREA

Kyoto

Hakone

To the United States →

Port
Arthur

Dalny
(Dairen)

Shimonoseki

Kobe

Osaka

Tsingtao

Yellow
Sea

Pusan

SHANTUNG

Straits of Tsushima

Nagasaki

PACIFIC

OCEAN

N

To Hong Kong, Europe

FORMOSA

| 0 | 100 | 200 | 300 | 400 miles |

| 0 | 200 | 400 | 600 kilometers |

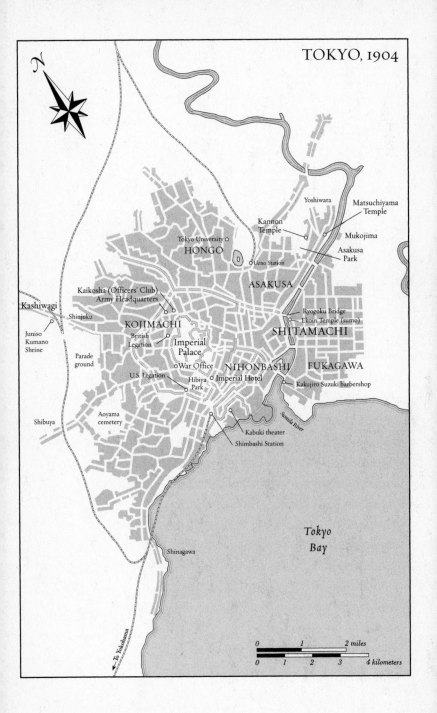

TOKYO, 1904

N

Kashiwagi

Juniso
Kumano
Shrine

Shinjuku

Parade
ground

Shibuya

Tokyo University ○
HONGO

Ueno Station ○

Kaikosha (Officers' Club) ○
Army Headquarters

KOJIMACHI

British
Legation

Imperial
Palace

U.S. Legation ○
Hibiya
Park

Aoyama
cemetery

War Office

NIHONBASHI

Imperial Hotel

Kabuki theater

Shimbashi Station

Shinagawa

Kannon
Temple ○

ASAKUSA

Yoshiwara

Matsuchiyama
Temple

Mukojima

Asakusa
Park

Ryogoku Bridge
Ekoin Temple (sumo)

SHITAMACHI

FUKAGAWA

Kakujiro Suzuki barbershop

Sumida River

Tokyo
Bay

To Yokohama

0   1   2 miles

0   1   2   3   4 kilometers

Sword and Blossom

ONE

RETURN TO BALLYMOYER

Swift and faithful.
· Hart family armorial motto,
Celer atque fidelis, granted 1883 ·

When Captain Arthur Hart-Synnot came back to Ireland on a bright summer morning in July 1906, and walked down the gangplank of the overnight boat from Holyhead, he had not seen his father for two and a half years. The major general had received his telegram and was there to meet his eldest son and accompany him on the train for the last stage of his five-thousand-mile journey back from the Far East. A family of soldiers who had spent years in India and the farthest outposts of the British Empire, the Hart-Synnots were accustomed to the long sea journeys, extended personal separations, and occasional periods of great loneliness that military service required of them. As the train steamed close to the shore, passing the oyster beds along the ten-mile fjord that cut deep into the coast and divided County Down from Louth, and the sun caught the wooded slopes of the Mourne Mountains on the other side of the water, they began to catch up on family news.

At Newry Station the coachman was waiting with the old black landau. Once the luggage was transferred, the captain and the general were driven up the narrow country road, past the low stone walls and scrubby hedges that divided the small fields of South Armagh, gradually gaining height on the two-hour journey to Ballymoyer. When they reached the lodge and turned into the gates, a crowd of estate workers and staff from the house were waiting for them, with a banner strung across the drive welcoming Captain Hart-Synnot home.

Arthur knew many of the faces from his childhood, and some had served under his father in the Irish Brigade in South Africa. They cheered and waved, grabbed the shafts beside the two horses, pushed the carriage from behind, and helped turn the wheels up the long gravel avenue that ran through the parkland towards the house. This was not a family used to displays of affection in public, but Arthur stepped down and embraced his mother and his sisters on the porch. A brass band played, and a little later the family and guests sat down to a noisy lunch with many toasts. The captain made a speech in which he said how happy he was to be back home with friends and family.

Only four years before, his father had been given a similar hero's return when he came back to Ballymoyer from the Boer War. Since then he had retired from the army and devoted his energies to the estate that his wife, Mary, had inherited, and which he had known since their marriage. With seven thousand acres of low hills, moorland, and small tenant farms, seventy miles north of Dublin, the property was one of the largest in the county of Armagh. The Synnots had made their money in the linen trade and mining and, unlike many other Irish landowners, had always been resident landlords. General Hart added his wife's surname to his own to become General Hart-Synnot, confirming his place among the Anglo-Irish gen-

try. The general was eager to show Arthur the improvements he had
begun to make on the estate demesne, the home farm that was not
rented out to tenants, knowing his son shared the same love for the
place he would one day inherit.

The original stone manor had been built in the eighteenth century in a gentle valley at a point where three brooks, after racing
down from their own glens, reached flatter land and joined together
to continue as one fast-running trout stream. In the early nineteenth
century a more imposing house in the classical style, with a stucco
façade of three stories and a colonnaded porch, had been added
onto the earlier, rougher building, and the two were linked with
creaking corridors and staircases. The library, the smaller bedrooms,
and the servants' hall were in the old section at the back, but the
principal bedrooms, drawing room, and dining room were in the
grander addition, looking across the lawns and parkland to stands
of beech on the hillside. Over the years the gardens had been landscaped and replanted, and the streams channeled and directed over
weirs, but the sound of rushing water could still be heard all round
the house, and gave a calming, almost drowsy background noise.
For Arthur's return, both parts of the house were full, with relatives
who had come to greet him and would stay until the following day.
The celebrations did not end till after dinner, when the general directed a fireworks display on the lawn. That night Arthur must have
wondered how he was going to tell his family what had happened to
his personal and emotional life on the other side of the world, and
how he wanted nothing more than to put Ireland behind him as fast
as possible and get back to Tokyo.

Two and a half years earlier, before he left for the East, Arthur
had known almost nothing about Japan, and his ambitions
were centered on the army. The military connection was hard to
ignore at Ballymoyer. Portraits of mustachioed ancestors in full

uniform were hung all over the house, along with their swords and honors. Military biographies and campaign histories filled the library shelves. Arthur's grandfather General Henry Hart had edited *Hart's Army List,*[1] the annual compendium setting out names, rankings, and organization that was indispensable to army messes and clubs around the British Empire. His father was a major general who had fought Ashanti tribesmen in West Africa, the Zulus in Natal, the Egyptians at Tel el Kebir, and a whole range of recalcitrant natives in India and Afghanistan. His father's brother Reginald was another major general, the better known because while still a young officer he had won the Victoria Cross, for crawling up a dry ravine in Afghanistan to rescue a wounded soldier, under withering fire from Afridi tribesmen shooting at him from behind rocks.[2] Uncle Reginald's book, *Reflections on the Art of War,*[3] laying out his forthright approach to "push-on" soldiering, was an inspiration to young officers. His father's other brother, Uncle Horatio, was a colonel with the Royal Engineers. In 1883, the three Hart brothers had jointly revived a coat of arms once used in the family, with a stag's head and rampant antlers over the motto *"Celer atque fidelis,"* meaning "Swift and faithful."[4]

The soldiering tradition conditioned Arthur's outlook and made him the sort of man he was. No one ever thought he would do anything else but become an officer. Family custom put him into the army, and family connections assisted his career through it. When Arthur left Sandhurst in 1890, he went out to India as a subaltern. He joined the 1st Battalion of the East Surrey Regiment at Dum-Dum, near Calcutta, where his father was the colonel, and saw his first fighting in the mountains along the India-Afghanistan border, on a march to relieve a British force besieged by Pathan tribesmen in Chitral. When his Uncle Reginald, also serving in India, was sent to quell yet another rising by the Afridis around the Khyber Pass, he asked to have his nephew attached to the expedition.

After eight years in India, Arthur returned to England to go to

Staff College, coached for the examination by his father. By this time his younger brother Ronald had, in his turn, just joined the East Surrey Regiment, and his father had come home to be a general. The British Empire was at its apogee. When Queen Victoria came to review her troops on the Aldershot parade ground in the summer of 1899, General Fitzroy Hart was able to ride past his sovereign at the head of his brigade, in plumed helmet, immaculate uniform, and highly polished boots, on a magnificent seventeen-hand Waler horse that belonged to Arthur, with his two sons jogging along beside him as members of his staff. At moments like this, when the pomp was at its most splendid and the military bands at their most stirring, it was not surprising that British rule over much of the world seemed so natural, or that families like the Harts could derive so much of their identity from it. A few months later, when that mastery came under challenge in southern Africa, and the Boer War broke out, professional soldiers like the Harts welcomed the chance for some sustained action against a more challenging enemy than the primitive tribesmen they usually found themselves up against. The war could bring honors and promotion. Arthur, his brother Ronald, his father, Fitzroy, and the seventeen-hand Waler all sailed for Cape Town in 1899 as part of the first Expeditionary Force, impatient to get there lest the fighting end too quickly. The only regret in the family was that Uncle Reginald, now in India, could not be released to come along, too.

Once they reached South Africa, Arthur's father commanded a brigade made up of Irish battalions, and insisted that standards of turnout were maintained in the field. The writer Arthur Conan Doyle described General Fitzroy Hart as a "dandy soldier," who conducted operations by the book. Troops advancing in close order, and coming under fire, had to wait for an exact signal before spreading out to extended formation. On one legendary occasion he drilled his men for half an hour before leading them into battle against an unorthodox and wily enemy who had no interest in parade-ground drill at all. Fitzroy's bravery was unquestioned. "His personal disregard for danger was notorious and reprehensible. 'Where is General Hart?' asked someone in action. 'I have not seen him, but I know where you will find him. Go ahead of the skirmish line and you will find him standing on a rock' was the answer."[5]

For Arthur and his brother Ronald, junior enough not to be tainted by the early failures of the high command, the Boer War brought the opportunities they hoped for. If the British Army was ill prepared and amateurishly organized, it was also spirited and chivalrous. This would be seen as the last "gentleman's war," fought by volunteer soldiers who knew their generals, not by vast conscript armies locked in by machinery and run by distant bureaucracies. The bugle calls in the tented camps on the veldt, the scent of dry grass, the long rides by mounted infantry over country that stretched to the horizon under the African light, brought moments of high exhilaration. The battles were mostly short and sharp. Arthur, now a captain, took part in the dash to relieve the besieged diamond town of Kimberley and was at the critical battle of Paardeberg, where the main Boer force was trapped in a dusty riverbed in the heat of summer, and attacked and pounded until they surrendered. He was wounded twice. Ronald spent most of the war acting as personal military assistant to his father, as his aide-de-camp. By the end both brothers had won the Distinguished Service Order for gallantry, and all three members of the family came through safely. The much-loved horse was the only casualty, killed by Boer rifle fire while Arthur was astride it during an action near Pretoria.

Arthur Hart-Synnot was among hundreds of other young officers who sailed back to Europe in the summer of 1902 suspecting their adventures on the high grassland marked the end of an age for the army they had known. An inquest was already beginning, asking how 60,000 scrappy farmers with bullock carts and hastily acquired weapons had been able to humiliate the British Army, so that a force of nearly 500,000 men was eventually needed to deal with them.

Great reforms in military organization and equipment were expected, and for Arthur it was a time to take stock and consider where his career might be heading. He belonged to a respectable but not fashionable county regiment. He had spent years living in dusty cantonments in India or under canvas, alongside men from backgrounds like his own. The rewards of army service came more from the comradeship and opportunities for sport than from the pay, and he needed his small private income to supplement his captain's earnings of £230 a year. He had learnt to understand hierarchy, obey orders, and conceal his private feelings and emotions behind good manners and a stiff reserve. If he let matters take their natural course he could stay on with his regiment, locked into its little firmament as it rotated periodically between India and England, and between postings at home, unless another war disrupted the pattern. Throughout this time he would have to wait patiently for his next promotion. It had taken him ten years to become a captain, and it would be another ten years before he could expect major, and few lieutenant colonels in charge of a battalion were under forty-five. The only way to break out of the strict regimental seniority system was to become part of the structure of command, rising through divisions, corps, and armies to the headquarters staff at the War Office that ran the British Army as a whole.

Arthur had already passed through Staff College, and his DSO and record in South Africa improved his chances of getting into the fast stream. He had good connections, and was already seen as a man with energy and intelligence, in an officer corps that still included a high proportion of genial and dashing dimwits. While he waited for a suitable posting, his Uncle Reginald, now the major general in charge of the Thames District, acted as his patron again, and Arthur went to be his adjutant at the barracks in Chatham. There he could impress senior officers who came to visit and keep his ear to the ground for opportunities. Meanwhile he continued to measure his military career against his father's at the same age and

to look to him for approval and advice. With General Fitzroy's return to Ballymoyer, at the end of thirty-eight years' service, his own
time in the army was over, and from now on he hoped to keep in
touch vicariously, giving what help he could to his son.

Arthur may also have compared the progress of the private and
personal side of his life with that of his father. He had reached the
age of thirty-two, and was still unmarried. He was accustomed to the
bantering, all-male atmosphere of the regiment and had met few
women, except when he was introduced to the daughters of the
Protestant ascendancy at parties in Armagh country houses during
home leaves. By contrast, his father had been married by the time he
was twenty-four to Mary Synnot, a well-born Anglo-Irish girl. With
a smart sense of military symmetry, his Uncle Reginald had also married at the age of twenty-four, also choosing a girl called Synnot, his
brother's wife's sister.

As someone who thought of himself as a plain soldier, Arthur
did not feel the need to keep abreast of every international develop-
ment or the shifting balance between the great powers. From the
nursery onwards, he and the sons of British military families like his
own were brought up on a series of simple assumptions. At school,
Sandhurst, and in the army, the onward advance of the British Empire was taken for granted. The superiority of the Anglo-Saxon way
of doing things was incontrovertible, and it seemed unlikely that the
British had much to learn from others. The recent experience of
the South African war had dented this self-belief, and just as it led
to questions about how the army was organized, it fueled wider
concerns about whether the whole British Empire was too tightly
stretched. Britain had avoided alliances or entanglements with other
countries, believing that as long as the Royal Navy controlled every
ocean no one could stand in her way. Other powers were now resent-
ing this dominance, establishing empires of their own, and building more battleships, and the United States was starting to take a
more forceful part in world affairs.

On the parade grounds of military towns like Aldershot or Chatham the outward bluster and confidence were undiminished, but at the highest levels it was already acknowledged that the nineteenth-century posture of haughty isolation could no longer be maintained. Over the past few years, through secret correspondence and discreet missions, approaches had been made to a number of European countries, in particular to Germany, exploring the possibility of a mutual defense pact that would bolster each side if attacked by a third power. In the back of the British mind all the time was the vulnerability of India, the pride of the empire, to an attack by a stronger and expanding Russia.

By the time Arthur was back from South Africa, Britain had acquired an ally. The details emerged in February 1902, and the news was the more stunning because the alliance was not with a European nation, but with a country until then hardly acknowledged as a major power at all. Britain's new partner was to be one of the "yellow" races, Japan. To those in the know, who were aware of Japan's recent rise, who had followed her defeat of China in 1895 and her military and industrial buildup, the link was understandable and perhaps masterly, but the general public were mystified. They thought of the Japanese at best as a source of fans and furniture, silk fabric and screens, and at worst as a bizarre people, whose small stature, conical hats, and risible inability to pronounce English consonants had earned them a place in light opera and music-hall songs. In the following months, as both governments tried to explain the agreement to their home populations, the British took the line that, though it had to be conceded that the Japanese were Asians, not Europeans, they deserved the status of honorary Anglo-Saxons. They were held to be hardworking, plucky, and also from an island nation. When a Japanese Navy squadron visited that summer, the *Daily Telegraph* remarked on "the close resemblance of the English Jack Tar and the sturdy Jap."[6] Count Tadasu Hayashi, the Japanese minister in London at the time of the alliance, was so absorbed in British life that he joined the Freemasons. The Japanese were told they should aim to be "the England of the East," and a Japanese artist painted the draped figure of the marine goddess Yamatohime with one arm around her opposite number, Britannia, both looking mistily into the future they were expected to share.

It was at this point, as Whitehall departments began to work out what might now be required, that the alliance had an impact on the career of one of the smaller cogs in the imperial machine, Captain Arthur Hart-Synnot, DSO, still on the lookout for his next posting at his uncle's headquarters in Chatham. The treaty said that if either Britain or Japan were to be attacked by a single country, the other ally would remain strictly neutral. If one partner was attacked by two enemies, the other would be obliged to join in on its ally's behalf, though the military or naval assistance would be rendered only in the Far East. The possibility that Britain might one day have to undertake a joint military operation with the Japanese brought an alarming realization of a very practical problem. How would they talk to each other?

The War Office put out the word and invited applications from men willing to be sent to Tokyo to learn the language and discover how the Japanese Army worked. Only a very few were wanted. The postings would not suit a married officer, or anyone for whom polo, cricket, or the social side of soldiering was the main attraction. Candidates needed intellectual capacity and sticking power. The scheme carried a career risk, of being cut off a long way away, while contemporaries advanced themselves at home, but Arthur Hart-Synnot secured the backing of his uncle and patron and applied. Arthur did not know what his chances were, but liked the idea of a challenge after twelve years in the army. He was already a good linguist, with fluent French and some German and Hindi. He was a bachelor, with no female attachment that might have detained him. In the autumn of 1903 he learnt that he had been selected.

The first four officers to be chosen were drawn from the cavalry, the infantry, the artillery, and the engineers, so that each could study the matching wings of the Japanese forces. They left for Tokyo just as Arthur, part of the second group of four, started a preliminary course under J. H. Longford, who had served as consul in Yokohama for many years before becoming the first professor in Japanese at London University. Arthur's new interest in the Far East came just at the moment when the region was attracting more attention. A smoldering quarrel between a newly confident Japan and imperial Russia over their competing interests in the territory of their weaker neighbors, China and Korea, had flared up and might soon turn into war. Both wanted the chance to develop forests and mines, both wanted to develop the fertile plains of Manchuria and the right to run railways, and both wanted ice-free harbors on the Pacific for their navies. When Russia occupied Manchuria and built a base at Port Arthur, which the Japanese had expected to have for themselves after their victory over the Chinese in 1895 but were then denied, Japan made repeated protests and called on Russia to withdraw. St. Petersburg ignored them, refusing to believe that a small, upstart nation could possibly dare to confront a European power with the largest army in the world. It was to prove a devastating misjudgment.

Meanwhile Arthur passed a preliminary language test, and booked a sea passage to Japan for January 1904, before crossing to Ireland to join his parents and sisters for Christmas. Ballymoyer was as peaceful and quiet as ever, except for volleys of gunfire from the shooting parties who went out to decimate the pheasants. On Christmas Day, the family walked to St. Luke's, the small gray stone Protestant church across from the village school, where earlier Synnots were buried, and whose stained-glass windows had been given by his grandfather. In the elegant Ballymoyer drawing room, still lit by lamps and candles because the old house had no electricity, with logs burning in the marble fireplace, he and his father talked about the possibility of war in the East and Japan's chances against Russia. It would be a David-and-Goliath struggle, but senior British officers like General Hart-Synnot had heard nothing but good reports of the Japanese Army.

Every day there was more news of the crisis. In Tokyo a War Council had been formed. Because of strict censorship there were no details of military mobilization, but forty troop transports were rumored to be ready to sail. Reports from around the world suggested the systematic thoroughness with which the Japanese were preparing. In South Wales orders had been placed for tens of thousands of tons of the best steam coal, to be shipped immediately to Japanese Navy coaling stations. Marine engineers from Scotland were traveling out under contract to work in the repair yards if warships were damaged in action. In Burma the Japanese were buying stockpiles of rice. In the United States they placed an order for thousands of bicycles from a company in Connecticut, and agents were seen buying wagonloads of cavalry horses in the West. When the British foreign secretary, Lord Lansdowne, said war now seemed inevitable, many were enthusiastic at the prospect that their traditional enemy from the days of the Crimea would be attacked, and the Russian bear biffed, always provided they were not drawn in themselves by the terms of the alliance.

After saying goodbye to his parents and unmarried sisters, Arthur came back from the isolation of rural Armagh, and the smell of peat fires and wet leaves, to the hustle and lights of wintertime London, where the chill air was acrid with coal smoke. He had two weeks to make his final preparations for the journey. London was still the largest city in the world, with a population three times the size of Tokyo. In the financial district of the city, where early intelligence might make the difference between huge profits and sudden losses, banks and insurance companies were following the war news closely. In the West End, crowds who would find it hard to locate the Yellow Sea were flocking to the capital's exuberant range of theaters and entertainments for New Year escapism. Alongside the pantomimes, and a jungle spectacular in which Indian elephants hurtled down a water-slide into a vast tank, the newest sensation was a lavish Japanese play, portraying the fantastical country that audiences had come to expect.

Darling of the Gods, written by David Belasco and John Luther Long and first produced in New York, was a tragic love story, replete with ferocious samurai, tittering geisha girls, temple dances, sword fights, and ritual suicides. The play, wrote one reviewer, "brings the life of Japan, with its odd manners and customs, its tobacco smoking and sake sipping habits, its salaams and quaint forms of politeness, into the heart of the metropolis. It is a play to see again and again."[7] Though troupes of Japanese actors had already come to London and shown audiences the genuine article, the five-act drama on Drury Lane was performed by an English cast. London actresses with white makeup and rosebud mouths played Japanese girls and geishas, furling and closing their fans and speaking their lines in birdlike fashion. The actor-manager Beerbohm Tree took the part of Zakkuri, the Emperor's cruel and scheming minister. A senior Japanese diplomat in London was invited to the first night and tactfully declared the production charming, but allowed himself a few caviling criticisms. Japan's two religions, Shintoism and Buddhism, had been rolled into one. The sets and pagodas looked Chinese rather than Japanese. The clothes were the wrong color, and the mannerisms exaggerated, with too much bowing and scraping. "In Japan a person bows to another at meeting and parting, but in the play they may be seen performing genuflections at every moment, almost after every word."[8] The plot involved a samurai's obsessive love for a girl he could not marry, though in a lyrical and much-admired last act their souls met in paradise.

A more sober view was promoted by the Japan Society in London, whose members included those with Japanese connections as well as earnest enthusiasts who wanted to learn more about Britain's new ally. Three days before Arthur left London, a Mr. Kadono gave a lecture about women and female education in Nippon. He described a nation where women practiced self-restraint, self-control, and self-effacement in their daily lives. "They are taught to be loyal to those they hold dear and superior to them. Thus taught, the Japanese girls and women have developed that resignation and disinterestedness which sometimes takes the form of serenity and dignity."[9]

Arthur was eager to see this country for himself. He visited his bank and his military tailor, left instructions for his mail, packed his luggage, and made final calls at the War Office. On 19 January 1904, he took a cab to the East India docks, and went on board the 5,500-ton *Wakasa Maru,* owned by the Japan Steamship Company, the Nippon Yusen Kaisha, which ran a fortnightly passenger-and-cargo service between Europe and the Far East. That afternoon the ship sailed down the Thames and out into the Channel on a voyage scheduled to take forty-seven days, calling at Suez, Colombo, Singapore, and Hong Kong before reaching Japan.

Because of alarm about the war, the number of passengers was reduced, with only twenty in first class. They included planters returning to Malaya, a schoolmaster bound for China, and a few Japanese going all the way to Yokohama, the port for Tokyo. Another of the army language officers, Captain Everard Calthrop of the Royal Artillery, was traveling out at the same time. By now the full difficulty of learning Japanese was clear to them. The language mixed four different writing systems and required the learning of at least three thousand Chinese ideographs. In their cabins and in the small saloon they went on working at their books and practicing their characters, or *kanji.* Calthrop wrote in a letter home, "I am able to get in a good deal of time at the language, but don't make much progress as a conversationalist. I know 540 characters, but I forget the old ones almost as fast as I memorize new. It is good training for the memory."[10] Since there was no way of hearing when or if war had broken out while the *Wakasa Maru* was at sea, and fearing that unspecified enemies might attack his vessel at any moment, the captain ordered the ship's name painted out, and the shipping line's "NYK" marking on the funnel covered over, as they passed through the Mediterranean.

When the anonymous ship reached Colombo, on 10 February, they learnt that the war in the East was under way. Three days earlier, the Japanese had made a preemptive attack on the Russian Pacific fleet at Port Arthur, when torpedo boats raced through high seas to damage two battleships and a cruiser. To achieve the maximum surprise they mounted the raid without declaring war beforehand, a move *The Times* of London was to describe appreciatively as "masculine."[11]

The *Wakasa Maru* went no farther than Ceylon. With the war having started, the captain claimed he could not expose his passengers to the risk of Russian attacks, and they were put ashore. Arthur and Captain Calthrop had to find their own passages with other shipping companies for the remainder of the journey. Desperate to reach Japan as fast as they could, they split up, each believing he could make better arrangements. Both hoped they would be able to put aside the language studies they had been sent out for, and proceed to the front immediately as observers for the War Office. Calthrop boarded a French boat, of the Messageries Maritimes, going via Saigon, and wrote to his mother, "It is a race now to Japan. This boat will get there first if all goes well, but the French steamers not infrequently break down."[12] Arthur sailed on the *Java,* a larger P&O liner. He was leaving the familiar world of Britain and the raj for a society that had intrigued, infuriated, and entranced many visitors before him, and would change his life.

TWO

DAI NIPPON

*But how sweet the Japanese woman is! All the possibilities of
the race for goodness seem to be concentrated in her.*
· Lafcadio Hearn, 1891[1] ·

I n March 1904, as Arthur's ship plowed through the China Sea
on the final leg of a long journey that had taken even longer because of the war, his head was full of all he had been told about
Japan, the books he had read, and the many generalizations and
contradictions they contained. *Japonisme* was still the fashion of the
time, and Japanese design, crafts, and fabric were widely admired.
From the 1860s onwards, a succession of Western travelers had
given rapturous accounts of a land of quaint clothes, fragile houses,
wooden temples, tripping doll-like women, and a green countryside
of thatched villages. *Darling of the Gods* was only the latest in a long
line of plays and entertainments to mine this exotic seam. Gilbert
and Sullivan's *Mikado,* and a flush of popular songs and novels
about geishas, reinforced the idea of what one Victorian visitor described as "Elfland." Alongside this Arcadian fantasy was a growing
awareness of another Japan, rapidly industrializing, trying to catch
up with the West with painstaking thoroughness. However fascinated he may have been by the myths and culture of "Old Japan,"

Arthur Hart-Synnot knew the army was sending him out to engage with the new, with its British-engineered railway system, its clattering textile mills, its Prussian-trained army, its arsenals belching smoke into the sky as they turned out gun barrels, and its shipyards sending new destroyers down new slipways.

The many British and American visitors who had published accounts of Japan seldom omitted a description of their first view of Mount Fuji, which came a few hours before the ship reached Yokohama. This was almost compulsory, and done in varying degrees of purple prose. The American journalist Elizabeth Bisland excelled at the moment. "A delicate gray cloud grows up along the edge of the water, and slowly a vast cone like cumulus, a lofty rosy cloud takes shape and form, gathers clearness of outline, deepens its hue of pink and pearl, melts softly into the gray beneath, soars sharply into the blue above, and reveals Fujiyama, the divine mountain . . . and when the gray clouds about its base had resolved themselves into land we found they were the green hills of fairyland. . . . We had come to Fan Land—to the Islands of Porcelain—to Shikishima, the country of chrysanthemums."[2]

Arthur was denied this encounter, as the weather was cold and blustery, with the shoreline hidden by low clouds as the *Java* steamed slowly into Tokyo Bay, passing navy warships and small craft in the mist, and tied up at the shipping company's buoy off Yokohama. Steam launches bustled alongside to take passengers to the Customs House on the Bund, and from the train that took him the eighteen miles up to Tokyo it was possible to glimpse a tidy countryside, with vegetable plots growing onions, cabbage, and white radishes, and the brown, banked-up rectangles of stubbled rice paddies, before the train entered the suburbs, passed the fine municipal gasworks, and reached the Tokyo terminus. There he found fairyland on a war footing.

Though Japan had been at war for only six weeks, preparations had been under way for much longer. At the station, lines of flags were strung above the approaches, and every few minutes the dense crowds at the roadside broke into shouts of *"Banzai!,"* the Japanese equivalent of "Long life" or "Hurrah," as soldiers in blue uniforms arrived to board the troop trains. Military bands, complete with glockenspiels, played marches on the platform to send them off. Fourteen special trains a day were heading along the Tokaido line towards Osaka, picking up more soldiers as they went west towards the ports of embarkation for the war. Mobilization was proceeding with impeccable staffwork. Ships had been requisitioned. Crates of ammunition, lengths of railway track, and timber were piled high at the docks. A small flag flew at the door of each family whose son had been called up, with a sign saying "Gone to the war." Appeals for donations to a special fighting fund had been posted on public buildings all over the country, and citizens nailed small slips of wood to the hoardings with their names and the amounts they were pledging. In their patriotic fervor, families bought garish-colored pictures of the first naval engagements around Port Arthur, or cut photographs of soldiers from the magazines and placed them in the *tokonoma,* the small shrine alcove in every home. Shops sold children's dresses in a printed cotton design showing submarine mines exploding. Women wore pins mounted with small model battleships in their hair, and the ladies of Japan's most aristocratic families put on white nurse's caps and long aprons to roll bandages in the Red Cross Hospital in Shibuya. They were to keep this up every day until they reached the target of 180,000 bandages set for them by the army medical service. The attention to detail was almost microscopic.

Arthur went straight to the British Legation, with the simplest address in Tokyo at number 1 Number 1 Street, where he found he had lost the race. Captain Calthrop had reached Tokyo three days before him and was already investigating the possibilities of getting to the war. The hopes of both men were soon dashed by the military attaché, Colonel Hume, who affected surprise at their arrival and ruled out any chance of going to the front on the grounds that a team of more senior officers would be coming out from Britain to observe the fighting, escorted by Hume himself. Hart-Synnot and Calthrop were sent on to John Gubbins, an old Japan hand who was in charge of language teaching for young diplomats. He was more welcoming, though he said that a year was far too short a time to learn the language. He passed on the names of some teachers used by the legation, told Arthur what would be expected in the qualifying exams he would have to take before he finished, and left him to make his own arrangements.

Returning to his hotel by rickshaw, Arthur was pulled along tree-lined streets that followed the moat of the old Edo castle. Across the dark water, behind a wall of massive and tightly fitted granite boulders, lay the new palace built for the revered Emperor Mutsuhito, whose reign had been given the name "Meiji," meaning "Enlightened Rule." Mutsuhito had become emperor in 1867, and in his time Japan had made the extraordinary transformation from an isolated island nation to a modern state. He was following the war closely, and was said to be writing up to six poems a day, in the traditional tanka style, about the privations his troops were enduring:

> *The night it is far spent,*
> *The insects keep a glowing hum*
> *In what unsheltered places now*
> *My soldiers do they spend their night?*

A respectful courtier translated some of Mutsuhito's poems for a foreign readership, describing them as "imperial effusions."

> *Even while seated on my balcony,*
> *I gaze at the moon shining bright,*
> *My thoughts carry me far away*
> *To the scene where battles rage.*[3]

Arthur was on his own, in an alien and confusing city of nearly two million people. Having spent years in the organized and all-providing world of the army, with the enforced comradeship of the Officers' Mess, he now had to provide for himself and organize his own days. His appetite for a period of cerebral study was already reduced. The greatest conflict of the new century was taking place a few hundred miles to the north, on the plains of Manchuria. As a professional soldier, he wanted to get there as soon as possible and see the action. Still hoping to reach the front later on, he engaged a teacher, and started to look for somewhere to live. Calthrop was first to set himself up with a house, and Arthur thought of sharing with him. But Calthrop feared two Englishmen together would slow each other's progress, so Arthur stayed on at the Imperial Hotel.

In his first few days, as he ventured out to make calls at the Japanese Army Headquarters, he saw the new face of Tokyo, the capital of an emerging world power, Dai Nippon, "Great Japan." The work was still in progress. All the appurtenances of a capital on European lines were being imposed on a sprawling old city whose monotonous streets of low-built unpainted wooden houses, weathered to a dull gray, had been called a "wilderness of huts"[4] by an earlier visitor. The skyline was changing as three- or four-story "foreign-style" buildings in red brick and stone were erected for ministries and government departments, many designed by the English architect Josiah Conder. Thick skeins of telephone and electricity wires sagged from utility poles. Tokyo had a new imperial university, museums, and hospitals. Men in top hats and frock coats went to work in offices and banks. Electric trams ran up and down the rebuilt European-style shopping street, the Ginza, where it was possible to buy pianos and French fashions, but Western faces were still rare, and Western women even rarer.

Most Europeans and Americans who came to do business in Japan based themselves in the old treaty ports, at Nagasaki, Kobe, or Yokohama, which had a Western population of 3,500, of which 1,600 were British. The British community in Tokyo numbered fewer than 200. Though the diplomats at the British Legation kept the language officers at a slight social distance, the officers were asked to receptions in their first few weeks, and Arthur put on his dress uniform to attend a garden party given by a prince. The Japanese Army invited them to visit the Staff College and watch exercises on the parade ground at Aoyama. The army also allowed them to use the Officers' Club, the Kaikosha, the imposing building near Army Headquarters, furnished in the heavy German style, which provided a meeting place and dining rooms for Japanese officers when in Tokyo.

As reports of Japan's first victories came through, newsboys ran down the streets, bells tinkling on their belts, with special editions of the papers. The Russians had completely underestimated an enemy they had mocked as "yellow monkeys," but the Japanese knew they were facing a far stronger enemy, with almost unlimited men and resources. The Japanese government did all it could to involve the public and encourage a spirit of self-sacrifice. On several days during Arthur's first few weeks, streets were closed off and the sound of wailing pipes and muffled drums was heard approaching, as solemn funerals were mounted for men who had died in the early stages of the fighting.

Detachments of troops escorted a gun carriage bearing what remained of Commander Takeo Hirose, a newly minted hero who had been in charge of a bold attempt to sink four old merchant ships in the narrow approaches to Port Arthur, as the navy tried to lock in the remains of the Russian Pacific fleet. Having steered his own vessel to the right position, and sunk it, the commander managed to escape by torpedo boat. He then returned three times, through stormy seas, braving Russian searchlights and gunfire, to try and rescue a junior fellow officer who had been left behind, before being killed himself by a shell.

The watching crowds were the more moved because it was known that the coffin on the gun carriage contained only a small scrap of Hirose's flesh, not much bigger than a coin, that had been retrieved and brought back from Port Arthur in a bottle. A few days later, a longer parade, of fourteen white draped caskets, enclosing almost equally small fragments of the crews of two warships blown up by Russian mines, passed the Imperial Hotel on the way to the cemetery at Aoyama. White-robed Shinto priests carrying fans and mysterious ritual articles, and a navy band playing Chopin's "Funeral March," escorted them slowly towards the Japanese Valhalla.

Arthur could by now measure his own first impressions against what he had studied in London. Like many others, he was first disoriented and then struck by the cleanliness and order, and the level of education and civility of the Japanese he encountered from day to day. This was a city where visitors were looked after with assiduous care. Railway clerks and telegraph staff were courteous. Government officials and army officers appeared modest and self-effacing. His colleague Everard Calthrop wrote home to his mother: "One important conclusion I have come to is that . . . they are more civilized than we are. I always feel a barbarian in their company, their feelings are more delicate than ours and in consequence they show more regard for other people than we do. They are cleverer in the art of pleasing."[5]

That the Japanese were more cultivated was a familiar claim for a number of British and American writers so impressed by Nippon that it had come to represent an ideal. The New York journalist and critic Henry Finck, in his book *Lotos-Time in Japan*,[6] had judged Japanese civilization superior under a whole list of headings, including the relations that existed between parents and children, politeness, contempt for display of wealth, their frugal enjoyment of life, and their patriotism. He claimed that even Japanese criminals were more cultivated than their American equivalents, having visited a prison where former thieves and burglars worked peaceably alongside each other to produce delicate cloisonné ware. The scene was unimaginable in Sing Sing.

Not all subscribed to this rose-colored view. At least one reviewer took issue with Finck, harrumphing that "civilization . . . is something else than courtesy, however sincere, the arrangement of flowers, however exquisite, or the readiness to die for one's country right or wrong."[7]

Other visitors praised Japan's capacity for thorough planning, her respect for technical education, and her grasp of steam engineering, but after all this earnestness no aspect seemed to capture the imagination of Western men so much as Japanese women. It was a time when males of a certain class could write in an unembarrassed fashion about the relative appeal of women from different backgrounds and nationalities. Finck pronounced: "Nowhere on four continents have I seen eyes, black and brown, more lovely in colour and shape than in Tokyo or Kyoto; nowhere hands and wrists more delicately moulded; nowhere arms and busts more beautifully rounded; nowhere lips more refined and inviting. . . ." Douglas Sladen, the British author of *The Japs at Home,* was impressed by the cleanliness of the women and "their delicate figures, slender necks, and thin, refined looking faces."[8] Sladen was pleasantly surprised when he found that "Even the lower classes have exquisite hands and feet." The *musmee,* or unmarried young girl, was a particular inspiration to Sir Edwin Arnold, who settled himself in Tokyo, lived and dressed in the Japanese style, and wrote vignettes of everyday life for British and American magazines. He described "the pretty, lively, laughing Japanese girl" with her "happy, winsome face." One of his poems included the verse:

The Musmee has small faultless feet,
With snow-white tabi trimly decked,

Which patter down the city street
In short steps slow and circumspect. . . .[9]

Whereas Sir Edwin was attracted by the way Japanese women pattered, with a little shuffle so the wooden *geta* clogs did not fall off their
feet, the refined Douglas Sladen thought this the one feature that let
them down. "These clogs, combined with the petticoat that pinions
their knees together, give women a most ridiculous gait, something
like a weak-minded girl's on roller skates for the first time."[10]

Just a few visitors felt that women suffered by comparison with
their equivalents in the United States or Britain—in the suppression
and oppression of wives by their husbands, and in their lack of individual rights—and concluded that the way the Japanese treated
their females was one of the great blots on their civilization. Such
judgments tended to be made by Western missionaries and visiting
American women, but to many conservatives it was American women
that were the problem. Sir Ian Hamilton, a suave British general
who arrived in Tokyo just after Arthur on his way to Manchuria,
kept a diary he was to publish the following year. "Asiatic women still
guard the secret of what Western women show signs of losing. Men
have always been selfish, but now an appalling danger confronts civilization in the shape of the American selfish woman and her imitators
in Europe."[11] Hamilton trilled about Japanese women, whom he had
found the most pleasing in the world. "Looks may be a matter of
taste, but charm is not. The smile of the Japanese girl is an enchant-
ment. She looks exquisitely good. . . . There is something childlike
about her, and yet she is so thoughtful, and they say, so brave. There
is something else. She is intensely, essentially, feminine."[12]

Most Western visitors spent their time in the central and western parts of Tokyo and the better-class residential districts
of the Yamanote, the high city, uptown. Streets had been widened

into boulevards to make a new axis leading to the palace, and if Arthur crossed the courtyard of his Western-style colonnaded hotel and walked out between the cast-iron railings, he could stroll in Hibiya Park, just completed on the model of parks in Berlin or Paris, with a European café, formal flower beds, gravel paths, and a cast-iron bandstand.

Life was changing far more slowly a mile or so to the east, in the Shitamachi, the "low city," the working-class area on the flat land that stretched to the Sumida River and beyond. The wards of Asakusa, Fukagawa, and Honjo were still a maze of unpaved roads, dusty in summer and so muddy during the rainy season that they were almost impassable except with high *geta* clogs, which raised the feet four or five inches off the ground. The meanly built, plain two-story houses, each with an identical-sized shop on the ground floor, opened directly onto narrow streets that had no pavements. Upright signboards or strips of flapping blue cloth displayed the owners' names, and whether they sold vegetables, tin basins, bolts of cloth, or paper and string, the prevailing smell was of dried cuttlefish and kerosene. The Shitamachi streets were livelier and noisier, retaining more of the character of Edo, the name the old city had carried before it was renamed Tokyo in 1868. Night markets stayed open till late. Vendors moved through jostling crowds hawking roasted sweet potatoes, bean curd, or fresh flowers, and the few foreigners who penetrated this far were always impressed by the itinerant blind shampooers who walked the streets offering their services with a distinctive low whistle. On holidays and summer evenings, crowds flocked to Asakusa Park, both the religious and the entertainment center of Tokyo's eastern districts. At the Buddhist temple, dedicated to Kannon, the goddess of mercy, the great hall was lined with lanterns and incense sticks placed as offerings, and it was possible to buy charms to ward off sickness or help women in childbirth. In the temple grounds, running to fifty acres, were the amusements of old Edo, a lively and raucous parade of jugglers, storytellers, puppet shows, and performing monkeys, with modern additions that included an aquarium, shooting galleries, and photographers' studios. To one side of the temple was a landmark of the Shitamachi, the twelve-story Ryounkaku, meaning "Rise Above the Clouds Tower," and by far the tallest structure in Tokyo. For a few pence it was possible to climb the wide internal stairs and look out over the city from the viewing platform at the top, across the miles of gray roofs to the mountains to the west, and south as far as the Boso Peninsula on the other side of Tokyo Bay.

Kakujiro Suzuki kept a barbershop on a long street in Fukagawa, close to the timber yards on the far side of the river, where older customers still expected to have not just the face, but nose, shoulders, neck, and any bald part of the head razored daily to produce a glossy sheen on the skin. Suzuki had raised a family of seven, with three boys and four girls, before handing on the shop to his eldest son, Seijiro. His youngest son, Haru, was in the army, and Masa Suzuki was his youngest daughter. She was numerate, shrewd, and intelligent, but her ambitions were governed by the conventions of the time. In Shitamachi, women worked hard, and helped fathers or husbands in the family shop or business, but however competent and essential they might become, they remained submissive and deferred to men. When she helped her mother serve meals as a child, Masa knelt at a distance while her father and brothers ate. Whole areas of conversation were limited to the males in the family, and women were expected to talk to other women on subjects suitable for women.

When Masa left elementary school at the age of fourteen one of the last lessons she received was on "the duties of a man and of a woman," which her teacher drew from the government textbook for moral instruction used in every school in Japan. It explained that their responsibilities were not the same, and each must not forget his or her own proper sphere. Whereas men were to be specially active, girls were to be specially gentle. Girls were taught the importance of frugality, self-sacrifice, care of extended-family members, and support for a husband. According to the Ministry of Education the object of female education was to make "good wives, and wise mothers."[13] Women had no political rights, and no vote, and to keep them from any newfangled distraction, the Police Security Regulations of 1900 specifically prevented them from joining political organizations or attending political meetings.

It was normal and expected for marriages to be arranged by parents through a go-between, and once married a woman could not buy or sell property, enter into debts, or start legal proceedings without her husband's consent. Masa was known as a local beauty, and when she was twenty Kakujiro Suzuki contracted for her to marry a paper wholesaler from the commercial district of Nihonbashi, across the iron Ryogoku Bridge. The match with an older and wealthier man was good for the Suzuki family, and Masa soon had a daughter, but within a couple of years her husband decided he wanted a divorce. Separation was easily achieved for men, who could cite grounds that included "not respecting the mother-in-law" or "talking too much." The rule was that in all settlements children were automatically allotted to the father. The paper merchant took their small daughter into his family to be looked after by his new wife. Masa was dumped and discarded. Because she now carried the stigma of divorce, and was past the usual age for marriage, the chances of her family's being able to arrange another husband for her were slim. By April 1904, she had gone to live with her second-oldest brother, Yokichi, who had opened his own barbershop in Kojimachi, the higher-class district of government offices and embassies to the west of the Imperial Palace.

In earlier years, all Masa Suzuki would now have been able to expect was a life of domestic drudgery, more dependent on her family than ever, but the prospects for young women in the city were changing in one respect at least. Many more were going out to work for wages, in jobs that had not existed twenty years before, and not just into the textile mills and factories where so many girls from the country were now laboring. The war with Russia, and the call-up of hundreds of thousands of men, increased the need for women workers. Masa applied for a job as a clerk at the Kaikosha, the Army Officers' Club, which faced the long cherry-tree-lined slope that ran up to the Yasukuni Shrine, where Shinto priests watched over the spirits of Japan's fallen soldiers from wars past, and expected a great inrush of souls from the present one.

For Arthur, an amateur botanist who had studied the plants in India and took much pleasure in his parents' garden at Bally-moyer, the heightened Japanese awareness of nature was something else to be admired. This was a people who followed the passage of the seasons closely, not just in the countryside but in the city, and seemed more aware of the natural world around them than any Londoner. The sight of a particular flower or leaf, or the lines of a tree branch, or a limpid moon on a summer night, generated real enthusiasm and could prompt viewing parties and outbursts of po-etry. The whole city waited for the days in the middle of April when the cherry trees burst into their great blaze of color. In May, crowds admired the banks of azaleas and the long drooping clusters of pur-ple and white wisteria flowers trailing over garden trellises and around teahouses. In June they paid homage to the irises, and in November the chrysanthemums. The most sublime experience of the year was reckoned to be found in July, when thousands made their way through the darkened streets in the early hours of the morning and waited quietly by the lily ponds in temples and parks. At around three a.m., if they were lucky, they might catch the sound of the white lotus flowers opening for the first time, with a very slight popping noise, an exquisitely gentle report to be discussed and compared with other years.

Arthur Hart-Synnot joined this cycle of the seasons in March, when the white plum blossom was out. On a fine day in early April, he was with other officers admiring the peach blossom at the Officers' Club when he saw a girl with a group of others in the garden, also looking at the trees. Wearing a kimono, Masa Suzuki had the features that attracted so many Western men to Japanese women, an open smile, a rather modest downcast look, and a delicate, almost childlike complexion. She was twenty-six. Arthur thought she was beautiful and told his family later that he was smitten immediately. Masa must have been pleased by his attention, as he tried out his very basic early Japanese. The mustached captain, whose height of over six feet was unusual in Japan, was the first foreigner she had ever spoken to.

That April, Japanese staff officers, who continued to walk across from Imperial Headquarters to eat at the Officers' Club and admire the peach and then the cherry blossom, were planning more death and destruction for the Russians. After the first few weeks of the war, in which the navy had finally managed to lock the Russian fleet inside Port Arthur, the First Army landed in Korea and moved north to engage the main Russian force. Final details were put in place for another army to land on the Manchurian coast, with the aim of seizing the neck of the peninsula on which Port Arthur stood. Strict censorship was in force, but the Kaikosha was the easiest place to see the official bulletins, pick up the limited gossip that was on offer, or get an economical meal, and Captain Hart-Synnot called in regularly. Masa Suzuki gave him a new reason for going. Though not as gregarious as his fellow officers, he liked female company. He continued to seek her out, they made light conversation, and she answered his questions about Tokyo and helped with arrangements he was having to make.

At the end of April, the war moved into a new phase when the First Army crossed the shoals and small islands of the Yalu River to attack the Russians. The victory, the first time an Asian country had defeated a European army using modern weapons and tactics, was reported round the world and gave a boost to Japanese confidence. As their strategy became clearer, the authorities finally agreed to take the first group of foreign observers, who had been languishing in Tokyo hotels with their kit packed, across to the war. The party included Italian, German, French, and American officers, but the British, as the allies, sent the largest number, including General Sir Ian Hamilton; Colonel Hume, the military attaché; and two of the first four language officers who had arrived in 1903. The new intake of students—Captain Calthrop, Captain Yate, Captain Piggott, and Captain Hart-Synnot—were left behind to their own devices, each still hoping he could get to Manchuria eventually.

Arthur had by now begun to see Masa Suzuki outside the Kaikosha. Some of the other language officers also met Japanese girls. It was easier to meet young women of Masa's type, who had slightly more independence because they went out to work and earned a small wage, than girls who, in terms of the almost equally stratified British and Japanese class systems, might have been reckoned their social equals. The better-educated daughters of Nippon were more constrained by the etiquette that governed relations between the sexes, tied more closely to the home and the acquisition of ladylike skills, and more closely watched. For the Shitamachi girls, the foreigners were interesting and daring. For the British captains, the Japanese were so different from anyone they had encountered before, and so exotic, that any contrasts in background were unimportant. For the moment, the language gap made these friendships even more tentative and unreal. The only questions that could be asked and answered were on the simplest level. None of the officers had yet reached the point where he could have anything resembling a normal conversation, so the spring began with picnics and outings.

With the distraction of the opening stages of the war, and the possibility of getting to Manchuria himself, Arthur was slower than some of the others in setting himself up and starting to study seriously. In other countries where the British Army sent bright young officers to learn a language, including Russia and Germany, the custom was for them to board with a well-chosen family, go out to lessons, and get speaking practice by taking part in the daily comings and goings of a household. In Japan this was thought impractical. Even if any Japanese could be found who was willing to have an unmarried foreigner living at close quarters in the flimsy environment of a Japanese house, it was presumed the officer would be unable to survive a life spent almost exclusively on the tatami matting without benefit of chairs or tables, and the dynamics of family life were quite different. Instead, the second batch of arriving Tokyo language students were advised to rent houses of their own, add some European furniture so they could be comfortable, and get an experienced teacher to come in for a couple of hours a day of formal lessons. They were also recommended to find a young male university student to live in, help run the house, engage a servant, and be available for constant language practice in return for his board. Another British officer explained this role with a reference to Kipling. "This 'student' is, in fact, a private secretary and confidential adviser as regards things Japanese, and a most faithful companion. The relationship is similar to that of the 'guru' and 'chelah' in 'Kim.'"[14] By May, Everard Calthrop had found an eager young man, and Captain Piggott, who seemed to exist on a different level because he was so well connected, had employed the impecunious son of an aristocratic family.

A part from the paper wholesaler, the men Masa had encountered up to then had been limited to her family, the well-shaved shopkeepers and traders who were their neighbors, and, more recently, the Imperial Army officers at the Kaikosha, mostly drawn from old samurai families. To almost all of these she was a lowly presence, expected to hover in the background or take orders with a display of willing obedience and humility. Arthur Hart-Synnot listened to what she had to say, was serious-minded, and seemed more

interested in gardens and botany than in drinking and entertainment. In her limited time off from the Kaikosha, she began to show
him parts of Tokyo he might find it difficult to get to, not just the
temples and parks on every visitor's list, but the "low city" she had
grown up in. She took him to Asakusa Park and the working-class areas on either side of the Sumida, where country boats still unloaded
straw-wrapped bales of rice brought round from the other side of
Japan to the row of rice stores along the bank. Despite the coming
of the railways, the Sumida was still busy, with fishing boats returning from Tokyo Bay, lighters delivering charcoal and vegetables, and
long rafts of lumber from the inland prefectures floating down to
the timber yards. Masa saw how Arthur appreciated all this and
seemed interested in the smallest details of daily life, and at an early
stage she took the well-tailored officer back to see her brothers and
her mother, with whom he sat on the floor and drank green tea. She
also helped him explore the different areas in which foreigners
would usually look for somewhere to live, in Ushigome and Kojimachi, to the north and west of the palace. With so many Japanese
officers away on active service in China, many houses were available.

At twenty-six, Masa was competent and more worldly-wise after
her experience with the paper wholesaler, and she liked Arthur. So
when the Englishman she had known for only a few weeks suggested she should leave her job and keep house for him, and offered
to pay her a better wage than she could ever earn at the Kaikosha,
she was shocked and flattered. She also knew that one thing could
be expected to lead to another, and there would be more to this role
than housekeeping and language practice. Even if they had not slept
together by this stage, proximity under the same roof would make
such a step easy and inevitable. The relationship was moving into
waters that were deeper, though already well charted. Unmarried
foreigners had been posted to work in Japan for nearly forty years,
and in the foreign settlements at Yokohama and Kobe there was
nothing unusual about girls of a certain sort living with Western

men. For the men the liaisons brought companionship, an antidote to loneliness when they were so far from home, and a sexual partner. The more conscientious, who were trying to learn the language, would count the additional benefit of having what was known as "a sleeping dictionary." For their part, the women had a chance to share the comforts and privileges of expatriate life, and put aside money for the future, even if they were scorned by their Japanese neighbors. Both parties accepted the reality that they would be together only for the duration of a posting. The girls tended to come from families on the fringes of the community, with connections to restaurants, the geisha quarter, or the licensed brothels that served the foreign settlement. These were not the sort of people that Masa's family would approve of, and becoming an Englishman's mistress was not what Masa had contemplated when she went to work at the Kaikosha. She may have been intrigued and tempted by Arthur's proposition, but needed to get her family's agreement.

Though they were against the idea of her going to live with a foreigner, Masa finally persuaded her brothers to give their consent. They were impressed by Arthur, and were flexible enough to see advantages in the short term for both Masa and themselves. She would be off their hands, away from home, and financially supported. She might pick up knowledge and connections that would help them in the future. She could influence where he took a house, and this would be a temporary arrangement, since the Englishman was only going to be in Japan for another eleven months.

Masa took Arthur to Mukojima, on the far side of the Sumida, in Honjo, where an avenue of cherry trees ran along the embankment beside the river for nearly a mile, attracting cheerful crowds to its rows of teahouses and refreshment booths in the weeks of the best blossom. To Arthur's eyes it seemed an exotic corner of old Japan, and it was also discreet, a place where they would attract little attention. They rented a house, and the heir to Ballymoyer brought his clothes and possessions across from the Imperial Hotel. It was a cold April, and on one day flurries of snow fell just as the blossom was falling from the trees. However picturesque, Mukojima was also a long way from the center of Tokyo, on the wrong side of the river.

Within a few weeks, they moved again, finding an old house that was more convenient, looking across to Mukojima from the Asakusa bank, on a bluff of high ground above one of the ferry crossings. The house was next to the Matsuchiyama Temple, and in the nineteenth century the woodcut artist Hiroshige had depicted it at night, under a full moon, with boats arriving by lantern to go up to the Yoshiwara, the pleasure quarter of Edo. From the screened veranda Arthur and Masa looked out on the river traffic, and on the boathouses of the Imperial University, whose rowing club came to practice for regattas on this section of the Sumida. The rent was around thirty yen, or fifteen dollars, a month.

The other language officers were living in a more English style in more salubrious areas of the Yamanote. Down in Asakusa, Arthur experienced Japanese life to the full, with its pleasures and its drawbacks. His privacy was limited. The neighbors took a close interest in the unusual household, and Masa's brothers visited frequently. The public baths were a minute away, across a small children's playground at the rear. Masa employed a maid and took control of the cooking, fanning the charcoal in the brazier in the small kitchen when she wanted to heat a pan. Arthur adapted to the everyday Japanese diet, in which rice and pickled vegetables took the major role, bread, milk, and red meat had no place as yet, and grilled eel was a luxury. By cutting himself off from his own countrymen as much as possible, he hoped to make faster progress with his Japanese. He continued to wrestle with the awesome complexities of a language in which the end of a clause was where verbs were placed, and in which sentences could be so long and involved that the introductory details could be forgotten by the time the final verb was reached. The system of honorifics, by which the status of the person to whom you were speaking governed the form of words used, added pitfalls to almost any communication. Many teachers believed that, once past the mid-twenties, the Western brain could never grasp all this, and store the thousands of ideographs that had to be recognized and written. Arthur had a good memory and was careful in his attention to detail. He was a natural linguist, already fluent in French and with some German and Hindi. He studied for hours each day with the teacher who came to the house, worked with cards for each *kanji* character, and tried to memorize the correct order of pen or brush movements which made each one. Some characters—such as *tama,* meaning a bullet—required just five strokes:

玉

Other words needed over twenty upright or angled strokes. The word for "battleship," *gunkan,* had to be built up painstakingly with two characters and a total of thirty strokes:

Arthur called Masa "Dolly," and the daily chatter with her meant his speaking Japanese advanced more quickly than his written.

Arthur and the other language officers were asked to come to the legation to help type up the reports now arriving from the British officers in Manchuria before they were forwarded to London. At the end of August, the Japanese inflicted a further defeat on the Russians at Liaoyang, on the railway line between Port Arthur and Mukden. The significance of what was happening did not escape the observers. After a day in which he had watched the Russians fleeing north, Sir Ian Hamilton wrote in his diary, "I have today seen the most stupendous spectacle it is possible for the mortal brain to conceive. Asia advancing, Europe falling back, the wall of mist and the writing thereon."[15] Hamilton put the victory down not to strategy or tactics, but, rather, "the souls of the Japanese troops which triumphed over the less developed, less awakened, less stimulated, spiritual qualities of the Russians."[16] The Japanese faith in their own fighting spirit, or *Yamato-damashii,* was greater than ever.

Arthur could not cut himself off from the expatriate community altogether. He was invited to tea parties given by the wives of diplomats, and his stock rose when it was discovered he played cricket. He scored eight runs for a Tokyo team captained by the legation counselor, George Barclay, against the Yokohama cricket club. Off the cricket pitch, Arthur Hart-Synnot was already seen by his fellow officers as something of a lone player. He was thirty-four, and his private life was his own business as long as it did not cause any scandal or embarrassment. Whereas the virtuous Captain Calthrop could give return tea parties to the diplomatic wives at his house in Ichigaya, this was not an option for Hart-Synnot, about whose domestic arrangements it seemed best not to ask.

Living with a local woman was common among those in trade or business, but it was not what was expected in the diplomatic service or the military, where attitudes were less tolerant and different rules applied. In the British Army, affairs between officers and Asian women were condemned in India, Malaya, and Hong Kong, lest they subvert the imperial authority. Though Japan was certainly not part of the British Empire, officers were not expected to cross the boundaries of race regardless of where they were serving. Though some at the legation, including Gubbins, knew what was going on, the degree of disapproval of his fellow officers probably reflected their own place in the subtle social hierarchy that existed among them. Jardine and Adams (in the cavalry) felt a cut above Vincent and Calthrop (Royal Artillery), who would think themselves superior to Hart-Synnot, who, as an infantryman from a county regiment, was the sort of person who might be expected to move in with a Japanese barber's daughter. Questions of propriety apart, the differences in class had as much to do with this disapproval as the issue of race.

Masa and Arthur were getting to know each other better all the time, and they could start to say more to each other as Arthur's language improved. Though the war news was followed closely, and thousands of wounded soldiers were being cared for in temporary hospitals at Shibuya, on the western outskirts of Tokyo, this did not interrupt the calendar of the Tokyo year. In early May, the spring wrestling tournament was held as usual at the Ekoin Temple, just across the Ryogoku Bridge. Over the summer, there were festivals and fireworks, when the Mukojima teahouses were lit with red and white lanterns, and strains of music came across the water from the pleasure boats. At the end of July, when Arthur Hart-Synnot was exposed to the enervating humidity and heat for the first time, they left the city on a rail journey to Hakone and the mountains and lakes around Mount Fuji, though it was impossible to avoid the war even here. The Japanese Red Cross had taken over whole villages as convalescent centers. Invalid peasant soldiers sat about quietly, wearing heavy white kimonos with red crosses on the sleeves and tall white caps like chef's hats over their shaved heads, and the hot-spring pools were filled with men who had lost arms or legs.[17]

Arthur and Masa took walks and saw gardens and waterfalls together. A shy man, who admitted he found many Englishwomen of his class to be brash and forward, he liked Masa's quiet style and modest manner. After years of loneliness in India and South Africa, Arthur had found someone he wanted to spend all his time with. For her part, Masa Suzuki had now met someone who treated her differently from any man she had ever come across. Each found the other physically attractive. He admired her unlined and serene face, and her trim figure wrapped in the kimono she always wore. She saw the Englishman as handsome, strong, and urbane, and was awed by his knowledge of a world beyond Japan.

Then, just as the alliance was strengthening, new orders came from London. In early December 1904, Arthur was instructed to stop his language studies and leave Tokyo to join the military observers in Manchuria, where one of the British team had been taken

sick. The decision to send Hart-Synnot, as against Calthrop or Piggott, was probably due to his service and greater experience in South
Africa, and the others were envious. This was what Arthur had
wanted nine months earlier, but now his feelings were mixed.

With Arthur due to leave in a few days' time, their relationship reached another stage in a trajectory that others had
passed along. Just as the attractions of Japanese women had caught
the Western imagination and been written about, so the affairs between Western men and Japanese women had been going on for long
enough to be dealt with in books and plays. The loosely autobiographical novel *Madam Chrysanthemum,* by Pierre Loti, told the story of
a French naval officer's temporary marriage to a Japanese while stationed in Nagasaki and suggested the callous attitude that was common among Western men. When they parted, the officer gave his
girl silver dollars, and took his leave with unabashed frankness. "Let
us part good friends. Let us even embrace, if you wish. I took you
for my own amusement, and though you may not have been a total
success, you gave me what you could: your little body, your respect,
and your quaint music. All in all you have been sweet enough in
your Nipponese way. And, who knows, perhaps I shall think of you
from time to time, in a roundabout way, when I recall the glorious
summer, the pretty gardens, and the music of the cicadas."[18]

A few years later, John Luther Long wrote a story for a New
York magazine in which another naval officer, Benjamin Franklin
Pinkerton, left Japan declaiming his love for the pregnant Cho-Cho-
San, whom he had been living with, and promising to return to her,
but then betrayed her and married an American girl. His story was
adapted for the stage in the play *Madame Butterfly* in 1900, by the
same David Belasco who was later responsible for *Darling of the Gods.*
Arthur Hart-Synnot would have known of Loti's novel, and would
probably have been aware of the play, which was produced in Lon-

don in 1900. What he may not have known is that just as he was arriving in Japan, in 1904, Puccini's version of the Madame Butterfly story was being performed for the first time at La Scala in Milan, and was about to ride the wave of *japonisme* into opera houses all over Europe and North America. Its sublime and emotionally charged story would reinforce the romantic view of old Japan, and give new life to the geisha clichés of Japanese women. The real-life liaisons were more prosaic, and few Japanese women were as naïve as Cho-Cho-San.

Arthur was not callous and Masa was not a geisha, but she must have worried that with his departure for China for an indefinite period her role would be over, and she would be discarded once again. Both were aware of the precedents and the pattern of most such encounters. Though Arthur had no idea how long he would be away, he tried to convince her that she was not just another mistress, or "temporary wife." He promised to continue to send her money so she would not have to work. In a long talk before he left, he begged her to trust him and wait for him until he came back. On a cold December evening, she saw him off at the station, and he left on the twelve-hour rail journey to western Japan. When the train reached Osaka next morning, he sent his first postcard, from the hotel where he stopped to wash and breakfast. "Have arrived in Osaka. Am so sad to be apart from you. I think about you all the time."[19] A few hours later, he reached Kobe, where he was to board the ship, and sent off his second message of the day. "I am very sad after leaving you. Give my regards to your mother and all the others. Hart-Synnot."[20]

The passenger liner *Tosa Maru,* taken over by the army for the duration of the war, sailed that afternoon with nearly a thousand troops on board. By next morning, it had made its way through minefields in the channel that separated the main Japanese island from Kyushu and was crossing the Straits of Tsushima towards Manchuria in a snowstorm. On board, Arthur wrote the longest letter he had ever sent in Japanese, with some difficulty. "We arrived at Shimonoseki early this morning but did not stop. Now it is midday and the shore of Dai Nippon is gradually disappearing. I worry about you every day. Please take care of your health. Please give my regards to Mrs. Kokura. I was sorry to trouble you with moving my possessions to Davidson's house. I have felt sad since I left you. I fear my writing is very poor. You may not be able to read it. Today is the 16th and snow has started to fall. I feel sad that the distance between us is getting bigger. I shall not forget you. Goodbye from the *Tosa Maru,* Hart-Synnot."[21] They did not know when they would see each other again.

THREE

THE PROMISE

I shall not break the promise.
We will be very happy after the war is over.
· A.H.-S., December 1904[1] ·

Though Arthur had said he would pay Masa an allowance while he was away, it made no sense for her to keep up the house next to the Matsuchiyama Temple, overlooking the Sumida River. She did not want to move back in with her brother Yokichi, to be ordered about by his wife, and so she returned to the district where she had grown up and found a smaller place to rent. Since there was not enough room for Arthur's possessions, she took them across to the house of the young diplomat Colin Davidson. She may have returned to help her eldest brother, Seijiro, in the barbershop, where all the talk among the Fukagawa customers was about the bitter struggle still raging around Port Arthur.

The public had been waiting for the Russian naval base to fall since the summer. They expected it to be taken so quickly that the Tokyo city council had set up a committee to plan celebrations for the capture back in June. In reality, the siege proved costlier and bloodier than ever expected. General Nogi, the Japanese commander, ordered assault after assault against the Russian trenches and fortifications that ran across the neck of the Liaotung Peninsula and protected Port Arthur from the rear. The attacks were launched across stony hillsides crisscrossed with barbed wire, metal posts, and spiked fencing, in direct line of fire from the Russian positions. Nogi's soldiers were scythed down so quickly that survivors had to pile up the corpses of the fallen to make cover from which they could shoot. Tokyo newspapers regaled their readers with the heroism of men giving their lives for the Emperor willingly and almost nonchalantly, in wave after wave of "human bullet" attacks, but the tactics were disastrous, and Nogi was criticized by other generals for throwing away Japan's precious manpower in futile suicide attacks. The lesson was that having the moral advantage was not, after all, enough. The allegedly superior souls of the Japanese troops, and their fighting spirit, were not sufficient when they faced greater firepower from well-dug-in positions.

By November, frontal assaults having failed, the Japanese had turned to more traditional siege tactics. They dug angled trenches or "saps" that provided cover, and worked them closer and closer to the enemy positions. They chipped tunnels through the rock to place mines and waited for the arrival of larger guns that would finally be able to break up the eight-foot-thick concrete of the Russian forts. The huge new siege guns finally reached Manchuria from the Osaka arsenal and were dragged from the railhead along wooden plankways by teams of five hundred soldiers pulling on ropes. Once miniature railways had been built to move the equally massive shells, they started to pulverize the fortifications. After renewed infantry attacks and thousands more casualties, the Japanese took the crucial 203 Meter Hill at the beginning of December, and were at last on the heights above Port Arthur, with the amphitheater of the base spread out below them. By the end of the year, all Japan was waiting for news and expecting Port Arthur to be taken at any time. Masa was waiting to hear from Captain Hart-Synnot, but after the first postcards sent when he sailed from Japan, nothing arrived at the house she had taken in Fukagawa, in a backstreet close to the lumber yards.

Though other British officers were at Nogi's Third Army Headquarters, Arthur was sent two hundred miles north, to join the Second Army. When they first arrived, during the summer, the British observers had been impressed by Manchuria, with its rich dark soil, groves of trees planted for shade, and flat fields of millet and soya beans. General Sir Ian Hamilton described it as "a white man's country, worth a seven years war to possess."[2] Now, in the North China winter, with temperatures below zero Fahrenheit, the country looked less desirable. Every tree had been axed down for fuel, and the villages were scorched and battered. The fields were scarred with abandoned trenches and littered with broken wagons and horse skeletons from the fighting that had passed through a few weeks before. The ground was hard-frozen to a depth of two feet.

Arthur joined a group of a dozen officers from five countries, most of them older and senior in rank, sharing a house in a dirty and half-destroyed village. The observers had become a quarrelsome and fractious group, frustrated by the Japanese passion for secrecy and unwillingness to let them get as close to the action as they wanted. They spent much of their time reading, drinking, and playing cards, and complaining of severe headaches: the charcoal braziers the Chinese servants brought in every few hours provided the only heating, but gave off dangerous carbon monoxide fumes. On Christmas Day, 1904, after a Christmas Eve dinner including French wines and delicacies sent from Tokyo, Arthur sent Masa his first proper letter from the front: "I have been feeling lonely since I left you, and I have been thinking about you every day. I am in a place called Shi-li-ho. All the other officers are under the same roof, so it is a little crowded, but that cannot be helped. It is extremely cold and everything is frozen outside. Yesterday I received a letter from the bank. I will be sending you money every month and I had told them to send it to the house, but you will have to go and pick it up yourself. I shall write to them again, so that you get it by post next time, but it may be delayed this month, so I will put some money in with this." Having dealt with practical arrangements, he grew more soulful. "I have not received a letter from you but I am sure you have not forgotten me, and I remember you very well. Give my regards to your mother and Miss Owaka. I will always remember you. I shall not break the promise. We will be very happy after the war is over. Please take care of yourself. Sayonara. Hart-Synnot."[3] Outgoing mail was censored, so he had to be discreet, and even when he had written he had no idea how long letters would take to get to Tokyo, or whether she would be able to read them when they arrived.

The end of the war looked a little closer one week later, when Port Arthur was finally taken. News of the Russian surrender, on 2 January 1905, was greeted as a New Year present for the Emperor, and the long-planned parades and celebrations were held all over Japan. On the Ginza, the trams were festooned with flags and lit up with thousands of small electric bulbs, and Masa and the Suzuki family saw the torchlight processions pass through the streets of Fukagawa and Asakusa and the fireworks soaring over the river. The Japanese achievement was hailed abroad, nowhere more than in Britain, where the papers paid tributes to a brave ally. For the British this was a proxy war, and the humiliation of John Bull's old foe was something to celebrate. British schoolchildren were awarded a special holiday.

The foreign military observers made a slow train journey, along a track just converted from the five-foot-wide Russian gauge to the narrower Japanese gauge, down to Port Arthur to visit the recent battlefield. They were photographed with General Nogi at his headquarters in their winter furs and then taken up to the remains of the forts and to 203 Meter Hill, eerily quiet after the months of shattering bombardment, where the Japanese were still collecting the dead. With new snow on the ground, Arthur rode past the charred

warehouses and splintered railway wagons to the harbor, where all
that remained of the Russian Pacific squadron was a line of masts
and tangled superstructures, the waves lapping over the rusting
decks. With these ships now sunk, the question was when a reliev-
ing Russian force of forty-five vessels, including seven battleships,
which was making the long journey down from St. Petersburg, round
the Cape of Good Hope, and across the Indian Ocean, would finally reach the Japan Sea to try and avenge them. Meanwhile, the
Japanese Navy lay in wait and practiced its gunnery, and General
Nogi's army was free to move north to join the attack on Mukden,
the largest city in Manchuria, where the Russians were strengthening their defenses.

When Arthur had no time to write at length, he sent brief postcards. One showed Russian prisoners of war being well treated by
Japanese nurses. Another was of a cat, on the back of which he just
wrote, "Greetings from Manchuria, Hart-Synnot,"[4] but nothing
was reaching him in the other direction, and he began to sound anxious. "I left Tokyo a month ago today, but I have not received any
letter from you, so it is worrying for me."[5] He referred to the presents they had given each other before his departure and the lock of
Masa's hair he was keeping. "The thing you gave me is my most precious possession and I will keep it forever. Darling, Hart-Synnot."[6]
Arthur wrote his endearments, incongruously, on an official letter
form showing the bombardment of some railway yards, part of a set
specially produced to commemorate the victories. He asked her to
send him some traditional *makigami* paper and envelopes of the
sort they had bought together at a stall near the Yasukuni Shrine,
close to the Officers' Club.

In Tokyo, reminders of the war were everywhere. Outside the Imperial Palace, a collection of captured Russian guns, wagons,
swords, and rifles was on display. In the amusement park around

the Kannon Temple in Asakusa, the war could be seen in waxwork models of the generals, and battle scenes constructed of chrysanthemums. An entirely new attraction drew the biggest crowds, as small theaters showed the first jerky moving pictures from Manchuria, and then the first films of wrecked Port Arthur. After the run of victories, and the realization that Japan was winning, morale rose at home, and the government worried that overconfidence was setting in. To keep up the martial spirit, officers at the front wrote letters to their old schools, and schoolchildren followed the campaign on classroom maps. The Women's Patriotic Association asked mothers to make savings at home and economize for the war effort. Newspapers published patriotic poems provided by their readers. The ability to write classical Chinese poems, or the thirty-one-syllable Japanese tanka, was seen as a desirable accomplishment among serving army officers themselves. One officer imagined he saw a fallen samurai on the snow:

As the silk brocade
Turns crimson red
White snow falls
On the sleeve of his armor[7]

General Nogi wrote his own poem about 203 Meter Hill:

The 203 Meter Hill, steep though it may be
Is surely not unclimbable
Young men know perils need to be overcome
If glory is to be won
Bullets fall and blood pours
And the hill changes shape
Look up and pray to the mountain
Where your spirits rest[8]

. . .

In mid-February, Masa finally learnt that Arthur had received her first letter, sent just after his departure from Tokyo. They had started to reach him at the end of January, and then a backlog arrived quickly. With military attention to record-keeping, he counted them in. "I have received three letters from you in two days so now I am very happy. The following letters have arrived so far: 13 December, 17 December, 7 January, 13, 16, 21, 25, 27 January, and 1 February. I can understand all the letters you have sent, but perhaps you don't understand mine because of my poor Japanese. It is very cold here, with a little snow, though Port Arthur had even more snow than here. I have had a letter from Mr. Davidson, who says you went to see him in Kojimachi and that you were not well, so I am worried about you. Please look after yourself. As soon as the war is over I shall return to you. I don't know when that will be, but I have been thinking about you every day. Give my regards to your mother. I send you my best wishes, Hart-Synnot, to Dolly."[9]

If Arthur's letters from Manchuria seemed rather formal and bald, this was in part due to his inborn reticence but also to the limitations in his vocabulary and inability to express more complicated ideas in Japanese. His writing of the *kanji* characters was still uncertain, and he did not always choose the right word.

Masa was writing more often than he was. Before he wrote to her again, nine days later, he had received three more messages from her. "On the 15th I received the letter dated 20 January, and yesterday I received your letter dated 4 February, and today the 6 February. Thank you so much, I am very happy when the letters arrive. There is no news to give you. It has been very cold. The north wind in Manchuria cuts into you like a sword, but I can protect myself with a fur coat. In the morning there is always a mist but by noon it has gone and it is usually sunny. Today it snowed heavily. Please take care of yourself. The precious thing you gave me is kept in a safe place and nobody in the world knows where it is except you and me. Thank you for the *makigami* paper and envelopes."[10]

Arthur and the observers were waiting for what was expected to be the conclusive land battle of the war, south of Mukden. The Japanese needed a quick victory before they ran out of men and money, and knew that warmer weather would soon set in, leaving the rivers uncrossable and the roads impassable quagmires. The Russian forces were building up fast, with the Trans-Siberian Railway operating more smoothly. The Russian commander, Kuropatkin, already had more than 300,000 men in and around Mukden, and his forces would soon far outnumber those of the Japanese. Throughout February, the Japanese moved in their own troops and supplies, until they had five armies to the south and east of Mukden, and thousands of guns in position, including the eighteen great siege howitzers laboriously shifted from Port Arthur. As the two sides watched each other along a front of trenches that now extended more than 150 miles, this was acknowledged to be a new type of warfare, in which the strongly dug-in defense had the advantage over the attackers. It was the method needed to get round the apparent stalemate that the foreign observers wanted to see.

For six weeks in the late winter and the spring, Arthur's military training and professional zeal came before everything else again. He was, after all, his father's son. Preoccupied with the battle ahead, he wrote less frequently to Masa. At the end of February, with the attack about to start, the Second Army Headquarters moved. "Yesterday we left Shi-li-ho, and rode our horses for seven miles through a snowstorm to a village called Kou-tzu-yen. Tomorrow we will be moving on again. I expect the big battle will be starting shortly. I doubt that I will be able to write to you, but I will try my best. This place is very cold and dirty and really unpleasant, so I don't feel like writing a long letter."[11] A blizzard was blowing from the northeast, and the observers were billeted in half-destroyed houses with no windows.

When the offensive began with an ear-splitting artillery bombardment on 1 March, Arthur was with the headquarters of the 5th Division of the Japanese Army. In the report he made later to his own War Office, he described the events of the first morning, as he saw just one engagement among thousands of similar actions taking place on either side of him. Now, writing in his own language, his account could be more fluent than anything he had been able to put across in his basic Japanese. "About 9 a.m. I found a shrine in the front line of the village of Liu-tiao-kao, it stood in a small mud walled enclosure about twelve feet square; from there I got a splendid view of the operations. A very heavy artillery engagement was going on, the field batteries and the village itself were under a tremendous fire. The Russian ranging was perfect, and at times the batteries were quite hidden by the dust raised by the rain of shrapnel bullets and pieces of shell."[12] He could see the deep Russian trenches, with a parapet of sandbags and firing slits, a couple of hundred yards away.

At ten o'clock, the Japanese troops started to move forward into the no-man's-land. "The infantry attack was made in a manner almost exactly similar to our own system, that is to say line upon line of men extended to five or six paces. . . . The infantry advanced over flat and bare fields with no cover of any sort, under a perfect storm of bullets; fortunately for the Japanese the shooting of the Russian infantry was wild to an extraordinary degree, bullets flew all over the place, most of them high up in the air, they pattered about in the village, flew over the guns, and fell like rain on the plain about a mile behind us."[13] Later in the day, the Russian shooting improved, and the men he was following took severe casualties from machine-gun and rifle fire. "The whole surface of the ground between Liu-tiao-kao and the line from which the Japanese had started was literally strewn with the bodies of the killed and wounded, amongst whom the stretcher bearers walked in the coolest possible manner in spite of the flying bullets. Wounded men walked back from the firing line by scores, and the strangest thing of all was that nobody seemed to be in a hurry, or in the least bit flurried. . . ."[14]

Arthur followed the injured to a dressing station below a bridge, close to where lines of army horses were tied up under the shelter of the bank. "The wounded men lay on the ice bearing their pain without a murmur, while the vicious little Japanese horses fought and kicked each other within a few feet of them; great shells screamed overhead or burst close by with a fearful noise. One 12 cm shell pitched just beside the bridge . . . and the explosion was deafening, while everyone was covered with dust and pieces of stone. The doctors took no notice of these disturbing elements, but worked away untiringly. . . ."[15]

With his ability to speak the language and move about the battlefield with only an orderly, questioning officers about what was happening from hour to hour, Captain Hart-Synnot's descriptions were vivid and personal. Entering a village that the enemy had left hurriedly, they found piles of military stores burning away and an abandoned Russian field bakery complete with stacks of rye bread. "The loaves were enormous, measuring 10 x 9 x 6, and weighing at least 12 lbs each. The bread was frozen and as hard as flint, but we were glad to get it, for we had nothing else that night, and the baggage was miles behind; so we thawed it by the fire and found it very palatable; it was black and coarse, but, with a little salt sprinkled on it, was excellent."[16]

Though he was a privileged observer rather than a combatant, Arthur was in his element again. Manchuria proved that the months spent in a more bookish life in Tokyo had not reduced his appetite for soldiering, and in his head he was making comparisons with South Africa and India all the time. The fighting was on a scale greater than anything he had seen before. When they reached the hard-frozen channels and rivulets of the Hun Ho River, he compared it to the Ganges, "if one can imagine intense cold prevailing instead of intense heat. There are the same great weary stretches of sand, the same sort of banks, and the same sort of scrubby jungle, but here instead of mimosa thorn, almost all the growth on the banks is willow."[17] He followed the fighting for ten days, as the Japanese overcame the Russian defense lines with a combination of cunning feints and a flanking movement to the west, and fought off several fierce counterattacks.

The task for the observers, who included German and French officers, was to note the points that would be relevant in any future European war. Arthur recorded everything he saw, from the organization of field hospitals to the effect of shrapnel as compared with high-explosive shells, and the formations of men used when attacking machine-gun posts. He was shocked by the Japanese carelessness over water supplies and failure to dig latrines, which would never have passed muster with his uncle, General Sir Reginald Hart, author of the standard work for British officers, *Sanitation and Health*. He thought the Japanese were slow in pursuit and lacked effective cavalry, but he admired the thoroughness of the planning, the way orders were issued and carried out, and the phlegmatic calm of the commanders. He observed that in flat country it was necessary for the generals to be dangerously close to the front line, putting them well within enemy artillery range.

After days of fierce fighting, in which 17,000 Japanese were killed and another 53,000 were wounded, many more than on the Russian side, a dust storm blew through. The artillerymen could no longer see their targets, and advancing troops lost their bearings in a brown haze. The wind that carried the dust came from the southwest, and the temperature rose rapidly. By the next day, the frozen Hun Ho River was starting to melt, with a narrow strip of fast-flowing water, and could not be crossed. By that time the Russians were fleeing north in a disorganized rout, and the titanic battle had been won. Arthur was with the 5th Division when it marched into Mukden and bivouacked by the light of the burning railway station, which had been set on fire by the Russians as their last trains pulled out. The Japanese managed to find barrels of frozen salmon that had been left behind. Arthur could identify with the soldiers, most of them peasants from the villages. "Almost every soldier had possessed himself of one, a treat indeed for a fish-eating race, and as they sat round their fires they toasted the fish on their bayonets and were thoroughly happy; this night of peace was a great change to them after the horrors of the past ten days."[18]

Much later, one of the other language officers wrote of Captain Hart-Synnot, "Except for Calthrop, he was probably more in touch with Japanese ideals and thought than most of his contemporaries or successors."[19] His few months in Manchuria, and his experiences during the climactic fighting, reinforced the empathy with the Japanese he had already started to develop in Tokyo. To other observers the Emperor's soldiers were "brave little men," sometimes "fanatical little men," but always depersonalized stereotypes. To Arthur they were the neighbors he had come to know with Masa in Asakusa and Fukagawa, the farmers he had met on their walks beyond Mukojima, and Masa's youngest brother, Haru, who had been called up. Arthur's feelings showed through the thirty-page account of the battle of Mukden he submitted to the War Office. He concluded: "By far the most remarkable feature in the Japanese Army is the wonderful feeling of devotion to the Emperor and their country that pervades all ranks and arms. From this feeling springs the marvellous bravery of the incomparable infantry and all the many soldierly virtues that are so marked in this wonderful army."[20]

Another perspective came from one of the language officers who never went to Manchuria. Captain Calthrop spent his time in Tokyo preparing an English–Japanese dictionary of military terms for use by the two allies. After the battle of Mukden, he wrote home: "Again, the Japanese successes in battle are extraordinary, due to the devotion of their soldiers and officers, who have but one idea, their profession and a fanatical wish to die for their country, and to whom wife, children, parents, art and a thousand other things that interest us, and probably distract our minds from soldiering, are nothing. But to me the army is not everything."[21]

. . .

M asa's uncertainty about whether or when the British captain would return continued into May. The war was not over, and much of the Russian Army had managed to escape—instead of being encircled and decisively destroyed, as the Japanese had hoped to do. All attention had shifted to the final stages of the long voyage of the Tsar's Baltic fleet. The straggling procession of warships had reached as far as Formosa, and was heading north in the hope that it could get through to the Russian base at Vladivostok. Arthur spent several weeks in the dirty, run-down walled city of Mukden, where the mud season was beginning. There was little for the observers to do except ride over the recent battlefields, and inspect the captured Russian supplies. They met Marshal Oyama, the Japanese commander. They visited the crumbling palace of the Manchu dynasty, which had ruled China for the last three hundred years, and rode out to see the imperial tombs, in a fir wood three miles to the north. They were billeted in houses in the compound of a Buddhist temple just beyond the city wall. Arthur caused an alarm one morning when he knocked over a lamp in the cramped room he was sharing. In a few moments his papers were on fire, and then one whole side of the house was in flames. Major Aylmer Haldane, the senior British officer, was next door and just managed to drag all his documents and reports outside before they were destroyed. Japanese soldiers extinguished the foreigners' blaze.

In early May, Arthur and Captain David Robertson were sent back to Tokyo. As they left Manchuria through the Japanese Army's principal supply port at Dalny, they saw more examples of the legendary attention to detail that had sustained the victorious campaign. Lines of transport ships were at anchor, waiting to unload ammunition, food, and fodder onto the quays. The supplies were piled up neatly beside the railway sidings, ordnance of different calibers in lightweight crates with special markings, sacks of rice tied with white string, sacks of barley with red string, oats with green, a quartermaster's dream. Meanwhile, anything with possible value had been collected from the battlefields and brought back to Dalny, and coolies sorted through heaps of worn boots, broken rifles, and used brass shell cases to be sent back to the home islands for repair or reuse. When Arthur reached Japan, he passed through the same quarantine procedure as all those returning from the war, taking a compulsory bath, and handing in his clothes and heavy winter furs for fumigation, to destroy any plague-bearing Chinese fleas.

A rthur and Masa's joyous reunion came in the middle of May, after five months of separation. Arthur had kept his promise, she had kept herself for him, and Masa's trust had been justified. Once they were together again, it was she who had to reconstruct the life that they had enjoyed in the previous year, and find a new place to live. The house at Matsuchiyama—in the Asakusa neighborhood, where everyone knew each other's business and neighbors gossiped as they soaked themselves in the public bathhouse—was no longer available. Arthur may have wanted a little more privacy, and Masa may have wanted to make a break from the Shitamachi, where so many people knew her, where so many of her family lived, and where not all approved of her liaison with a foreigner. She went across the city to the far western side, around Shinjuku, and looked at houses for rent, while Arthur wrote up his Mukden report at the legation and tried to reestablish his own position with the War Office. After living rough for so long, he had to reaccustom himself to the urbanities and stiff dress code of official Tokyo, and made courtesy calls at Army Headquarters to announce his return. He renewed contact with the other language officers—Piggott and Calthrop, who had stayed behind, and Captain Jack Somerville, who had just arrived. He saw his friend Colin Davidson again, a young diplomat who was also involved with a Japanese woman.

On 28 May, Major Roundell Toke, the acting military attaché, with John Gubbins and Davidson from the legation and Captain Hart-Synnot, crossed the Ryogoku Bridge to the eastern side of the Sumida River on an outing to see the spring wrestling tournament at the Ekoin Temple in Fukagawa.[22] Until a few years before, women had been banned from watching the sumo, but though they were now admitted, Masa stayed at home. As the group of Europeans sat in the temporary planked seating and watched the wrestlers squat on their heavy haunches until the umpire dropped his fan as the signal for a bout to start, the greatest sea battle since Trafalgar was drawing to a close in the straits between Korea and Japan, near the island of Tsushima. Arthur and his colleagues stayed at the sumo through the afternoon, as vendors moved among the spectators with oranges and rice crackers and the crowd talked among themselves, breaking into a roar when one of the wrestlers forced his opponent to touch the ground or heaved him out of the sawdust ring altogether. By the time the wrestler Umegatani, who weighed 158 kilos, had beaten his popular rival Hitachiyama, and emerged as the champion, the Russo-Japanese War was all but over.

Back at the legation that evening, reports started to come through of the two-day battle in which Admiral Togo's fleet had annihilated the Russians at sea. The Japanese Navy had outmaneuvered the Baltic fleet and then turned their guns on them with a sustained blitz of accurate shell fire that sank twenty-two Russian ships, including four new battleships, and took the lives of nearly 5,000 sailors. Other ships surrendered. In the whole action, Japan lost only three torpedo boats, and 117 men. With this epic naval victory, Japan had confirmed her status as a world power to be reckoned with, and had shown that an Asian country could be a match for Europeans. Though Japan had triumphed, the cost had been extraordinarily high: 90,000 Japanese lives had been lost during the war, and the nation was almost bankrupt; the government had taken out massive loans abroad, most of them in London, and raised taxes at home. Both Japan and Russia now wanted a settlement. President Theodore Roosevelt offered to act as mediator, and talks were to start in Portsmouth, New Hampshire, in August.

The house Masa took Arthur to inspect was ten minutes' walk beyond the Shinjuku railway station, down an unpaved road that followed a gentle slope by the boundary fence of the Tokyo metropolitan waterworks and reservoir. The Juniso pond was another beauty spot from the preindustrial era before 1868, when it had consisted of a shallow wooded valley with ginkgo and willow trees and azaleas, and a celebrated waterfall next to the thatched Kumano Shrine. Whereas Matsuchiyama had been within the old city of Edo itself, known to everyone because of its place on the route into the Yoshiwara, Juniso was more remote, an hour's walk from the city bounds.

In 1905, modern Tokyo was coming closer. Land had been taken for the new reservoir, and the railway skirting the west of the city was close by. The stands of bamboo and the paddy fields were being broken up by building plots and new houses, but Juniso was still a local attraction and a place for excursions. In contrast with the stiffness of official Meiji Tokyo, and the bourgeois character of the new villa districts west of the palace, the area had a raffish charm. Juniso was anonymous and out of the way, and if Arthur and Masa wanted to get on with their lives by themselves, then this was a better place to be than the long-established community of Asakusa.

Once again Masa managed to find an older house with a special character and charm, shaded by trees, where they could hear the bell of the Shinto shrine. Hiroshige had depicted Juniso in his *One Hundred Views of Edo,* just as he had the temple at Matsuchiyama, where they lived before. Having found this secluded hideaway, they were even happier when Arthur heard that his time in Tokyo had been extended, so that he could stay till May 1906.

FOUR

TOGETHER IN SHINJUKU

My darling, darling, the queen of my heart.
You are the most precious person in the world.
· A.H.-S., 1906[1] ·

Arthur had said they would be happy when the war was over. It was not quite over, and the Japanese government was making great efforts to prevent any word of the peace negotiations from reaching the soldiers in Manchuria, lest their fighting spirit be sapped, but Arthur and Masa were now reunited back in Tokyo. In the summer of 1905, Arthur put away his uniform, wore a loose cotton *yukata* around the house, and went back to the familiar routine of the previous year. A teacher came out to Juniso each day. Masa and Arthur talked as much as they could, and she looked after the cooking and cleaning with the help of a maid. Arthur gave Masa and her family the presents he had brought back from China and showed the photographs he had taken during the war. They mounted these in an album, and he wrote identifying captions: "Chinese Mandarins and Captain Tanaka"; "Village children in Shi-li-ho"; "Japanese infantry advancing." Masa made a cloth sleeve from old kimono fabric to protect the cherry lacquer cover. Arthur displayed a shell case he had picked up from the Mukden battlefield as a souvenir.

For someone who had just come from the blood and thunder of the greatest land battle the world had ever seen, the company of the serene Masa, and the uncluttered interior of the house with its white paper shoji screens, must have had a calming effect. From across the veranda came the sound of summer insects, oars splashing on the lake, and the murmur of conversation from the teahouses. In 1905, crowds still came out to the Juniso pond to picnic, feed the carp, hire rowing boats with prows in the shape of swans and dragons, and visit the creaky teahouses built out on stilts from the bank, just as they had in the days before the Meiji restoration, when the city was still Edo.

Arthur's Japanese studies were as demanding as ever, and he still used small cards to help him memorize the thousands of *kanji* characters he needed to learn, but his own writing was improving, and his brushstrokes were defter and faster. When they wanted to get away from the house, they could walk out into the countryside to the west, just as they had explored beyond Mukojima when they were living on the other side of Tokyo. Sometimes they took the train along the valley of the Tama River, which came down from the hills through fruit orchards and mulberries grown for silkworm breeding. At Hino, where stone steps led down to the Tama, they did what all visitors to the small village came to do, hired a boatman who took them cormorant-fishing on the river. The skill of the fisherman lay in half throttling the bird's neck with a cord, and adjusting it so the cormorant could swallow only small fish, and the large ones stuck in the gullet and could then be disgorged. The freshly regurgitated trout were cooked to order at the teahouse on the bank.

Arthur was emotionally engaged with both Masa and Japan. Letters from his father and brother brought news of Ballymoyer, where the future of the estate was threatened by a government scheme that was forcing big Irish landlords to sell off land to their farming tenants. His uncle, and fellow officers in the East Surreys, told him of the reforms that were shaking the British Army, but after eighteen months in the Far East, all this seemed increasingly remote. He was reinstalled with Masa, his Japanese had improved rapidly, and he was not due to return until the following May. For a while they were under no pressure, and any possible questions about the long-term future could be put off.

Though they were some way from the heart of Tokyo, the journey into Kojimachi was easy. A new tramline from Shinjuku ran to a stop near the northwestern corner of the palace, a few minutes' walk from Masa's brother Yokichi, and from the British compound. With the war work done, the British Legation left him alone, and there were few reasons to call in. Arthur did not play cricket that summer, and was not part of the fashionable social set that played tennis at the club in Azabu. Though most foreign residents might have regarded Juniso as a little louche, even shabby, the easygoing atmosphere appealed to other young Englishmen who were involved with Japanese girls. They included Colin Davidson, who had been a Foreign Office language student while conducting an affair with Otomi-san and was now working at the legation, and the newly arrived Captain Geoffrey Salmond. Major Roundell Toke, who was still acting as military attaché while Hume was away, came out to Shinjuku to see his girlfriend Oharu-san. They could stroll round the lake, admire the waterfall that cascaded over the rocks into a shallow pool with maples on the bank, and call on Arthur and Masa at their house by the shrine.

Toke was at the more rakish end of the expatriate spectrum, pursuing all the diversions Tokyo had to offer. Aside from his liaison with Oharu-san, he was fascinated by the geisha, the professional women who could be hired by men to entertain at a gathering or a dinner with dancing, singing, and flirtatious chat, though they did not offer sexual services. His particular weakness was for *hankyoku,* young girls who were still training to be geishas. In his private diary, the officer listed his legation lunches and engagements with ministers and generals, and also jotted down the names of the *hankyoku* he had encountered or hired, Chiyoko-san, Tsuneko-san, Tonko-san, or Kinta-san, with an occasional note. "Met a very nice Hankyoku named Toyoko, aged 14," and, a little later, "Narikoma. Age 15."[2] He was entertaining company and got on well with the more romantic Captain Hart-Synnot. None of the other Englishmen had relationships as established or intense as Arthur's with Masa, but they formed an identifiable group, more integrated with Japanese life than the starchier diplomats in Tokyo or the Western businessmen in Yokohama.

In July, as the temperature and humidity rose, and the mosquitoes around Juniso became ferocious, Arthur and Masa left to see more of Japan. They traveled first to the opulent and richly decorated tombs of the Tokugawa shoguns at Nikko, and the mountainous spine of Japan north of Tokyo. From Nikko they took two-man rickshaws, with a puller between the shafts in front of them and a pusher behind, up the steep and twisting road that led to Lake Chuzenji, 4,100 feet above sea level. Overlooked by a sacred mountain and surrounded by forested slopes, the seven-mile-long lake had been adopted as a summer resort by foreign diplomats getting away from the heat, and the British minister had a house by the shore. First secretaries and attachés fished for trout from boats as they might have fished a loch in Scotland, or raced small yachts over the dark-greenish water, while Japanese pilgrims came to climb to the top of Nantai-zan or just went as far as the temple at its base. Arthur and Masa kept to themselves. They were staying in a Japanese inn at Lake Chuzenji on Masa's birthday, 18 July, and for Arthur's birthday the following day. Masa was now twenty-seven; Arthur, thirty-five.

Coming down from the hills, they took a long hot train journey farther north, to Sendai, two hundred miles from Tokyo. They changed to a branch line that led out across the bright-green rice paddies to the Pacific shore and caught a small steamer. For two hours they sailed through some of the most beautiful and tranquil coastal scenery they had ever seen, passing hundreds of small islands capped with gnarled pine trees, their sandstone sides eroded and pocketed by the sea, across to the village of Matsushima. This was the old Japan again, and Arthur and Masa stayed in another small inn for two weeks, looking out over the bay, where breezes filled the square sails of the fishing boats that cut in and out of the islands. They went out to the sacred island of Kinwazan, where wild deer grazed, and from whose summit it was possible to look back over the whole archipelago. They fished for mackerel at Aikawa, and swam in the clear sea from beaches of white sand. Matsushima seemed as far as it was possible to get from the carnage of Mukden. Their Arcadian summer, living for the moment, undistracted by any responsibilities, gave them a kind of happiness neither of them had experienced before. They were not just physically passionate, but believed they shared the same aesthetic sense and the same sensitive spirit.

The return to Tokyo was jarring, and Arthur saw a side of Japanese life he had not seen before. Through the war months, he had watched a disciplined people accepting the leadership of their rulers without a demur, but by September, they had reached the limits of their tolerance. When the details of the peace with Russia came from the conference at Portsmouth, New Hampshire, they seemed so favorable to the Russians that there was general outrage. From the balcony of his state apartments inside the palace, Emperor Mutsuhito could hear a new sound, his angry citizens milling and clashing with mounted police on the other side of the walls, as an estimated 30,000 forced their way into Hibiya Park to hold a protest rally the authorities had banned. The police fired their pistols into the air, and troops were ordered in to guard the palace and government buildings. The ugly disturbances continued into a second day, when crowds set fire to trams and police boxes, and the rioting spread to Yokohama and Kobe. Demonstrators demanded that the Cabinet resign and called on the Emperor to refuse to endorse the treaty.

Only the arrival of torrential September rains finally dowsed the protests. Tokyo remained under martial law for two months. Censorship was imposed on the newspapers, which had shared the sense of indignation and condoned the protests. The feeling was that Japan's case had been sold down the river by a government bowing to American pressure. They had been led to expect that Russia would pay a large indemnity to compensate for the vast costs incurred, the 90,000 lives lost, and the sacrifices made, but the Russians had steadfastly refused to pay a single ruble. Under pressure from President Roosevelt, the Japanese had finally given way. Japan was to withdraw its troops from Manchuria, as were the Russians, though Japan would take over the remainder of the Russian lease on the Liaotung Peninsula and Port Arthur.

Arthur and his fellow British officers suddenly found themselves more popular in Tokyo, while American residents were shunned. With anti-American feeling rising, the Japanese government stressed the continuing British alliance, and the secure bulwark it provided against any threat from Russia in the future. Though the 1902 Anglo-Japanese Alliance still had two years to run, it suited both London and Tokyo to revise and widen it. With the new pact, the Japanese gained an assurance that Britain would send her navy if Japan were to be attacked by Russia in a war of revenge, and would support Japan's control of Korea. For the British the scope was also extended, so that Japanese troops could be sent to Britain's aid if the Russians were ever to attack India. To Arthur Hart-Synnot, who had spent years on the North-West Frontier, the possibility of "that wonderful army" appearing in the Khyber Pass and along the Himalayas, to help prop up the British Empire, was further evidence of how fast his world was now changing.

To mark the second alliance, the British Legation was upgraded to an embassy, and a round of Anglo-Japanese events was held to mark a visit by the Royal Navy. Thirteen warships of the British Pacific Squadron steamed into Tokyo Bay to take part in the Emperor's postwar naval-victory review. Admiral Togo's victory at Tsushima and the renewal of the alliance were conflated and celebrated together. Tokyo was adorned with pictures of King Edward VII and Emperor Mutsuhito, newspapers printed verses from the British national anthem, and the mellifluous talk about the two island nations was renewed. Over two days, four thousand British sailors were brought up from Yokohama by train and taken to Hibiya Park, where city officials plied the bluejackets with beer and sake and entertained them with acrobats, jujitsu, and sumo wrestling. Officers were given a Japanese dinner at the Maple Club, attended by a full company of geishas. Editorials found the date auspicious. "It is a strange coincidence," the mass-circulation newspaper *Jiji Shimpo* wrote, "that this ceremony of congratulation and welcome should synchronize with the centenary of the Battle of Trafalgar which made England mistress of the ocean, just as the Battle of the Sea of Japan gave Japan command of Far Eastern waters. There seems to be something more than chance in this concurrence of dates, something that draws the two countries very close together. Their union enormously powerful; absolutely invincible at sea, and too strong to fear any enemy on shore."[3] Britannia and the Japanese maritime goddess Yamatohime were still arm in arm.

At a ball in Yokohama, guests toasted Britain's Admiral Nelson, and the man Japanese saw as the reincarnation of Nelson, the plainly dressed and modest Admiral Heihachiro Togo. At the Kabuki theater thirty girls dressed in costumes bearing the Japanese and British flags performed a specially conceived dance, *Chiyo-no-chigiri,* said to convey the goodwill and respect of the two peoples for one another. A Japanese count said that the alliance was a combination of *bushido,* the samurai warrior's traditional code of honor and self-discipline, and "British gentlemanhood."[4] Arthur attended the

British Legation's garden party, largely organized by his friend Toke. He put on his full-dress uniform again, with his DSO, and drove in a carriage to the Imperial Palace, where the British observers who had been in Manchuria were presented to Mutsuhito. When he returned to Masa, he could tell her that he had bowed to her Emperor.

The warm flow of Anglo-Japanese sentiment had hardly slowed when Prince Arthur of Connaught, Edward VII's nephew, arrived from Britain in a battleship to confer the Order of the Garter on the Emperor of Japan on the King's behalf. Once again schoolchildren were taken to the roadsides to wave flags, gardeners created tableaux celebrating the alliance out of chrysanthemums, demonstrations of the tea ceremony and jujitsu were lined up, and squads of geishas were hired at government expense. When the day came, Prince Arthur's aristocratic assistants advanced across the parquet of the imperial throne room carrying red cushions with the many items of insignia the Order entailed, while a band played "God Save the King" softly behind a screen.

The Emperor was already wearing the embroidered tunic and white breeches of a Japanese field marshal and several decorations of his own, and by the end of the ceremony had been further burdened with a large black plumed hat with a white feather, a blue velvet cloak with a jeweled cross on his left shoulder, and a twenty-four-piece gold collar with a pendant of Saint George slaying the dragon, in addition to the diamond-encrusted garter itself. At the high point of the protracted ritual, Prince Arthur, who was twenty-three, buck-led the garter round Mutsuhito's left thigh. While doing so, he pricked his finger on the pin, leaving a small bloodstain on Mutsu-hito's breeches. In a less elaborate ceremony, Marshals Yamagata and Oyama and Admiral Togo were awarded the Order of Merit, another exclusive British decoration. The number of holders was limited to twenty-four, and a foreigner had never been included. Now there were three Japanese. Admiral Togo, whose self-effacement was well known, chose to wear his medal with the words "For

Merit" turned inwards, worried that having the inscription ex-
posed might be thought boastful and un-Japanese.[5] The exchange of
Anglo-Japanese decorations reached as far as the military observers.
Major Haldane was awarded the Order of the Sacred Treasure,
Third Class, while Arthur came away with the more modest Order
of the Sacred Treasure, Fourth Class.

Apart from these court distractions, and the need to attend the
New Year military review, which was turned into a five-hour-long
victory march-past for the Japanese Army, Arthur spent the whole
winter out at Shinjuku with Masa. Since entering the army, he had
never lived such a domesticated, civilian existence for as extended a
period. Masa had never lived with a man, or kept a house with this
degree of authority and independence, for so long. The winter was
cold, with snow and sleet for much of February. On the road out of
Tokyo, the lines of wagons that took night soil, collected from every
house each day on a malodorous dipper-and-bucket system, rolled
through mud and slush on their way to the farmers. The teahouses
were shut up, and a raw wind blew across the water. Fierce drafts
were a feature of all Japanese houses, and Arthur and Masa kept
warm round the hibachi brazier. Both were settled into Tokyo life,
with its customs and conventions, its respect for the seasons, and
periodic reminders of great natural forces that might strike at any
moment. Small seismic tremors were common, and, like all Tokyo
dwellers, Masa and Arthur were used to them, but at the end of
February, Arthur experienced his worst earthquake so far, and the
strongest shock to hit Tokyo for five years. It rattled the shutters,
and shook the whole house for over four minutes, agitating the surface of the Juniso pond so that the water lapped angrily against the
banks for a long time afterwards.

Arthur and Masa had known each other for nearly two years.
They had overcome the period of separation, and were moving to a
new stage. For her part, Masa was being regarded as a person in her
own right, by a man who wanted to know her views and opinions

and was energetic and amusing. She had never met anyone with such wide and eclectic interests. Arthur could regale her with his adventures in India and South Africa, tell her about country life in Ireland, and discuss botany or Asian religions. He was insatiably curious, and the questions he asked, and the traveling they had done together, were helping her see her own country with new eyes.

For Arthur, the general's son, brought up in the repressed tradition of Victorian public school and military service, Japan and the months with Masa were having a liberating effect. He had watched Japan from the start of the war to its conclusion, respected the national character, and believed that Japanese patriotism had something to teach his own country. On a personal level, the values and attitudes he saw in Masa Suzuki's extended family impressed him too. These were people with only a fraction of the physical space and financial resources his own relatives enjoyed in Britain. They lived simply and frugally, caring for one another through a network of mutual responsibilities. Other foreigners might have found the extreme intimacy of Japanese family life oppressive, but Arthur could see how much support Masa drew from it. Her brothers came out to see them at Juniso. Masa and he went in to Fukagawa to see her mother, who teased him because of his size and sometimes stumbling Japanese, but was always kind.

If all the Anglo-Japanese claims were to be believed, Arthur and Masa's relationship should have been the very embodiment of the alliance, but in practice it was something to be covered up. Masa could not appear at the official functions that Arthur was required to attend, and there were strict limits to what they could do together and where they could be seen, because of who she was. Masa would not have been accepted in Tokyo polite society, nor was there any shared social life with the army officers from samurai families that Arthur had met in Manchuria and Tokyo.

Japanese women were not expected to be part of their husbands' professional world. Arthur's senior officer in Manchuria, Major

Aylmer Haldane, described going to the house of a Japanese friend, Captain Inoue, for dinner when he came back from the war. "We sat down, or rather squatted tailor-fashion, for me a rather painful pose, on the floor of the room which as in all Japanese houses, was covered with beautifully made mats of fibre. The wife of my host did not at first appear, and when at length she did it was only to perform the menial function of pushing along the floor from the adjacent kitchen the plates bearing the eatables we were to consume. The meal had evidently been prepared by her; and when she emerged from the kitchen she made a deep obeisance and disappeared. As I felt it awkward to accept this subservience on her part I made a gesture of protest, but Inoue made a sign to be silent and ignore the lady."[6] Masa was not expected to push plates like this, and she acted with Arthur in a way that Japanese men, and other women, might find almost shockingly forward.

In the eyes of foreigners in Tokyo, Arthur's relationship with Masa could be explained as a short-term physical affair that suited them both, of a sort many had engaged in before, and with money as one of the inducements. If the couple were now starting to think of what might follow beyond this, they were bound to look at the precedents, each from his or her own perspective. Arthur knew there were long-lasting partnerships between European men and Japanese women that fell outside the normal definitions of man and mistress, or "temporary wife." He had come to know Captain Frank Brinkley, owner of the English-language *Japan Mail* and for fifteen years the Tokyo correspondent of *The Times* of London, who was so attuned to local life that other foreigners believed he had gone native and was too pro-Japanese in his reporting. Brinkley had lived with a Japanese woman for a long time, then married her in 1884, and brought up a family in Tokyo.

Western-Japanese marriages were exceptional, though a few unions were celebrated as especially romantic. The well-born Mitsuko Aoyama had seen the deputy minister of the Austro-Hungarian

Legation fall from his horse on an icy winter day in Tokyo in 1891 and had gone to help him up. Count Heinrich Coudenhove-Kalergi, thirty-two, was entranced by his seventeen-year-old rescuer, but when he asked her father for her hand in marriage the father refused and for a while banned Mitsuko from his house. The Austrian persevered and eventually took Mitsuko back to Vienna as a countess. Another German-speaking diplomat made an easier match in 1904, while Arthur was in Tokyo, when the German military attaché Count Alexander Hatzfeldt-Trachenberg married Miss Hana Aoki in a society wedding at the Roman Catholic cathedral, with the cream of the Japanese aristocracy and most of the *corps diplomatique* in attendance. A soprano sang "Ave Maria," the British minister was one of the witnesses, and the well-connected Captain Piggott served as an usher.

Their different racial origin ought not to have prevented Arthur and Masa from marrying if and when that point was reached, but Britain and Japan had something else in common, a rigidly hierarchical class system. Miss Aoki was the daughter of a viscount, who was close to the imperial family. She had a German mother, and moved in sophisticated international circles. Masa came from the lower class and was the daughter of a tradesman. Arthur knew that the differences in their backgrounds were an obstacle, even if other prejudices, on both sides, could be overcome. He knew the gossip about the much-respected Sir Ernest Satow, the British diplomat who had been involved with Japan from the earliest days of the Meiji restoration. Satow had lived with a woman, Kane Takeda, when he was in Tokyo in the 1870s and '80s, and she had two children. Because of his position in the Foreign Office, and her background, he had to leave her behind when his posting ended and he was sent to Bangkok in 1882. When he returned to Tokyo as the minister in 1895, he was overjoyed to be back with his common-law wife and two sons, Eitaro and Hisayoshi, but the minister's Anglo-Japanese alliance still had to be kept secret.

Masa was conscious of their class differences, and equally aware of the attitude of her own family, who would have to give their approval if Arthur were ever to ask her to marry. The Suzukis were not as sophisticated or as worldly as the Aokis. They would want Masa to stay in Japan, because that was the only place they could imagine she would be safe and secure. As the more realistic and down-to-earth of the two of them, Masa may have assumed that she would, despite all Arthur's assurances, eventually be left on her own.

Time was running out, and in April, with only seven weeks before Arthur was due to return to Britain, they went to Hakone again, sixty miles from Tokyo. They changed from the train to a light electric tram, and finally to rickshaws for the hour-and-a-half journey up the valley to the village of Miyanoshita. Arthur took Masa to the expensive Western-style Fujiya Hotel. They had to be discreet, because the Fujiya was much used by Tokyo's foreign community and popular with visiting British officers, who compared Miyanoshita to Simla and the Indian hills. They used the baths, fed by hot natural springs with traces of soda and salt, and walked along wooded mountain paths to waterfalls and boiling pools where sulfurous fumes rose off the water. They climbed up to viewpoints with small teahouses, from where they could look out over the valleys and hills to Mount Fuji. Both knew that this idyll was about to end and wondered what would happen next. For a second time, Arthur told Masa that he would continue to support her, that she should keep herself for him because he was coming back, and she should trust him.

Arthur was playing for time. He hoped they could keep living together, without ever having to address the question of marriage, or whether Masa could be persuaded to leave the country. He planned to return home, see his parents at Ballymoyer, and then get back as soon as he could. His Japanese was now better than that of any of the other officers he had come out with except possibly Calthrop, and he believed the War Office would recognize his value and let him have another posting in Tokyo.

In their time together, Arthur and Masa had visited many gardens, and in his last few weeks they went to the nurseries in Yokohama and bought plants and bulbs to be shipped home to Ballymoyer. The enthusiasm for Japanese plants was another facet of *japonisme* in Europe and America, and several nurseries had a well-organized trade in the supply and dispatch of lily and iris bulbs, shrubs, and dwarfed trees. They bought porcelain, silk, and jewelry as presents for his family. Just before he was leaving, at the beginning of May, Arthur heard good news. It was announced at the embassy that Colonel Hume, the military attaché, was leaving for Constantinople. The job that Arthur believed he was qualified for, with his working experience of the Japanese Army, his contacts, and his language, was becoming vacant.

Masa did not come down to the ship at Yokohama, perhaps because she would have found parting in front of others, in a country where a public embrace was out of the question, too painful and difficult. Arthur's language teacher was there to see him off, with friends from the little group who had spent so much time together. Colin Davidson and his woman friend, Otomi-san; Captain Geoffrey Salmond and his girl, Otsuru-san; and Major Toke were all on the dock. At noon, when the ship was pulling away, he followed the Japanese tradition and threw a small ball of paper to Otsuru-san, with a farewell message to be passed on to Masa, which just said, "I am leaving now, sayonara." Masa Suzuki was in Juniso, already clearing the house by the shrine. Her sense of economy was so developed that she felt it was foolish to waste the higher rent on a place that was larger than she needed. Next day, she moved to a smaller and plainer house in Kashiwagi, closer to the main road that led out of Tokyo.

Ships leaving Yokohama for Europe via Suez had first to steam for nearly seven hundred miles along the southern coast of the main Japanese island and through the Inland Sea, making long halts to take on passengers and cargo at other ports before they finally put Japan behind them and headed west. The fact that the railway covered the same route in a fraction of the time made it possible for mail to overtake the ship, and be posted from the vessel en route, so, by the time the *Sanuki Maru* left Japanese waters, the lovers' correspondence that had started in Manchuria had already been resumed, and Masa and Arthur had exchanged seven letters and three postcards. Arthur's first letter was posted from Kobe. He did not leave the ship to visit Kyoto, only an hour away, as many other passengers did. "I am not interested in going anywhere without you. I do not care about anything else. I feel lonely away from you. The ship is rolling fiercely, making it hard to write. My dearest treasure, please take care. I am thinking about you all the time. To my darling Dolly, Arthur."[7]

At Moji, where they stopped for thirty hours to take on coal, Captain Hart-Synnot left the first-class deck and went down to join the almost naked laborers on the dock. "All day yesterday I helped to load the coal, so it was the equivalent of hours of exercise. But I did not enjoy it very much and went back on the ship. We will leave at noon today and this will really be goodbye to Japan. I am very sad, and will write from Shanghai. I am very worried about you and you must look after yourself because you are my most precious one. To my dearest, Arthur."[8] The letters continued from Shanghai and Hong Kong, where his friend Captain R. J. Woulfe-Flanagan, an Irishman who had been in the first group of language officers, joined the passengers. He posted more letters from Singapore, and from Kelang, on the coast of Malaya. In his fourteenth letter, he told her it was too hot to sleep in his cabin. "I am sleeping on the upper deck every night, and think about you watching the stars. It is 17 days since I parted from you but it cannot be helped. I will return to Japan as soon as possible. Did Otsuru-san give you the small note I threw when I left?"[9]

They reached Colombo by the middle of June. While the ship took on more coal, Arthur had a haircut, bought Masa a sapphire pin, and made a quick trip to Kandy, in the hills. He was already on his twenty-fourth letter of the voyage. "I cannot tell you how beautiful the Botanical Gardens are. There are countless trees, plants, and flowers that grow all through the year. I wish I could come here again with you. After lunch we came back by the 2 o'clock train. The mountains on the way were magnificent. We shall come and stay in Kandy for ten days."[10] There were many similar references to the trips he hoped they would make in the future, just Arthur and Masa, with time to discover exotic places on their own, as they had in Japan. "I am thinking about my darling all the time. I would be fine if we could see different countries and people together. It would be so wonderful to travel with you. At night, in the moonlight, the sea turns a silver color. It is so beautiful that I cannot really describe it in words. At times like this I get away from everyone else and think about you."[11]

Masa was by now settled in her new street, and Arthur pressed for more details about how she was faring. "I would like to hear about the new house. What sort of neighbors do you have ? It must be convenient because it is so near the tramline."[12] Once Arthur's ship left Japanese waters, the communication was in only one direction. He was able to tell her about other passengers, the routine at sea, the weather, and shore excursions with Captain Woulfe-Flanagan, but there was no way she could tell him what was on her mind, or what was happening to her, until the *Sanuki Maru* reached Marseilles, where post that had traveled overland across Russia would be waiting for the ship.

They docked in Marseilles on 7 July, and the shipping line's agent brought on a sack of mail for the passengers. There were several letters from Arthur's family in Ireland, and a letter from Tokyo. Masa told him she was pregnant with his child. She had suspected this might be the case even before he left, and the baby was due at the end of November.

The full implications for Arthur took some time to sink in. He wrote back to her immediately, but his first letter on hearing the news suggested he was stunned, almost denying the new situation. After just a sentence, exclaiming *"Banzai!"* and saying how happy he was, he moved on quickly to describe his visit to a Colonial Exposition in Marseilles, various sightseeing trips he had made around the town, the state of the weather, another haircut, and a clock that he wanted to buy for her. Only then did he return briefly to the news of the baby. "Please look after our darling for me. You are my treasure. We will look after the little one, and if he or she is like you we will love it even more. I will never forget you. I am very pleased you trusted me. I will always be honest with you. On 18 July it is your birthday and I will think of you all day."[13] He saw the baby as an extension of Masa, and because he loved her he would love it. In his first reply he did not seem to acknowledge how Masa might be worrying, or the effect this would have on the Suzuki family, or how their future together would now be more complicated.

By late July 1906, Arthur was back in Ballymoyer with his family, for the first time in two and a half years. After the triumphal return, the progress up the avenue, the band, and the fireworks, he wrote to Masa to describe the day. "The house was full of relatives and friends and local people. I was embarrassed but I made two speeches of thanks. I have been wanting to write all the time, but it is very difficult as there are still so many people staying. I will try to write before they get up in the morning. . . . I am thinking about you all the time. I am so lonely on my own. I wish we could be together again soon and cannot wait to be with you. I will come rushing back when the baby is born. Give my regards to your mother. I will write again soon. From Arthur, to the queen of my heart."[14] Arthur unpacked the mementoes and plants, most of them bought with Masa. A Japanese storage chest was broken, but all the china and porcelain had survived intact. The Ballymoyer gardeners took the sacking and rice straw off the bamboos, camelias, magnolias, irises, and tea plants and planted them out.

Arthur spent three weeks in Ireland, walking the estate with his father, telling him about the war, and visiting relatives, but his family must have sensed a change in him. He was no longer pursuing his army career as single-mindedly as in the past. His father expected him to make the most of his Manchurian experience as quickly as possible, and angle for a staff job with an important command. It soon became clear that this was not at the top of his mind. Letters, layered with sober Meiji postage stamps, arrived at the house from Tokyo with great frequency. He told his family about Masa, and showed them pictures. His sister Beatrice thought Masa looked sweet, found the whole story touching, and helped him shop for her and post back clothes. His father and mother found his involvement with a Japanese woman harder to take, but may have assumed this was an infatuation that would pass. He told no one about the baby.

In the middle of August, Arthur went to rejoin the East Surrey Regiment, who were then stationed at St. Helier, in Jersey, in the Channel Islands. He hoped this would last only until he got the military-attaché job he was expecting to be offered, though as yet there was no news of this. As Masa's pregnancy went into its fifth month, he wrote more frequently, and sounded increasingly anxious about her. "How about money? I am worried you will hold back from telling me whether it is enough or not."[15] A few weeks later he was writing, "I am worried about the cramp in your legs. It is my fault as it is caused by the baby. I am so worried about you. As I expect you will not go to the doctor, I am even more concerned. It must be unusual to have cramp because of a baby. This isn't a reply to your letter. I just wanted to write briefly, to tell you how worried I am. On Sunday, when I have more time, I will write you a longer letter. From Sad Arthur. My darling, darling, Dolly." He tried to give her the long-term assurances she must have craved as she waited for the baby. "This will bring us closer together more than ever, so let us be close until we die."[16] He posted her small presents, including nail scissors and a stereoscopic viewer through which she would be able to see some of the places Arthur had been to, and sent her illustrated magazines.

Arthur's letters often echoed what Masa was writing to him. "You say so many nice things about me, but it is I who am the lucky one. We were always happy when we were living together. We will be happy again."[17] "I am very happy that you keep my photograph next to you in bed. I also have two of your photographs in my room. I put a fresh flower in front of them every morning. Before I go to bed I talk to you."[18] She told him the news from Shinjuku. Major Toke and Oharu-san were quarreling, and Masa was not going out much. "You say you do not visit many friends these days. That is good, as people like to gossip. Oharu-san must be the worst. Have Oharu-san and Major Toke got back together? I don't expect they have. My darling and I were closer than anyone else. It will be the same till we die. We are both so much in love with each other. I have given a lecture on the war in Manchuria to the generals and other officers here."[19]

He was bored by the slow pace of regimental life at the Fort Regent barracks in Jersey and told Masa he had not much work to do. "This place is famous for cows, potatoes, and flowers."[20] He bought a bicycle to get round the island, and was invited to dinner parties. "I am sad we are apart. English women are different from my darling, and I don't like them. There is only one woman for me in the whole world."[21]

The British and American fascination with Japan, which had been in its most romantic phase four or five years earlier, had changed in nature after the war, but several of the plays and musicals that had been part of the earlier craze were still doing the rounds of the provincial theaters. In September 1906, Sydney Jones's musical play *The Geisha,* which tapped the same seam as *The Mikado,* finally reached the small theater in St. Helier, having played for 760 performances in London. The story was about Mimosa, a Japanese girl, and an English officer who courted her. The lyrics of the best-known song were catchy.

A small Japanese
Once sat at her ease
In a garden cool and shady,
When a foreigner gay
Who was passing that way,
Said "May I come in young lady?"
So she opened her gate,
And I blush to relate
That he taught Japan's fair daughter
To flirt and kiss
Like the little white Miss
Who lives over the western water!

Arthur and a group of friends went to see it in St. Helier. The refrain at the end of the song continued:

For she was the Jewel of Asia—of Asia—of Asia
The beautiful Queen of the Geisha—the Geisha—the Geisha;
And she laughed, "It is just as they say, sir,
You love for as long as you can,
A month or a week or a day, sir,
Will do for a girl of Japan.[22]

There seemed to be no question of this being a little too near the bone. Arthur enjoyed it and wrote to Masa to say he had liked the music and hoped they could go to the play together next time. All his hopes still rested on getting back to Japan. "Tomorrow, 3 October, I am going to London to ask at the War Office about next year. . . . I don't want to stay in England but want to return to you. I would like to see my baby, but I would love to see you more than that. We will be parents next month. It is strange, isn't it? I hope our baby will take after her beautiful mother."[23]

FIVE

"CLOSE TO JAPAN"

*You have said some wonderful things in your letter. I am very
happy to read them. But I think it is I who am the lucky one,
because you love this man, wicked as I am.*

· A.H.-S., 1907[1] ·

Masa did not go out much in the last weeks of her pregnancy, and discouraged visitors. She did not like the
idea that her neighbors were whispering about her, as
an unmarried woman who had been made pregnant by a foreigner
who had then left the country. Her mother had moved into the
house in Kashiwagi to be with her, and her two elder brothers—
Seijiro, who was carrying on the family barbershop in Fukagawa,
and Yokichi, who had his own shop in Kojimachi—came to see her.
On 13 December, it was clear that the baby was due very soon, and
the next morning the neighborhood midwife was called. She spread
oiled papers on the mattress on the floor, and Masa's mother boiled
water on the charcoal brazier in the kitchen. The baby was delivered
in the small bedroom with Masa half upright, leaning against a
rolled futon and the wall. It was a boy, larger than most Tokyo ba-
bies, and the midwife washed him and wrapped him in a cloth.
Masa was kept in bed in the half-upright position, and not allowed

to lie down, for a further week, to help the circulation of the blood. It would have been possible to send an international telegram to Arthur telling him he had a son, but this would have cost an exorbitant 2.80 yen, about $1.40, per word, which was inconceivable for the frugal Suzukis. When Masa had rested a little, she wrote a letter to Arthur, and one of the family took it out to the post. The news did not get to him until forty days later.

The child had to be entered into the records kept for each household at the local ward office, and to get round any embarrassment or difficulty in the future, it was decided to register the very Western-looking baby as the second son of Yokichi Suzuki and his wife. This satisfied the system, and Yokichi then gave the baby over to Masa for adoption. Adoption within extended families was a common procedure to ensure a male heir for relatives who only had girls, to transfer a baby to a couple who had been unable to have children at all, or just occasionally to conceal illegitimacy. A week after the birth, the family celebrated the naming of the child, having decided together that he should be called Kiyoshi, using *kanji* from her elder brother Seijiro's name meaning "pure." Just over a month later, he was taken to the shrine by relatives, to ask the gods to protect him.

In the weeks that followed, Masa sat at the low table, when Kiyoshi was sleeping, and wrote letter after letter telling the father about his child. Meanwhile the mail brought more messages from a distracted Arthur, still waiting on tenterhooks. He wrote to her on New Year's Day, 1907. "I received your letter number 55 on 25 December. Thank you. I thought the letter would tell me about the birth of a baby but it didn't. It must be getting closer. Once the baby is born your heart and mine will be even more entwined. You once said we would never be able to have our own baby, but why? Our hearts were one from the beginning and will remain so until we die. I shall write again tomorrow. From Arthur, to my dearest."[2]

A few days later, Masa heard from him again, on paper with a delicate bamboo pattern. He had convinced himself that a daughter was on the way. "I cannot wait for your next letter. It must be the wonderful news, telling of the arrival of my daughter. How amazing that we are becoming parents. You said in the past many times that you could not have a baby, but now you have. I think you are happy, and it makes me happy. You and I are the same person."[3] A week later, another arrived, on the same traditional paper, this time with a background of morning glories. "Today I received letter number 56 from the queen of my heart. I thought it must be about the baby. Before I opened it I thought, is it a boy or a girl? It must be a girl, it must be a girl who looks just like my own darling, and I opened it, but it was not. I am longing for the news. You write so beautifully. Your letter is so precious because it has been written with my darling sweet's beautiful hands. I wish I could get back to Japan quickly. I wish I could be with you. Greetings to your mother. With my love and a thousand kisses to my own darling, darling Dolly. Sayonara, darling, darling, queen of my heart, from Arthur."[4]

For Masa the normal postnatal concerns of any new mother were compounded by the real uncertainty about when she might see the Englishman again. Arthur was writing to her in a way that was loving, positive, and confident, as if the fact that they were five thousand miles apart was a minor difficulty. In December, she had told him that there were matters she wanted to talk about but found it hard to put down in writing. He replied that he did not understand what she meant: "Why is it so difficult? I don't show your letters to anyone, so please write whatever is on your mind. Please let me know about money. If it's not enough tell me, then I will send it straightaway."[5] What Masa may have been worrying about was whether this thirty-seven-year-old bachelor, who was so passionate, romantic, and apparently devoted to her, really understood the demands of bringing up children, and all the long-term responsibilities that would come with fatherhood. He had always assured her he was coming back to live and work in Tokyo, but she feared this might be wishful thinking, and by now she knew that the military authorities, whether Japanese or British, took decisions in unfathomable ways.

It was not until the end of February that Masa finally received Arthur's response to Kiyoshi's birth, and he sounded happy, and immensely relieved. "My own darling, Dolly, my darling, queen of my heart. Today is a day for celebration. A truly, truly happy day. I have just received your letters 58, 59, and 60, and learnt that the baby is born and that my treasure is well after the delivery. I have been thinking about you day and night, because I know having a baby can be dangerous. Some nights I could not sleep for worry. I am delighted it was a boy, as that is what you wanted, and I, the wicked father, am also pleased as it is my darling's child. I wish I could see you now more than ever, and I would love to see my dearest and our baby. Sayonara from happy Arthur, to my dearest Dolly."[6]

Arthur was having to conceal all this excitement in his private life behind his normal dignified reserve and his parade-ground duties with the East Surrey Regiment in Jersey, but the new father gave nothing away to his fellow officers. The 1st Battalion was in the Channel Islands, while the regiment's other battalion was in India, under the rotating system that applied to all the county regiments. The 2nd Battalion was due to stay in the East for several more years, and the two would then swap over. Arthur had gone back to his regiment, as he was required to, hoping that news of the posting as military attaché in Tokyo would arrive soon and his stay in St. Helier would be brief. As the son of a former commanding officer he was liked and respected, and through the Christmas holiday season the eligible if rather enigmatic captain found himself invited to parties and dances on the small island, where the social circle was limited. The news that his baby had been born removed one source of anxiety, but he was now even more impatient to get confirmation of the job in Japan, where Colonel Hume was due to leave very shortly.

Arthur had made several trips back to London, a whole day's journey that involved a six-hour boat passage across the Channel to Weymouth and a train up to the capital. He could stay the night at his club, the Army and Navy, generally known by its nickname "The Rag," where members could dine at deeply polished mahogany tables lit by silver candelabra, under paintings of great victories of the past. From there it was a short walk along Pall Mall, lined with over a dozen other gentlemen's clubs then in their leathery heyday, to the War Office. He had reminded the section that dealt with Asia of his qualifications, and put the case for being sent back to Japan as forcefully as he could. But by the end of January they had still not contacted him, and he had to consider a new plan. He explained it to Masa. "As I still have not heard about the job in Japan I am wondering what to do. I have thought about it over and over again, and last night I wrote once more asking whether I was being posted to Japan or not. If not, I asked them to consider sending me to Hong Kong. If they can, I could be in Hong Kong for three or four years. It would be better than going somewhere else, at least Hong Kong is close to Japan. If I was stationed in Hong Kong I could take two or three months' holiday every year in Japan, and you could visit me in Hong Kong as well. How does this sound? I will write as soon as I hear from the War Office."[7]

Masa received the letter she had been waiting for in late March, and any fears or misgivings she had were swept away as she read it. Arthur was being true to his word. "Please be happy. I can come to my dearest. It is true. I cannot tell you how happy I am. I will arrive in Yokohama around 15 April. . . . I have written the same letter twice and I am sending one by America and the other by Siberia. I wonder which will arrive first. I am so happy that I can see you and our baby."[8] By the time she read this, Arthur had been back to Ballymoyer to say goodbye to his parents, who knew they might not see him again for three or four years, and was already on his way by the fastest route—by ship to New York, rail across the United States, and then another sea voyage across the Pacific. The news was not quite as good as both had hoped. He would be staying in Japan for only two weeks, because the job of military attaché, replacing Hume, had been awarded to a Major Boger. Though the War Office had given Arthur a much-coveted Asian posting, it was in Hong Kong, not Tokyo. He tried to downplay this. "Hong Kong is very close to Japan and so it will be convenient. I will be a staff officer. I will look for a house in Hong Kong. How do you feel about moving to Hong Kong? I will be able to take three months' holiday a year, so we can take many trips together. I wish I could kiss you, my dearest darling, but soon I shall be able to. Sayonara from Arthur, who is crazy with joy, to my dearest Dolly."[9]

Arthur arrived back in Japan in April 1907 on the *Tosa Maru* from Seattle. He had been away for nearly a year, and a country that had felt strange and baffling on first acquaintance now seemed familiar and safe, and his spirits rose. In the afternoon he traveled up to Tokyo and went straight to the house at 91 Yodobashi-Machi, in Kashiwagi, and was together with Masa and their son. After all the loving words and declarations that had traveled over the oceans between them for the previous eleven months, they must have been relieved to find they were as happy in each other's physical company again as they had ever been. There was no time to rent a larger place for such a short visit. For a few days, all three of them lived in the same small house under the same gray-tiled roof, and the need to feed and care for Kiyoshi meant Arthur got slightly less attention than in the past.

Arthur took photographs like any new parent, and they saw Masa's mother and brothers, and acquaintances from the previous year. Then he persuaded Masa to leave the baby, still only four months old, with her mother and took her off to Kyoto for a few days. She was able to enjoy the extravagant experience of first class on the train again, and the comforts of traveling with Arthur. In Kyoto they stayed in a high-class Japanese inn, the Matsunoya, near the south gate of the Yasaka Pagoda, close to the Gion, where geishas shuffled along the streets under paper umbrellas, and the Maruyama Park, where families were still picnicking under the cherry blossoms. The inn's upper rooms had narrow balconies opening onto a small and intricately landscaped garden behind. They walked through narrow lanes and up a long flight of stone steps to the nearby Kodaiji Temple, with its three-hundred-year-old garden and ponds shaped like a turtle and a stork, backing up against the wooded range of hills on the eastern side of the city. Farther along they came to the much larger Kiyomizu Temple, with its high balcony and magnificent views.

Every evening, once Masa and Arthur had used the Matsunoya's deep wood-lined bath and put on cotton *yukata*s, maids brought in an elegant *kaiseki* meal on lacquer trays, with soups, small pieces of grilled meat on porcelain dishes, pickles, mountain vegetables, sliced raw fish, and other morsels they could neither recognize nor name. For Masa, accustomed to rice and boiled vegetables in Kashiwagi, this was as rarefied and luxurious as it was exotic for Arthur. For the first time since the baby's arrival, they had time to themselves and could have long conversations. Masa heard Arthur repeat his long-term commitment. After Hong Kong, in three years, he still planned to come and work in Tokyo. When the time came for Arthur to leave, Masa consoled herself with the knowledge that he would be back for a much longer visit at the end of the summer. Arthur left hoping that she would join him in Hong Kong, once he had found a house. He wrote a few weeks later, "The time I was with you disappeared like a dream. I felt I was in paradise when I was with you."[10]

A rthur reached Hong Kong to find a line of Japanese warships at anchor under muggy gray skies, the blood-red disk with sixteen sharp sunrays flapping damply from their sterns. Nowhere were the effects of the Anglo-Japanese Alliance so visible as in the crown colony, the second commercial port of the British Empire and principal base for the Royal Navy in the Far East, where the Japanese were taking up part of Britain's imperial burden. London planned to keep fewer warships in the Pacific, and rely on the Japanese Navy to protect its interests, and this became even more possible once Admiral Togo had annihilated the Russian Navy at Tsushima. By the time Arthur arrived, the British had been able to withdraw all five of the battleships previously based on the China station at Hong Kong and move them to the Atlantic and the North Sea.

Japanese cruisers and destroyers were tied up at former British anchorages in the harbor and under repair in the dockyards. Because of these transfers, British government spending in the colony was falling sharply, affecting local business. British companies were still making fortunes in the China trade, and the directors of Butterfield and Swire, and Jardine Matheson, could be seen daily at the Hong Kong Club, across from the cricket ground. At the same time, more Japanese companies and banks were moving in, just as they were at Shanghai. Japanese businessmen played Go and met to drink at the Nippon Club, and a string of Japanese hotels had opened along Connaught Road. British residents in Hong Kong did not like what was happening. They were suspicious of the alliance and were convinced the Japanese were out to take their markets in China. In these circles it was generally held that the Chinese were pleasanter and easier to deal with than the Japanese, and represented less of a threat.[11]

Arthur reported to General Robert Broadwood, whose command covered the British Army forces based in Hong Kong and South China. A charming and likable cavalry officer who had made his name in the South African war, Broadwood was unmarried, and he and Arthur were soon playing golf and going out shooting together. Arthur was swept into a secret and high-level debate that arose from the Imperial Defence Council's concern about the security of the colony, after seeing what had happened to the Russian base at Port Arthur. He and other staff officers pored over maps of Hong Kong and its defenses and concluded that a completely new set of heavy guns was needed, pointing out to sea. Contingency plans were made to cope with every possible aggressor, including an American attack launched from Manila. As long as the alliance was in force, a Japanese attack could be ruled out, but the partnership might not last forever.

A War Office guide for new officers arriving in Hong Kong, published in 1907, gave detailed suggestions on the clothes and uniform considered necessary and warned that "spurs should be nickel plated to defy rust."[12] The damp climate, with high humidity and rain and fog for much of the year, meant that "after a few years of residence in the Colony the power of resistance to disease appears to become less . . . especially at the lower levels where European women suffer greatly from boils and blood poisoning."[13] Malaria was rife, and the rate of infection was higher among British soldiers than at any other posting. More than one in four contracted the fever while they were in Hong Kong. Arthur wrote to tell Masa how a fungal mold grew inside his shoes every night, and how he was suffering from boils, but asserted the weather would improve in the next month and he was hoping she would join him soon. "I am so lonely on my own. I will be so happy if you can come to Hong Kong. I will be happy wherever I am if you are with me, but unhappy without you."[14]

In his first months, Captain Hart-Synnot tried to avoid the worst of the sweltering tropical heat by getting up above it. At the end of the day he left his office in Headquarters House, in the heart of Victoria, the city that extended along the water's edge at the south side of the harbor, and walked in his khaki uniform to the tramway that ran twelve hundred feet up to the ridge of hills above. As the frail wooden car climbed up the steep track and the counterbalancing car descended, passengers could look out of the open windows over public gardens still devastated from the typhoon of the previous September, the worst in Hong Kong's recorded history, which had taken up to five thousand lives. From the top station, at Victoria Gap, narrow roads led along the ridge to the east and west, past fallen trees and tangled vegetation still not removed after the great storm, to the governor's summer residence and an army sanatorium, and a growing number of Western-style houses being built by Europeans on the hillside. Provided the cloud was high enough, it was possible to look out over the harbor far below, with liners and warships at anchor, and speck-sized fishing boats and steam launches crisscrossing the dull gray sea, and across to Kowloon, where the mist grew denser. The temperature could be ten degrees lower, with a cooling breeze blowing from the southwest that never reached the city below, because it was blocked off by the hills. Arthur stayed in the Peak Hotel, on a spur just across from the terminus, and began to search other parts of Hong Kong Island for a house to which he could bring Masa. It could not be on the Peak, because that was reserved for occupation by Europeans only.

I n August, just before his summer leave, Arthur sounded excited. *"Banzai!* I am on my way to my darling sweetheart, leaving on the 10th of this month...."[15] His *banzai* ideographs were enormous, stretching down half a column, with a huge ditto mark for a second *banzai:*

Masa met him off the ship at Kobe, having left the baby behind with her mother again, and they went straight to the Matsunoya inn for a few blissful days on their own. When he once more tried to persuade her to come and live in Hong Kong, she must have

pointed out the practical difficulties as she saw them. Kiyoshi was
still only nine months old. The climate would be bad for the baby.
She spoke neither English nor Cantonese, and the shops and markets would be strange to her. She would be uncomfortable in clut-
tered Western houses and was worried about how she would be
treated by Hong Kong's British community, who were notoriously
snobbish and hardly acknowledged the Japanese. Even if she was
willing to come, she could not leave her mother, and her older
brothers would object. Her younger brother Haru, the only one
who was not a barber, was Arthur's sole ally. He was considering
moving to Hong Kong himself, to find work in the growing Japanese settlement.

I
n the autumn of 1907, Masa was able to go out more. She sometimes came across the Englishmen and Japanese girls they had
mixed with in Tokyo in earlier years. Major Roundell Toke was continuing to see Oharu-san in Shinjuku, though it was a tempestuous
affair, and Captain Geoffrey Salmond was still with Otsuru-san.
Masa kept Arthur up to date with the gossip about these relationships. "So Otomi-san has had a baby boy and Davidson has gone to
see her in Kyoto. Things are lively these days!"[16] When Masa told
him about various Anglo-Japanese tiffs, Arthur wrote rather smugly,
"Other people have quarrels and disagreements all the time, and I
think it is horrible. We will not have a quarrel till we die. We have
said that to each other many times, haven't we?"[17] Both Arthur and
Masa eventually fell out with Davidson, over his treatment of
Otomi-san. "I knew you would hate to read Davidson's letters. He
told a big lie, and I said so in my letter to him. The rest is so unpleasant and complicated that we should forget it. It will be better to ignore him if you meet him in the street. We have had enough of
Davidson's affairs, haven't we?"[18]

Travelers coming to Tokyo from Hong Kong brought presents

from Arthur. When General Broadwood, who had become a good friend to Arthur and knew about Masa, went to Japan, he took her a parcel containing a mosquito net and some flannel cloth. Masa sent persimmons to Hong Kong when Toke was going there, and Arthur sent mangoes back, with instructions on how to deal with them. Masa was deeply conservative in her sense of a woman's role, but her horizons had widened since meeting Arthur. She was always interested in what Arthur told her about British home life and the women in his family, and was grateful when he sent illustrated magazines showing Western fashions and furnishings. Though Japanese women had far less buying power than their equivalents in the United States or Northern Europe, Western-style consumption was just starting in Japan. Tokyo household stores that sold paraffin stoves and vacuum flasks now began to offer the first affordable sewing machines.

The Singer company had begun to advertise widely. "In the twentieth century home, you must have a sewing box for the twentieth century. The sewing box of the twentieth century is the Singer Sewing machine. . . ."[19] In the autumn of 1907, Masa started to attend lessons at the company's new school in Yurakucho, in central Tokyo. For most of the women who went to the classes, the machine was a route to making their own dresses and clothes in the Western style. Masa preferred kimonos and never wore Western dress, but wanted to be able to make clothes for Kiyoshi, and could use the more intricate embroidery stitches to make the purses and cushions she had always made by hand. Arthur was as supportive as ever. "I hear you have been going to sewing-machine classes from early in the morning. It must be difficult, but interesting. When you become good at the machine I will buy you the best one there is. I will send you the money for the machine right away."[20] It may have been in the back of her mind that this was a skill that might one day stand her in good stead, if Arthur's remittances ever ceased. The Singer advertisements were headed: "Announcement for ladies who wish to find independent means."

While Masa studied the finer adjustments of the Singer, Arthur spent his free time, when he was not working with the general at Headquarters House, practicing jujitsu. Martial arts had enjoyed a vogue in Europe and North America as part of the enthusiasm for all things Japanese. A Japanese instructor was teaching the British Army judo at Aldershot, and a college of jujitsu had opened in London's Oxford Street. Arthur found a teacher in Hong Kong who showed him the falls and throws. Despite the anti-Japanese prejudice in Hong Kong, he was happy to proclaim his close identification with Nippon for all to see. He made friends with the senior Japanese diplomat in Hong Kong, Mr. Funatsu, and patronized Japanese traders and restaurants. He remembered to call at the consulate on the Japanese Emperor's birthday and leave his visiting card wishing Mutsuhito continued good health. When another English resident wrote a damning article in the local paper about his holiday experiences in Japan, criticizing the food, the overrated scenery, the high prices, and the indifferent train service, and described Tokyo as an "uninviting wilderness of poles and wires,"[21] Arthur rallied to the country's defense. He submitted his own, much longer article, which appeared in the *Hong Kong Daily Press* a few days later, setting the record straight. "Your correspondent has been at some pains to set forth, exaggerate and distort all his grievances. . . . Yet he has not one word of praise for this beautiful country or its wonderful people. He makes no mention of the unparalleled patriotism and love of country of the whole race, he ignores the splendid valour of its sons and the sweet and gentle unselfishness of its daughters; he has made no commendation of the energy and self sacrifice of a people which within forty years has raised itself from the barbarism of the middle ages to the proud position of a first-class world power in the 20th century." Arthur's panegyric, which appeared anonymously and was signed "An Ally," also showed his feeling that the Japanese had a certain moral superiority. "The wasteful and enervating luxury of life among the rich and the appalling squalor in the homes of the poor in Europe and the Americas—both terribly detrimental to the virility of a race—are unknown in Japan. Your correspondent . . . must remember he is among a people which has not yet been softened by over civilization and in a country where luxury has not yet become a necessity."[22]

With the end of the rains and the coming of much better winter weather, his fellow British officers were swept into a burst of luxurious social activity, with horse racing at Happy Valley, golf at the Royal Hong Kong Golf Club, and wild-fowling expeditions across to the New Territories to shoot snipe and grouse. Arthur complained he was having to go out too frequently. "Last week I had to attend dinner parties three times. On Thursday it was an admiral, and on Wednesday it was the governor's, and on Friday it was a ball. I don't like them, but I had to go."[23] His letters were as reassuring as ever, still gently pressuring Masa to come and join him. "In your number 4 you wonder why you have not received my letter, but you must not worry that I will forget you. There is not a day when I do not think about you even for an hour. I cannot bear being apart from you for long. I want to be with you more than anything else. If I find a house, what is there to stop you from coming to Hong Kong? I don't like thinking I might be alone here till next year. My heart was left with you when I fell in love. I will not love any other woman until I die, and I would like to be with you forever. As you are very clever, you must know how I feel."[24]

As he passed month after month at the Peak Hotel—in the best time of the year, when he had hoped Masa would be with him—his declarations became even more ardent. "From the day that I first saw you, I put my heart in your small hands, and since then there has been only one woman in the world."[25] He had not used the Japanese word *ai,* meaning "love," before, but now he wrote it regularly. Week after week, his assurances continued. "Our hearts will not change till we die and even beyond death. Our love for each other has not changed. I love you more than anyone in the world. You have my heart and you know it."[26] In Tokyo he had started to try to teach Masa some English. To help her, Arthur began to include words in the roman alphabet within the flow of *kanji* characters.

MY   OWN   DARLING   DOLLY   〈て ㏌∧ りハ|ハ∞ ₩ 宝 →

At other times, he sent a separate section in English, with his own Japanese surtitles.[27]

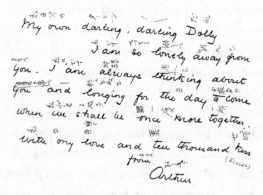

My own darling, darling Dolly I am so lonely away from you. I am always thinking about you and longing for the day to come when we shall be once more together. with my love and ten thousand kiss (kisses) from
Arthur

He still had to find somewhere for them to live, and saw a succession of places that were too big, too expensive, or unsuitable. He was worried how Masa would be treated by the neighbors in the central district, and went to see a house in the closest part of Kowloon, just a ferry ride across the harbor, where the Indian regiments were quartered. "At last I have found a suitable house. There are five rooms and another house for the Chinese servants in a separate part, as well as a stable. There is also a good garden. The owner wants 150 yen but he may take 100 yen. It may be a little hot but there is electricity so we can use a fan. I will go and see it again tomorrow."[28] He eventually decided against it.

After almost a year in the colony, Arthur decided on a more fundamental solution to the housing problem. He rode out from the eastern end of Victoria, beyond the Happy Valley racecourse, following the coastal road past the Naval Hospital and a sugar refinery to North Point. The hillside was steeper here and swept down to the shore, thickly covered with trees and tangled vines and undergrowth. Above the road, a few plots were being cleared, and he found a site where he could build a new house to his own design looking across the water to Kowloon. He would build her a Japanese-style house, in which she could feel at home, in a peaceful spot with a magnificent view. "I have been very happy for the past ten days. I will tell you why. I have decided to build a house for my darling, darling sweetheart. . . . Isn't it a wonderful idea to live together again in our own house? I wish for nothing else."[29] He spent days working out a design, and sent a first sketch plan to Tokyo. "I am planning to build the house like this. You can see the layout. There is a veranda all the way round. The widths of the verandas on the north, the east, and the west are 9 feet and at the back of the house it is 6 feet. It is good to have a wide veranda in a hot country. In my darling's house, we will put a hammock on the veranda. There will be five rooms. Your room will be the biggest with a length of 25 feet and a width of 20 feet. The other rooms are all 12 feet square. Inside the house there will be Japanese-style screens. All the windows will be made shoji-style."[30]

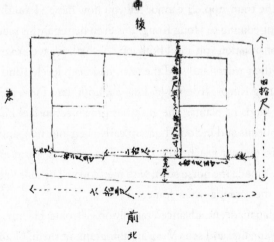

To get things under way, he moved down from the Peak Hotel, rented a temporary house nearby, and hired a gardener, who started to clear the ground. He found a Japanese builder who would construct the house for 2,500 yen, or $1,250, and thought, optimistically, it would take about three weeks. Masa's brother Haru came out to inspect the site, and was instructed to write a detailed letter to his sister about the area. Arthur told Masa how he envisaged things. "You, I, and your mother will be able to live happily, like before. If Haru wants, he can live with us, too. It will not be a good idea for you to be here in the hot season this year, but you can come in October. It will be wonderful to live together in our own house."[31] Not trusting Chinese workmanship, the builder wanted the house to be prefabricated in Japan, though this would take longer. Through the rest of April and May, Arthur went into greater detail, asking Masa if she wanted a Japanese wooden bath or a Hong Kong ceramic one, and about the placing of the kitchen and the servants' quarters. Meanwhile, Haru sailed back to Japan with the builder, and an envelope of Arthur's money, to order the frames and screens, wait while they were made in Moji, and bring them back.

The plot was less than three miles from the Murray Barracks, where Arthur had his office, and he could ride on horseback, or bicycle to the tram stop. "I cannot tell you how happy I am thinking about your coming to Hong Kong. It is even better as this place is in the sort of situation you and I both love."[32] Arthur gave progress reports on the garden, and said the lawn had been leveled and sown. "Your Hong Kong garden is looking beautiful and there are many different kinds of plants. The corn has grown seven feet high and there are beans and melons. I get up early every morning and swim straight in the sea just by the house. The water is warm and the other day I made the horse swim with me. You will be able to see the sea from the veranda when you come."[33]

The plan made, he advanced rapidly on all fronts. He hired three Chinese servants, and sent Masa a photograph of them. "I am buying household things bit by bit but I am not sure what to buy without you. When you come and see the things I bought, you may say, 'My goodness, we don't need this stuff.' But as I shall be so happy having you here, I don't care how much you tell me off."[34] The only thing left to be resolved was exactly who was going to live in the perfect Japanese nest he was building. "You wrote to say you wish you could fly to me. I am a really happy man. You say your love will stay the same forever. We have true love between us, we will never change. There will be no problem with your mother coming to Hong Kong but it will be difficult to bring Kiyoshi. It will be better not to have Kiyoshi in Hong Kong. People will talk. Let us discuss this fully when I am in Japan. I hope you will not be angry with me."[35]

After months of vagueness, Masa had now come up against the boundary line of what was acceptable and what was not for a British officer serving overseas. If living with a Japanese woman could be tolerated, provided he was discreet, and his fellow officers would turn a blind eye, it was another thing altogether to have a complete Asian ménage, with a child. When Masa pointed out the difficulties of leaving the baby, he was more specific and asked her to make a short-term sacrifice for a longer-term gain. "Let us discuss Kiyoshi when I come. It will be difficult for you to bring him to Hong Kong. People will gossip. Then the government will not be pleased and will not send me to Japan. If I were not in the army, this would not be a problem. I do not mind at all if people know about us, but it is silly to have a row with the government. Also, the climate in Hong Kong is not good for children. Please think about this and let us talk about the best thing to do. I always want you to be happy, so I will not refuse if you wish to bring Kiyoshi, but I would prefer it if you do not. Darling, my own dear sweetheart, you are not cross with me, are you?"[36]

Arthur's plan for the year was now laid out. He believed that once the house was finished the long periods of separation, which they had both borne since the end of his Tokyo posting, would be over. Masa would be in Hong Kong between November and April, and during those six months Kiyoshi would be left with her mother, or a child-minder if her mother came to Hong Kong also, as Arthur wanted. During the summer, Arthur would be able to spend two months in Japan. In that way, they would only be apart for four months of the year. Arthur exposed his true feelings about Kiyoshi's role in all this, in a letter he wrote at the end of May. "The 21st was a happy day because your letter came. Thank you. You wrote many things about little Kiyoshi. I am pleased to hear he is walking well. You do not like the idea of leaving him behind. I know how you feel but it will be better for the three of us not to bring him. If the government disapproves I will not be able to go to Japan later. I think the government will send me as a reward for the hard work I am doing in Hong Kong. That's why we have to be careful. Kiyoshi is a lucky child. I am a little envious of him. I said so before he was born. I am a selfish man so I want to have my darling's heart all to myself, but because of him I have only half, haven't I?"[37]

Masa allowed herself to be persuaded by the force of Arthur's arguments and finally gave way. She found a couple they could pay to look after her eighteen-month-old baby. "It is good news about Kiyoshi. You must feel relieved to know the Kuriharas are nice people. I am sure you will miss him. I am sorry about it but it had to be done. I know it is a burden for you to have to do things which you are not happy about for my sake. It is good that Kurihara's little child likes Kiyoshi. I will take lots of photographs of Kiyoshi when I am in Japan."[38]

Once Haru and the builder had returned with the materials, and work was under way, Arthur could leave for another summer leave in Japan. This time Masa was not prepared to meet him off the boat at Kobe and go immediately to Kyoto for another tryst at the Matsunoya, as he wanted. She insisted he come direct to Tokyo and see them there, and the three of them all took a house by the sea at Inage, a sea-bathing resort on the other side of Tokyo Bay. When he left Japan in September, his spirits were high, because there were only six weeks to go before Masa was due to follow. "I reached Hong Kong at seven in the morning. Miki and the carpenter came to meet me, but Haru wasn't there. He has a rash from poison ivy. He is better now but had stayed home. I went straight to the office but saw Haru when I got home, and he still had rashes on his hand and neck, but it is mostly gone, and he will probably be better in about ten days. The house isn't completed yet and will take another couple of weeks. Three of the carpenters are off work because of the fever. The other two, a carpenter and a plasterer, are working very hard. Today the roof will be completed. I am surprised at how big the house is—maybe it is too big, but it is a wonderful house."[39]

Though this time he had had to design and create it himself, Arthur had once again managed to find the traditional setting he liked for his life with Masa, a Japanese picture frame in which he could place Dolly, in some ways as much of a fantasy as the set for a Western play or opera. When the house was finished, still smelling of new pine, cedar, and fresh yellow-green tatami matting, it owed much to the places where they had lived, at Matsuchiyama and Juniso. It was flimsy by Hong Kong standards, and might not survive a typhoon, but this was a romantic as much as a practical project, and would serve until they could both be together in the real Japan again. "I will send Haru to bring you and your mother over here straightaway."[40]

Masa's mother declined the invitation, but Arthur still hoped the Suzuki family would come through. "In your letter you said your mother was too old to come to Hong Kong with you. If she does not come, please bring one of your nieces. You will be lonely on your own. It will be better for you to have some other woman with you. I think your mother will be the best person."[41] Masa arrived in

November 1908 without a woman companion, though her younger brother escorted her from Yokohama. Arthur showed her the sights, the Botanical Gardens, Government House, and the Peak tramway. They crossed over to Kowloon, and he took her farther along the road to the east of the island, past Quarry Bay to the village of Sau Ki Wan and the narrow Straits of Lyemun. Masa had never been out of Japan before, and must have been doubly struck by the strangeness, by the Britishness of central Victoria with its cricket ground and Europeans in straw boaters and white linen suits, and by the raucous din and careless dirt of the Chinese streets that were unutterably squalid to Japanese eyes. The colonial government had made great efforts to improve sanitation, and even tried to ban spitting, but it was the private view of the British that the Chinese were a hopeless case. The 1907 guide published by the General Staff, for officers only, said bluntly, "The complete ignorance of the laws of hygiene which characterizes all Chinese, and their apparent contempt for those laws even when apprehended, are well known."[42]

For six months, Masa and Arthur were able to pick up the domestic life they had led in Tokyo in the year after he came back from Manchuria. The difference was that Arthur, who had just been promoted to major, was no longer at home studying but out at work six days a week, and sometimes on military exercises in the New Territories or visiting Canton. He still played golf with General Broadwood and had to attend formal dinners at the army headquarters or HMS *Tamar,* where the British admiral was based. Masa found herself performing the duties that the British colonial wives, known in India as the memsahibs, traditionally performed for their men. She dealt with the garden and the servants, ordered the food and controlled the kitchen. She made sure the drains were disinfected, and directed the fight against the armies of termites who moved in on the light wooden building. Missing her mother and Kiyoshi, and confined to the house except for occasional trips into Victoria and the Japanese shops in Connaught Road, she found her principal source of company in Arthur's retinue of three indoor servants—Konwa, Sing Kee, and a houseboy—and Amoy, the gardener. She planted vegetables with Amoy and kept some chickens. She rented a sewing machine, to practice what she had learnt the previous autumn, and made a man's kimono-style dressing gown, or *yukata*.

As in Tokyo, most of Arthur's social world was closed to her, with the additional factor of the anti-Japanese feeling in the colony. He could not take her to garden parties or European dinners on the Peak, though he invited friends and bachelor officers to the house. Mr. Hewetson, who worked for the Admiralty dockyard, was a kindred spirit and often called for a meal or to play cards. Funatsu-san, the Japanese consul, came to visit. In May, the rains began again, the clouds lowered over the Peak, the mold returned to the shoes, and it was time for Masa to go back to Kiyoshi and her mother.

When liners left Hong Kong sailing east towards Yokohama, they sailed close to the island shore until they could pass out through Lyemun and set a course into the China Sea. From Arthur's veranda at North Point there was a clear view of the departing ships. After Masa had left, Arthur wrote a plaintive letter that had echoes of Puccini. "Darling, darling, I feel very lonely. When the ship passed by the house I could see my darling and I watched you with my telescope until the ship disappeared."[43] In the weeks that followed, he reported on what was happening at her house. The moonflowers had opened. The zinnias were flowering. The cucumbers had ripened. Nine chicks had hatched, and the white termites were not only massing under the house but gnawing at the roof.

With her confidence growing, Masa traveled back to Japan on her own, and found the other passengers surprisingly civil. Arthur thought they sounded too friendly. "I advise you not to write thank-you letters to the Western people you met on the ship. Also, you should not have let Mr. Perry take a photograph. Never let strangers take pictures of you."[44] Within a couple of months, Arthur joined her for his summer leave, and they went back to the seaside and rented a house on the Boso Peninsula. That autumn, Arthur finally succumbed to malaria, as was almost inevitable, and was sweating and in bed for five days, but he remembered to send Kiyoshi a Christmas and New Year present, and early in the new year, Masa was back for a second visit, of five months. Their little circle in Hong Kong was expanded when Norman, the twenty-two-year-old son of Arthur's uncle and mentor General Sir Reginald Hart, was posted to the East Kent Regiment, known as the Buffs, one of whose battalions was then in the colony. The young second lieutenant must have found his older cousin's exotic Japanese establishment—Arthur in his kimono smoking cheroots with Hewetson on the veranda after dinner, looking out over the lights of Kowloon; Masa swinging serenely in the hammock—strikingly different from anything he had encountered in the British Army so far. Norman was taken with Masa, and following the servants' example he called her "Mississisi."

Norman's arrival reconnected Arthur with his family. He had become so absorbed with the house project, and so convinced that after a couple more years he would be posted back to Japan, that Ballymoyer had receded in his mind. In his letters to Masa in 1909 and 1910, there were no references to the Irish house or family news from home. The estate was still going through a difficult period, with continuing negotiations over the sale of land to the tenants, and in Arthur's absence his parents were turning to his younger brother Ronald for help. Ronald had left the army in order to study agriculture for a university degree, and was trying out some of his progressive farming ideas in Armagh.

At the end of April 1910, while Masa was still in Hong Kong, Arthur was shocked and upset when he received a telegram telling him that his father, the bluff "push-on" soldier, had died unexpectedly. General Fitzroy had been in London to have a minor operation, but something went wrong, and he died in hospital with Ronald beside him, aged only sixty-five. When the general's coffin was taken back to Ireland, a gun carriage was waiting at Newry Station, and a detachment of soldiers from the regiments that had served in his brigade in South Africa escorted him back up the road to Ballymoyer. He was buried in the cemetery of the small church, in a grave lined with primroses from the estate. His brother General Sir Reginald Hart, with other relatives and friends, came over from Holyhead on the overnight boat with the coffin for the funeral, but Arthur could not be there. It was three years since he had said farewell to his father in the spring of 1907. Arthur had to decide whether to take compassionate leave and go back to comfort his mother and help sort out his father's affairs. Masa pressed Arthur to make the journey home, but he would have been away for three or four months, and he took a practical and unsentimental decision not to go. He would also have had to forgo his summer leave with Masa.

Masa went back to Tokyo, this time with Norman, who wanted to have a holiday in Japan, and Arthur watched his love leave once again. "1 June. The house looks deserted and is very empty. When the ship passed by the front of our veranda I was watching and I saw you with Norman on the deck. I went to dinner at Hewetson's last night. Afterwards we played cards and I won eight yen, and stayed the night. I shall write in this letter every day. 2nd. This morning it rained all day so it is a little cooler. There are many termites on the west side of the house, but fewer in the roof than before. 4th. Last night Hewetson came for dinner. At around 7:30 p.m. we found termites on the wall of the bathroom. We put candles in a bucket and killed thousands of them. There seem to be more this year than ever, and Konwa and Sing Kee are battling them every day."[45] Soon afterwards, he wrote her a complete letter in English:

My own little darling
Now you have gone
away from me I am
so very very lonely. I feel
as if I had been cut in
two pieces and the good
half has gone away.

Meanwhile, Cousin Norman was taken round Kobe and Kyoto by Masa. He came back bringing presents for Arthur, including a silk sleeping robe and a tablecloth. "Norman arrived at 5 p.m. yesterday and we had lunch together at the club. He seems quite taken by Japan and I thank you for looking after him so well. He showed me many photographs of the places we know."[46]

Though the periods of separation were much shorter now, Arthur never failed to let Masa know how much he missed her, and sent off a letter every Sunday, though they were written throughout the week. "12 June. Last night I went to the Seifuro restaurant with Funatsu-san. He had organized a Japanese meal but it was not very good. We were attended by two geishas but left by 11 p.m. I had a good talk with him. He told me the Nippon Club would like to buy our house when I leave Hong Kong. Hong Kong is very hot now, and there are a lot of mosquitoes. 13th. Today is a very hot day. On Saturday Funatsu-san and his wife and children will be coming for tea and on Sunday I am going for a walk with Hewetson. Luckily we have fewer termites at present. In the garden, the only good flowers are the zinnias and the cockscomb, and the love-lies-bleeding is now very large and pretty. I am sorry for my not very interesting letter."[47]

With less than a year of his Hong Kong posting to go, Arthur's plan to return to Tokyo seemed on course. His uncle and mentor General Sir Reginald Hart was still watching out for his interests, perhaps even more concerned for him now that his father had died. "Today I received a good letter from my favorite uncle, about going to Japan. He went to the War Office to ask about me. The man in charge of the department gave him good reports of me, and said that if I wanted to go to Japan he would be happy to recommend me as I have more than enough qualifications. My uncle also said I would be promoted to colonel next May. Don't you think that is good news! Don't tell anyone as this is not definite. This is a secret between us, but the news was so good I am telling you immediately."[48]

By now there was another secret between them. Masa was pregnant again. Arthur did not exclaim *"Banzai!"* as he had done when he heard she was pregnant before, and the references in his letters were very indirect. "You must take great care of yourself. You must not take bad medicines. It cannot be helped that you cannot come back to Hong Kong now. It is done. Let us talk when I return to Japan."[49] He still hoped they could travel together when he came to Japan in three weeks' time. "Where shall we go when I am in Japan? We have never been to Hokkaido. Shall we go there if you can manage this?"[50]

Masa was by now increasingly anxious, worried she would soon be left on her own with two of Arthur's children, and with no firm news about his posting to Tokyo. He tried to calm her down and showed some remorse. "I cried when I read that you had been to the temple in Asakusa to pray for us before the goddess of mercy. It is all because of me. You have been given much to worry about because of me. It is painful thinking about it. It is also hard for me that you will not be able to come to Hong Kong this October. I hate to be separated from you. It will be fine if I can go to Japan next year. I am sure I can."[51]

He added the by now familiar phrases and pledges. "I am thinking about my darling all the time. I have no real joy when we are apart. I wish we could be together and never be separated. There is no other woman like you in the whole world. You love me, and that makes me feel the luckiest man. Your love is my most precious treasure." At that point in the eight-foot-long letter, the columns of Japanese writing turned into roman characters.[52]

My own little darling you are the sweetest and gentlest and best woman in the whole world and I love you far more than anyone or anything Else in the world

He made no further reference to the new baby, nor did he return to the subject of her pregnancy in subsequent weeks. His next few letters told her about dinners and golf with General Broadwood, more Japanese visitors to the house, and continuing trouble with the termites and cockroaches. He listed the items he was planning to bring with him when he came to Tokyo, including soap and a box of ginger, and asked her if she needed a blanket. Though he was totally devoted to Masa as an ideal, Arthur did not seem able to put himself in her shoes or to see how the world might look from her point of view.

Once again Masa had the baby at home, with her mother and brothers looking after her in the weeks after the delivery. It was a boy, born in December like Kiyoshi, and for official purposes he was also entered as Yokichi's son and adopted by Masa. They decided to call him Hideo, meaning "brave." In the weeks before the birth, Masa had still heard no news of Arthur's Tokyo job, though the military attaché's post at the legation was now vacant, because Major Boger, who had held it since 1907, had just died of pneumonia. There had been similar uncertainty when Arthur was trying to get back from Jersey just after Kiyoshi was born, but the news that reached her from Arthur in early February 1911, when the baby was six weeks old, threw her into despair. After the good times they had spent in Hong Kong, and Arthur's optimistic assurances, it now turned out that his plan to come to Tokyo had failed.

A major difficulty had arisen. Arthur had received a telegram from his Uncle Reginald saying the job he had been counting on was not going to be possible after all. "Darling, as it is Sunday I can write to my dearest at last. I am sorry my last letter was so short, but I had the fever and did not feel well. There is no order from the government and I am worried that I will not be able to get to Tokyo. I had a telegram from my uncle in England to say that they cannot send me to Japan. He does not know the reason, but I wonder if the government knows about us. My uncle did not spell this out but I suspect this is what he is implying. It is a great problem not to know when I can get to Japan, if I cannot go now."[53]

After breaking the news, Arthur tried to be constructive and moved quickly to a solution, introducing a completely new idea. "I am thinking hard what would be the best thing to do. If I cannot go to Japan, why don't you come to England? What do you think about this? . . . It is inconvenient that we are living apart, otherwise we could discuss things properly. It is good that the baby is healthy and it must be hard work looking after two children. I miss my own little darling so much."[54] He wanted her to come to Hong Kong immediately and leave for England from there.

For Masa, at home with the two small children, Arthur's plan of action must have seemed sudden and totally impractical. She was still tired and weak from having the baby and in no state to make long-term decisions at the speed Arthur was demanding. She told him how worried she was by all this pressure, and he wrote back immediately. In his letter of 7 February, he made a new proposal. "I thought I must reply to you straightaway. You wrote that you could not sleep thinking about my idea of coming to England. It made me very sad. I feel so sorry for you. I am trying to think how we can be together. I don't know when we will be together again if I go back to England on my own. I love you. You love me, don't you? There is no mistake about this, is there? We will be unhappy if I am in England and you are in Japan, but if we are together we will be happy wherever it is. So you must come to England with me." For the first time he made a firm proposal of marriage. "English people value formality. Let us get married before we go. If we are married it will be forever and we will not be separated. The thought makes me happy. You must agree with me. You know my heart. I will love you and take care of you till I die. Even if we are far from Japan we will be happy because we are together. Your letter was truly my darling speaking. You are only concerned about me, and this is typical of you. You never think about yourself but always about this wicked other half. I will not go back to England alone. You must come with me, and I am sure you will agree because you love me. I pray that you will."[55] He did not mind if the marriage was Japanese-style or Western-style, but wanted them to get married in Hong Kong in March. "Please get things ready and come to Hong Kong as soon as possible. I cannot wait for you to join me. If you become Mrs. Hart-Synnot the government will pay your fare, too. Let us go to England together and we will be happy. We will not be parted ever again. If you need money please let me know."[56] Once again he broke into English.

My darling I love you. I love you so much

As always, their messages were overlapping, and for more than a month Arthur did not know how Masa had reacted to the marriage proposal sent on 7 February. Meanwhile, he kept on writing. "Darling, my dearest, I received your letters 32 and 33 yesterday. When I read the letters I could not stop my tears. The more I thought about your sadness the more painful it became for me. It is worse because we are apart. My own little darling, I cannot think of words to console you. If you accept my wish, I will never leave you. What will become of us if we are to be separated for a long time? I cannot bear to think about it."[57]

The letters he fired off that month were long, passionate, and increasingly frenzied. They flowed on across yards of rolled paper, small words of English seeded into the Japanese *kanji* characters. "Though the government will not allow me to go to Tokyo, they cannot stop us from being together. We will go to England together. I cannot live without you. At first it will be strange for you in England as everything will be different from Japan, but you will be fine when you get used to it. One thing will not change. That is my heart. If you do not like England I will leave the army after three and a half years and come back to Japan. So will you endure these three and a half years for me, darling? My wish is to receive your 'yes' reply as soon as possible. Darling, I am so happy thinking about us getting married. We cannot be separated, can we? I will not change my heart till I die. I will love my own little darling forever. You know this, don't you? I was sad reading your letter. It is unbearable to think how much distress I have caused you. I cannot bear to see your tears. I wish I could kiss your lovely eyes. I am moved reading your letter. There is no woman in the whole world who does not think about herself. You are only thinking about this wicked man. You say you will wait for me for five or ten years. This made me cry, and I could not read because of the tears. I am a very lucky man. Your heart is mine and it is the most precious thing in the whole world. . . ."[58] This was only the first half of the letter he sent on 24 February, which, when Masa unrolled it in Tokyo, ran on for another three feet. In one month he wrote ten letters, and sent her money to pay for the fare to Hong Kong.

The practical consideration that governed Arthur's response to the crisis, and limited his freedom of action, was his army pension. He explained to Masa that if he left the army now he would qualify for only £120 a year, but if he stayed in for a further three years he would receive £200. "When I leave the army I might be able to do something in Japan. Let us talk about it when we meet. I am hoping to receive your 'yes' reply as soon as possible. I cannot wait for your answer. Maybe you will come instead of the letter. This will be best. In Hong Kong they require fifteen days' notice before a marriage, so I hope to hear from you soon."[59]

Masa must have been so worried by his increasingly desperate tone that in early March she left the three-month-old baby and Kiyoshi with her mother and sailed to Hong Kong. They spent two final weeks in the house by the sea, and she tried to explain why she could not do what he was asking. She would neither marry him nor go to England, but was willing to wait for as long as it was necessary, until he could come and live with her in Japan.

SIX

UP THE IRRAWADDY

To tell you the truth, I would like to
go to Japan by telegraph wire.
· A.H.-S., 1912[1] ·

When Masa and Arthur said goodbye to each other at Shimbashi Station in Tokyo in May 1911, and Arthur left her to start his journey home by the fast route across the Pacific and the United States, it was their saddest and tensest parting so far. As Arthur's train rattled towards Yokohama, past the factories and workshops that now sprawled farther and farther down the line, their tall smoking chimneys made of iron because brick chimneys collapsed too easily in earthquakes, Masa made her way back round the western edges of the city to the unpainted wooden house she had rented in 1906, just after Arthur left her to go back to Europe for the first time. It was seven years since she had first met Arthur at the Kaikosha. For much of that time they had been separated, but whenever they were reunited each continued to find in the other someone unique and wonderful, and they were rapturously happy together. Masa was still upset by the way things had developed between them in the new year. Arthur had appeared not to understand why she could not leave and go to England with

him. Apart from the strong opposition of her brothers and her
mother, who were against the plan because they feared Masa would
face the same sort of discrimination they had heard Japanese met in
the United States, there were other difficulties. She would have to
leave her mother, who was increasingly dependent on her, and make
the long journey to Europe with a small baby and a four-year-old—
if indeed she was to bring them with her, a question Arthur had
never really answered.

During his brief stay in Tokyo, Arthur had continued to try to
persuade her to join him later in the summer. Arthur's attitude was
that the complications would sort themselves out. Once she was his
wife their situation would be regularized, the army would have to
pay for their travel back to Britain, and the question of where they
should live in the future would have to be resolved in the same way
as for any married major. Masa was also worried about her continuing dependence on Arthur for money, and had talked to him about
starting a business. He had said this was unnecessary and assured
her he would go on supporting her. "Darling, darling, we will not be
separated, but if we are, I will not allow you to do any work. As long
as I have money, you will have, too, as we are the same person. I will
not permit it."[2]

Masa ran a frugal household, using the sewing machine Arthur
had bought for her, and growing vegetables in the small garden.
Hideo, at five months, was sickly and needed looking after carefully.
In June, as the weather was getting hot, Kiyoshi came down with
a bad attack of measles and had to be dabbed with damp cloths
and dusted with talcum powder. He was an intelligent and good-
natured child, old enough now to take an interest in the picture
postcards that arrived from his father as he crossed the United
States on his way home, and wrote about the beauty of the Rockies
and the scenery he was seeing from the train. When Arthur stopped
at Niagara Falls, he sent Masa pictures and a tourist leaflet. After

three years in the Far East, he was suffering from culture shock, and complained that the Americans he had seen on the train and in Chicago were ill mannered and interested only in money. He did not like the viewing towers, or the rash of souvenir stands at Niagara. He complained that the falls themselves were "too large," and implied that the most visited natural wonder of the United States was no match for the smaller but more exquisite waterfalls they had seen in Hakone and Nikko during their trips together.

She could not write to Arthur while he was traveling, and all she received from him were cards and brief notes, so they were out of touch for several months, giving them both time to step back from the ferment they had just been through. Masa was fully occupied with the household in Kashiwagi, her mother helping her as well as her elder sister Yasu. Kiyoshi was taken to a local kindergarten every day, where he began to be inculcated into the cooperative and cozy values of the greater Japanese family, under the austere gaze of the Emperor, whose picture hung in a place of honor.

That summer the conservative system by which Japan was governed did not seem quite so firmly fixed, and the faintest whiff of challenge was in the air. A handful of Japanese radicals were importing socialist and even anarchist ideas from Europe. Other emperors looked less secure, in Russia and in China. The sensation of the previous winter came when police uncovered an incompetent plot to assassinate Mutsuhito. The news caused general alarm, the trial was followed closely, and twelve anarchists were hanged in Tokyo early in 1911. The shock was all the greater because one of those arrested, and executed, was a radical woman. Though the health of the Meiji Emperor was starting to fail, he was still keeping up his output of poems. In June, the Bureau of Poetry in the Imperial Household issued a thirty-one-syllable ode written by Mutsuhito to mark the coronation of his fellow monarch George V in London. In the official translation, the poem had a slightly self-congratulatory air:

When nation speaks to nation in tones
Of friendly greeting, 'tis a joy to hear.
When nations dwell in peace beneath the sway
Of wise, good rulers, 'tis a joy to see.[3]

This time Arthur's return to Ballymoyer, after four years away, was more subdued. He found his mother distracted and frail, still recovering from the shock of General Fitzroy's death the previous year, and leaving the daily management of the house to her unmarried daughters Beatrice and Blanche, known as "Dilly" within the family. Soon after arriving, he walked across to the small gray stone church beyond the stables and demesne farm, to see his father's grave. Much of the estate had now been taken over by the tenants who farmed it, under a government-financed scheme, though the compensation due the Hart-Synnots was yet to come. His younger brother Ronald was taking charge of estate matters and instructing the steward who ran the home farm. Within days, Arthur had a recurrence of the tropical illness he had contracted in Hong Kong. The bouts of shivering followed by fever, and then some days of remission, were familiar symptoms and an occupational hazard for those who served the British Empire in malaria zones, and he took to his bed, in the rambling old house he knew so well from his childhood.

Arthur found that his relatives and friends were more informed about Japan than they had been before 1904, and more realistic. Japan was now seen as a great military and naval power rather than as a quaint elfland. More than two million people had been to visit the recent Japan-British exhibition in London, backed by the Japanese government as a way of keeping up British support for the alliance. The exhibits included replicas of liners and warships, a display of railway trains and carriages, a teahouse, a Japanese village, and a model of Mount Fuji built entirely out of silk cocoons. Among the most popular attractions at the White City site were the two gardens built by Japanese gardeners specially brought over, along with miscellaneous craftsmen, calligraphers, cloisonné makers, an army brass band, and thirty-six sumo wrestlers. The official guide referred to "the striking similitude between the Japs and our own people. The resemblance manifests itself in manner, physical stamp, and shape of the head." The writer took this phrenological approach to the alliance further, claiming that the two races both had large proportions of the brain in front of and above the ear, and that "these structural conditions are indicative of considerable mental power. . . ."[4]

The opening of the exhibition had been held up by the death of Edward VII, but it had run on till the previous autumn. Now George V was about to be crowned, and the Japanese were still a presence in London. Just after Arthur got back to Ballymoyer, the two popular heroes of the Russo-Japanese War—General Maresuke Nogi, the victor of Port Arthur, whom Captain Hart-Synnot had met after the siege; and Admiral Heihachiro Togo, who had destroyed the Russian fleet at Tsushima—arrived to attend the King's coronation. They were cheered as they drove to Westminster Abbey in a carriage, with Colonel Haldane acting as their escort, and watched the ceremony from the north choir gallery, looking down on the array of crowned heads, princes and princesses of the royal blood, and the cream of the British aristocracy, who filled the nave in a crush of ermine robes and splendid uniforms.

Admiral Togo, a small and modest man with a white beard and a head with an interesting shape, spoke excellent English and had spent seven years in Britain learning seamanship as a young man. In the weeks after the coronation, he toured shipyards and met men he had served with on a Royal Navy training ship over thirty years earlier. The British establishment took the two distinguished Japanese to its heart. General Nogi attended Speech Day at Harrow School, sang the school song, "40 Years On," and heard the winner of the speech competition deliver a peroration about the siege of Port Arthur. Admiral Togo went to Hyde Park to review long lines of

Boy Scouts, along with Field Marshal Lord Kitchener and Sir Robert Baden-Powell. In a farewell message at the end of his two-month visit, Togo said he could not restrain himself from crying *"Banzai!"* for the British nation. "Having come back to this country after 33 years' absence, I have felt almost as if I had returned to my own native land after a long absence."[5] The Anglo-Japanese Alliance was extended that month for a third time. Togo said he was happy to have been in England for the renewal, "which I believe is the assurance of the peace of the world and of the everlasting friendship between our two nations."[6] The pact was to last for ten years, but Arthur wrote to Masa that he hoped it would last much longer. "It will be good for both countries. I hope the Anglo-Japanese Alliance will last forever."[7]

Arthur spent the days of the coronation in Armagh, where the degree of celebration reflected the religious divide of Ireland. In Protestant districts, the rejoicings were a chance to assert loyalty to the British crown and defy the nationalists who wanted an independent Ireland. In Protestant parts of Newry, houses were strung with bunting and Union Jacks, schoolchildren were issued Coronation Bibles, and fife-and-drum bands played at fêtes and tea parties. A few days later, the King and Queen came to Dublin to attend a service at St. Patrick's Cathedral. Arthur's mother and sisters went down to Dublin to see them, but Arthur, who was still suffering bouts of fever, stayed at home in Ballymoyer. Once again he set up a shrine to Masa in his bedroom and resumed a daily ritual. "I have put your drawings and photographs in a frame, and they are on top of the chest of drawers next to my bed. I put flowers by them every morning. This morning I put roses, pansies, and carnations. I speak to you in Japanese every day. I miss you so much."[8] He told her he liked Ballymoyer because of the countryside, but would enjoy it more if she was there, too. "When I go to bed I kiss your picture and keep it next to me. Darling, I hate to live apart like this. I want the day when we are together to come soon. I cannot bear living like this. When I see women here I think there is nobody like you, and I miss you even more. From lonely Arthur."9

June and July were the best months of the year in Armagh, when relatives liked to visit and friends of his sisters came to play tennis. Arthur did not like all this social activity. Writing in Japanese at his desk, within earshot of the well-modulated shouts from the tennis court, he confided his private thoughts. "Every time I see Irish-women, I think how my own little darling is so different from them. In this country upper-class women are selfish and trivial. To enjoy themselves is the most important thing to them. They are the exact opposite of my darling. This applies to my sisters as well. When they go out they always want me to go with them and I sometimes have to go against my wishes. I have had to go somewhere with Dilly for the past two days."10

Arthur's younger brother Ronald arrived for a month's stay with his fiancée, Violet, and her mother as chaperone. Watching the cou-ple together only exacerbated his sadness. "His fiancée looks very quiet and delicate, though not at all pretty. Once I get to know her better I will send a photograph. I envy my brother, and when I see him with his fiancée I feel so lonely. Why do I have to be so far away from you?"11 In the next few weeks, he talked more to Violet, the twenty-two-year-old daughter of a clergyman, and found her better company than some of his own female relations. Violet, for her part, was intrigued by her future brother-in-law, and his stories of Hong Kong and Japan, and the girl Arthur referred to as "Peachblossom." He wrote to Masa: "Yesterday my brother's fiancée came to my room and asked me about a lot of things. She saw the photograph of you standing on the bridge in Hong Kong and said, 'She is very beautiful!,' and she saw another picture with the straw hat and said, 'This one is also beautiful.' Then she asked me, 'Do you love the Japanese girl in the photographs?' So I replied, 'Yes, I do.' Then she asked me, 'If so why don't you get married?' and I said perhaps I would. This conversation made me even lonelier. Life here is much

the same every day. The weather is fine and I am sure you will like
Ballymoyer in the summer. It would have been good if you had
come with me."[12] Though he ended this letter "Greetings to your
mother and the children," his own family did not know about the
children, and their photographs were not on display.

With the candor that writing in an indecipherable language allowed, Arthur complained that Ballymoyer was turning into a hotel.
To get away from guests filling up the house, he spent hours fishing
for trout in the river that raced down through the glen and passed the
far end of the lawns in front of the house. Even this triggered Japanese memories. In the summer of 1905, he and Masa had been taken
out in a small boat by a fisherman off the Matsushima coast. "Do you
remember the mackerel fishing at Aikawa? You were the best at it.
When you come to Ballymoyer we will go fishing together."[13] Every
so often he referred to her refusal to come back with him, and almost
chided her for it. "I am always thinking, 'If only you were here with
me, I would be so happy.' Here you can do as you wish. We are not
formal. Had you come back with me you would have come to know
Ballymoyer by now and would be loved by all my family. Once you
came to Ballymoyer you would appreciate it like me."[14]

The local doctor advised Arthur that to get over the fever he
would need to extend his army leave, due to end in August. To try
and build up his strength, he took regular exercise, helping to mow
the grass and chop wood just as his father had done. Though he always protested that he was not enjoying his time without her, and
was only "half a person," his letters also conveyed the real satisfaction and pleasure he was deriving from this extended stay in Ireland. He told her about the flowers, the crops of strawberries,
gooseberries, raspberries, and currants that Ballymoyer produced
in profusion, and the peacocks pecking on the lawn. He sent her a
pressed spray of lavender. He carved the Japanese characters for
"Dolly" on a tree, and when he cut his thumb with an ax, drew a
small sketch of the wound.[15]

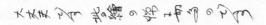

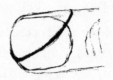

Towards the end of the summer, Arthur was spending more and more of his time on a scheme to make a traditional Japanese garden that might rival the well-known garden at another large Irish country house at Tully, in County Kildare. Arthur and the estate workers excavated a gourd-shaped pond, leaving an island, and diverted a stream to run into it over a waterfall. Around it they started to place the plants he and Masa had chosen at nurseries in Japan and shipped back as shrubs or bulbs in earlier years. They brought the lilies and irises out from the hothouse, to position them with the camellias, maples, bamboos, and palms in the dense style of planting that showed the contrasting structure of branches and leaves and would need to be pruned fiercely. Week by week he kept Masa up to date on the progress they were making. "For the last four days I have been putting a bridge over the stream. It was a difficult job, as I made it very solid. It will be strong enough for you to walk over when you come. I am sure you will like it when it is completed. All the time I am working I am thinking about you. Will she like this, or that? I am building this garden only for you."[16] He told her he had carved a symbol of the rising sun on the timber and called it "Nikkobashi" after the old medieval bridge they had seen together in Nikko, and included a drawing.

He developed an interest in beekeeping, and enthused to Masa about the Ballymoyer bees. The workings of the insect colony, and the need to anticipate the bees' behavior and manipulate and work with them, seemed to fascinate him. "My gardener is English and is used to bees. Irish people are afraid of bees and will not help him, so I am helping him and learning at the same time. I really enjoy it."[17]

Arthur was constantly looking forward to their life together, but there were inconsistencies in his vision. At times he seemed to assume Masa was going to change her mind and come to Europe after all, perhaps in a matter of months. "I am working very hard, so that we can go round the garden together."[18] At other times he referred to the life they would lead when he returned to Japan to set up house with her there. He put on a hat and veil to inspect the beehives again, and told her that on one day they had collected a record forty-two pounds of honey. "Bees are really wonderful and I like them. It is difficult but very interesting. When we are together in Japan let us keep bees."[19]

Arthur's uncertainty about where he would live with Masa, in Ireland or in Japan, reflected his dilemma and the question that still hung over his next posting. If he continued as a staff officer and was offered a job in London or elsewhere in Britain, then getting all the way to Japan during his leaves would be impossible, and Masa and the children would need to join him if they were to see each other. If he could get back to Asia, it would be possible to continue the unsatisfactory but nevertheless workable regime they had managed in Hong Kong, with each visiting the other for extended periods several times a year. Either way, they both believed this was a temporary problem. A date, March 1914, was fixed in both their minds. This was the time at which Arthur could leave the service with his pension, after five years as a major. After that, their lives disentangled from the British Army, they could live in Ireland or Japan as they chose.

In July, Arthur went to London to report once again to his War Office masters. He found the Tokyo post had been given to Major

Jack Somerville, a younger man who had come out to learn Japanese a year after Arthur, but could not discover whether stories of his relationship with a Japanese woman had been held against him. Though a return to Tokyo was ruled out, he picked up a valuable piece of intelligence, that a post would be coming free in Peking. With his knowledge of China and experience in Hong Kong, Arthur thought himself a strong candidate. "The military attaché in Peking is due to end his posting next December. They said I might be able to go to Peking to succeed him. What do you think about this? Also, there is no one in the War Office who knows about China, so I may be asked to be a staff officer. I do not want to work in London, but headquarters would be better than a regiment. Nothing is certain at the moment. I will tell you when I know anything. I am really fed up with the army."[20]

He was playing for time, hoping something would come up to save him from what would otherwise happen by default. If no other staff position were offered to him, then at the end of his leave he would have to rejoin his old regiment. A return to workaday duties after eight years in which he had been in the army's fast stream, first as a language officer, then working in Hong Kong, privy to the politics and secrets of the high command, would be a severe professional setback. What made the prospect worse was that his battalion of the East Surreys was now in one of the most inaccessible and unpleasant hardship postings of the British Army, at a small up-country base in the furnace of central Burma.

Though he was still not recovered from his malaria, Arthur received orders to go to Burma in September. At the end of August, an army doctor examined him and gave him another extension to his sick leave, and he still hoped he would be offered something else. No rescue came. Another officer was chosen for the Peking post. By October, Arthur knew the sentence to Burma was unavoidable, and appreciated the Ballymoyer autumn all the more. "Today is Sunday, so I shall write to my darling again. The Ballymoyer woods have been

beautiful for the past ten days. All the trees are turning red and yellow, but there was a storm the day before yesterday and most of the
leaves have dropped. In the autumn the leaves of Irish beeches are
just like Japanese maples."[21] He went out shooting rabbits and
snipe in the woods. "I talk to myself in Japanese when I am in the
woods alone. If anyone saw me they would think I was mad."[22]
With the Japanese garden nearly finished, he spent more time in the
house, working on family papers with his mother and going through
his father's wardrobes. "Luckily the clothes and shoes fit me very
well. I will keep them all. It would be silly to buy new when there
are perfectly good things. His shoes could have been made for me.
I do not know when I have to leave for Burma but it will probably
be at the end of the month."[23]

Accepting that no further postponement was possible, Arthur
packed his full kit, including tropical, winter, and full-dress uniforms, regimental helmet, pith helmet, many pairs of boots and
shoes, a tent, a foldable washstand, a small mirror, and his own sad-
dle and bridle, and sent them on to the ship he was due to board at
Southampton. He posted Masa a New Year present, a lace mantilla
bought in the Canaries on the way back from the Boer War, and kept
in a drawer at Ballymoyer ever since. Passing through London, he
called on his uncle General Sir Reginald Hart, and found his cousin
Norman staying with his parents. Norman understood Arthur's situation better than anyone else in his family, because of his time in
Hong Kong and his visit to Japan, and he came back to Arthur's hotel with him afterwards. "He asked me about you. I told him I was
going to bring you to England when I returned, and you agreed but
in the end you could not come because of concern for your family.
Norman thought it was sad, but said he wanted to be in England
when Masa comes. He said all of us including the family at Ballymoyer must look after her and Masa will get used to life in England
soon enough. He talked about you a lot, and asked me to thank you
for the Christmas card you sent."[24]

Norman already knew about Kiyoshi, and must now have learnt about Hideo, but there was no reference to the two children in Arthur's account of their conversation. As was often the case, he was focusing on the outcome he so passionately wanted, and putting the inconvenient details to the back of his mind. His ship left for India on 13 December. Trying to look on the bright side, Arthur told Masa that he would be entitled to ninety days' leave in 1912, and that he had now spent so much time at home with his family that he would be able to take all of it in Japan.

M asa's summer was not as peaceful as Arthur's. She and the two children sat out the torpid July and August heat, when women fluttered fans to generate a small breeze, clothes stuck to the skin, and the trams were almost intolerable. The Suzukis ate the traditional hot-weather foods—slices of watermelon, cold soba noodles—and bought cold drinks made of shaved ice from street sellers. At the time of Obon, the big summer festival when families honored their ancestors, she went back to Shitamachi to see the fireworks with her children and her elder brother Seijiro. There were no trips out of Tokyo to the sea coast or the mountains, no visits to hot springs or stays in comfortable hotels. Masa's only reminder of those privileged days lay in the photograph albums she and Arthur had made together, kept in the house at Kashiwagi, which showed one or the other standing against temple gates or squinting into the sun by the shore.

After the intense exchanges of the early part of the year, both went to great efforts to demonstrate that their feelings for each other were quite unaffected by the disagreement, and to show patience. Masa must have been helped by the continuing arrival of deeply affectionate letters from Ballymoyer. A little of the sense of what she was writing in the other direction can be deduced from some of his replies: "You say you get out my letters and read them again whenever you feel lonely. That makes me sad. I am such a lucky man to be loved by you like this." When he sent her presents, she told him she would be happy with a penny biscuit. "You always complain whenever I give you a present, but you know I can't buy you 5-sen biscuits here in Ireland."[25] Masa had known Burma was a possibility, and hoped, along with Arthur, that it could be avoided. She knew little about the place, except that the journey from Japan was longer and it would be far more difficult for her to reach than Hong Kong.

The journey out took Arthur Hart-Synnot thirty-five days, on the troopship *Plassy* to Bombay, then by rail across northern India to Calcutta, which he knew well, and a rolling, two-day sea passage across the Bay of Bengal to Rangoon. The ship passed the muddy shoals of the Irrawaddy delta and came into the main mouth of the river, where the flat shore was lined with rice mills and teak yards, and the smell of sawdust was heavy in the air. In the evening, Arthur visited the principal sight of the city, taller than St. Paul's Cathedral, and the center of Burmese religious life. "I went to the most famous pagoda, the Shwe Dagn, last night. It is a very high, glistening golden building so you can see it from miles around during the day. I wish I could show you these things because you would find them very interesting."[26] Burma was India's most remote and largest province. He was still 450 miles from his final destination, but instead of continuing up the Irrawaddy River by boat he took the train. Twenty-seven hours later, he reached Shwebo, a rough town in the central plain of Upper Burma. The 2nd Battalion of the East Surrey Regiment were based in a small cantonment with tin-roofed barracks for just over a thousand soldiers, a parade ground, and a flagpole. This was not Tokyo, or Hong Kong. Creaking bullock carts moved slowly along raised tracks between the paddy fields, lines of stooping men and women spread out putting rice seedlings into the mud, and boys herded buffaloes. Arthur was given a house beside the Officers' Mess, three rooms upstairs with a balcony, two large rooms downstairs, and a kitchen and stable in a separate shack at the rear.

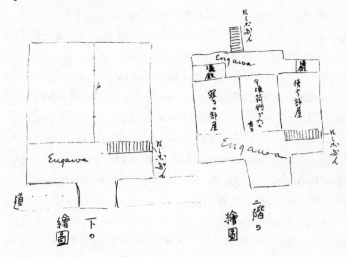

With his return to ordinary regimental life, Arthur's career had come full-circle. He was back in the same tight little military community, with the same respect for seniority and precedent, and the same silver and pictures in the mess, as when he first came out to India and joined the battalion on the outskirts of Calcutta at Dum-Dum. But whereas Calcutta was the second city of the British Empire, with over a million people and a liveliness he had appreciated as a young subaltern, Shwebo was a remote outpost with a population of 10,000. The army apart, the handful of British civilian residents included a deputy commissioner, a superintendent of police, junior officials in charge of irrigation and forestry, and a doctor. Aside from a few European bungalows, the houses were made from timber planks and roofed with palm thatch. Shwebo had no European-style shops, and the Europeans' only amenity was an improvised golf course. Battalions were rotated through from the larger garrison in Mandalay, the old royal capital of Burma before the British annexation, fifty miles to the south. There was little to do except maintain a presence, train the local volunteer militia, and be ready to deal with any trouble among the tribal peoples in the forested hill country that lay towards China.

Arthur's return was about the most interesting thing that had happened for his brother officers in many months. They knew of his record in Manchuria and his good War Office connections, and must have concluded that he had left them forever, destined for the upper echelons, like his father and uncle. Trying to make the best of things, Arthur bought a white horse, and found a Burmese who would teach him the language. He soon dismissed the Indian bearer he had hired in Bombay, who had escorted his extensive baggage across India, because he turned out to be a drinker. He took on a Burmese boy but complained he was equally unreliable. "I only have a bed, a table and chairs, and nothing else. All my clothes are laid out on the bare floor and it is very inconvenient. I am going to ask the colonel about my leave tomorrow."[27] He found he had little in common with his fellow officers, and they may have found him a little distant and austere. He continued to practice jujitsu. "I get up around 6 and have breakfast between 9 and 10. I can hardly eat because of the heat. Then I work till lunch. I study Burmese in the afternoon and sometimes go riding or play golf, but I am on my own a lot of the time. There is no one I feel close to."[28] He still broke into English every now and then. "My own little darling, please forgive this boring letter. If you could see Shwebo, you would not be surprised I have nothing much to tell you."

Arthur missed the companionship and activity of Hong Kong, and the poor postal service meant Masa's letters did not arrive for weeks, and then came two or three at a time. "I don't like Burma because I feel so lonely having to live away from you and letters don't arrive. I get lonelier as the year goes on. It is hard thinking what will be best for us. It is silly to quit the army now, yet it is also silly not to live with you. Darling, darling, what shall I do?"[29] By now these were rhetorical questions and no answer was expected, but he also tried to be positive. "I think we are happier than other people. Sometimes we have to be separated but our love remains the same, in fact it gets stronger. Darling, it would be better to die than to have your love die."[30]

He made a few friends among the local civilians, and played cards with the Shwebo doctor. He took up shooting again, going after wild duck in the lakes and waterways towards the river, where the paddle steamers of the Irrawaddy Flotilla Company throbbed past, carrying British planters and mining engineers, officials and missionaries, and the Burmese themselves, between Rangoon and Mandalay and the small towns farther upstream. Burma put special demands on all the Europeans posted there, with the debilitating climate and because its remoteness and poor communications left them on their own with little company for months at a time. The European population was small, and few of those who came out brought their wives. Live-in arrangements with non-European women had once been common across British India, but over the past fifty years Victorian prudery and "purity" campaigns had changed attitudes. In Burma the old practice carried on for longer, as it did in East Africa and Malaya and other more remote corners of the empire.

In outposts like Shwebo, it was almost standard for railway engineers or police officials to have Burmese "temporary wives" in the Yokohama sense, and several of the province's senior civil servants and police officers had married Burmese women legally.[31] In the years when Arthur was in Burma, the practice of "concubinage," as the imperial authorities in London now termed it, was becoming a much-talked-about issue. In 1909, the secretary of state for the colonies, Lord Crewe, issued a confidential circular that soon became known as "the morals dispatch," explicitly stating that such conduct was "injurious and dangerous to the public service."[32] Those already in the colonial service were to be put on notice that these "practices" were unacceptable, because they lowered officials in the eyes of the natives and diminished their authority over them. New recruits just joining were told that relations with a native woman would impair their capacity for useful work, and warned of "the disgrace and official ruin which will certainly follow from any dereliction of duty in this respect." The army was not party to this, and Masa was not a "native woman" in Lord Crewe's definition of the term, but the fact remained that the British Empire was becoming more racially prejudiced rather than less, and the official line on "miscegenation," or interracial sex, was tougher. In Burma many European men were either lonely or living in a way that was increasingly frowned on. If Arthur had ever brought Masa out to Burma, she might have faced a more formalized prejudice than among the British in Hong Kong a few years before.

Arthur made an expedition on army business up into the tribal country to the east, riding a mule through thick forest where it was possible to hunt leopards and tigers. He stopped at a ruby mine and bought Masa a stone that he had mounted on a ring by a local jeweler, and sent to her as a birthday present. By the middle of April, Shwebo was too hot for jujitsu, golf, shooting, or just about anything else; the sky was a burning gray haze, the corrugated iron roofs shimmered, and the birds were too enervated to sing. Arthur was used to heat, but the ovenlike conditions of central Burma were unbearable. "The temperature has been up to 104 for the past seven days and it is too hot to sleep. Although I miss you it is best that you are not here with me. You would die of the heat. I hate Shwebo but there is nothing I can do. It is difficult to write. I have to use another sheet of paper to stop sweat from spoiling my writing." The monsoon brought relief at the end of May, but then new trials, as Burma's extensive reptile population, rejuvenated by the rains, slid out of their shaded hiding places. Pythons, vipers, and cylinder snakes took their ease on the paths and tracks. "On the 13th it rained for two hours and the temperature came down from 108 to 76 degrees, but it is going up again. Shwebo is an indescribably horrible place. There are a great many snakes, so we have to take a torch when we go out at night."[33]

Back in England, Arthur's brother Ronald was now head of the agriculture department at the University of Reading, and had just married Violet. Arthur's new sister-in-law, who had so admired Masa's photograph, wrote to say she was sorry to hear Shwebo was "so dreary." The thought of Arthur and his Japanese girl continued to fascinate her, even at this distance. "Directly you come home you must come and stay with us, and we will sit on the floor and eat rice with chopsticks. Won't that be lovely?"[34] Violet knew Arthur was going to Japan for his leave. "I hope you will find Peachblossom very well and very beautiful. Don't forget to write and tell me all about her."[35]

M asa knew Arthur hoped she would be willing to travel to Burma, though once he saw the conditions in Shwebo, and experienced the climate, he realized this would be impossible. Her life in Tokyo was far more constrained than in the Hong Kong years. She was not spending five months of the year in a house with servants, and she now had two children, not one. Her mother continued to live with her and share the burden, and Masa wrote to Arthur about the children's progress. She gave him news of the Suzuki family and Tokyo, and the continuing hazards, from earthquakes, typhoons, and floods. The most common danger was fire, in a city still built largely out of wood and paper. In Kashiwagi the houses were farther apart and the risk slightly reduced, but in the old eastern sections, on either side of the Sumida, where the rest of Masa's family still lived, the lanes were narrow and the houses packed close together. In April, her old family home in Fukagawa, and the shop run by her older brother Seijiro, burnt down, and all his possessions were destroyed. It was the house where Arthur had first met the Suzuki family, and he sent his sympathy.

As the date of Arthur's summer leave approached, Masa received letters that showed his morale was picking up. "Darling, you must be careful. You may be nearly killed by the storm of my kisses when I see you. Are you afraid?"[36] Then, just before he boarded his ship, he wrote, "To tell you the truth I would like to go to Japan by telegraph wire. I will be with you in 25 days' time. I am mad with joy just thinking about it, you must be careful when you see me. Please tell your mother, 'The troublesome man is coming soon,' and also give her greetings from this troublesome man. From happy, happy Arthur."[37]

When Masa met him off the ship at Kobe in the summer of 1912, it is unlikely they allowed their private joy at being together again to be in any way affected by the fact that Japan was in a state of public mourning. The streets were quiet, theaters and public amusements were closed, playing music or singing was banned by a special decree, and white ropes and tassels were draped on public buildings to mark the passing of Mutsuhito, the Meiji Emperor, who had died while Arthur's ship was at sea. His reign had spanned the entire time in which Japan had emerged as a world power. The rituals that followed Mutsuhito's death continued throughout the six weeks that Arthur spent in Japan, as the Emperor first lay in state in the Imperial Palace on a platform covered with pure white silk, and was then moved to an *arakinomiya,* a temporary burial hall in the palace grounds, where his coffin stayed until the funeral, prayed to daily by the new Emperor and Empress.

Arthur, Masa, and the children left the gloomy atmosphere of Tokyo for a house that Masa had once again rented beside the sea. Arthur had asked her to travel with him as he had in previous summers, and leave the children with her mother, but Masa wanted them all to be together. Hideo was learning to walk. Kiyoshi, now five, appreciated having a father, and they spent days together in the garden and on the beach.

They were almost certainly back in Tokyo by 13 September, when the city shut down and the Emperor's funeral was held according to lavish Shinto rites. In the early evening five huge white oxen drew Mutsuhito's black hearse from the Imperial Palace, and a long procession set out towards the parade grounds to the west where the ceremonies were to be held, moving along streets lined with silver sand to hush the fall of footsteps, with the street lamps dimmed. At the head came three hundred men bearing pine-resin torches, beating drums, ringing bells, and carrying white flags, pennants decorated with the sun and moon, bows and arrows, shields, and wooden boxes. They were followed by princes and nobles, admirals and generals, the prime minister and Cabinet, and a Guards military band playing "Kanashimi no Kiwani," "Extremity of Grief." Army gun batteries fired every minute. Navy warships anchored in Tokyo Bay boomed out their own salutes, and thousands of temple bells tolled through the city.

Arthur may have been more personally affected by the news that came next morning. General Nogi, whom he had met with the other observers after the fall of Port Arthur in 1905, and who had recently been in London for the coronation and been presented to the King, had sat down on the floor of his house in Tokyo and thrust a sword into his stomach to commit suicide by seppuku. With his Emperor dead, he wanted to make amends for the loss of the tens of thousands of men he had sent to their deaths in the attacks on the Russian fortress. Nogi's action wrenched the public back to the Japan of the samurai code. The ritual suicide divided modernizers, who called the gesture stupid and unnecessary, from traditionalists, who hailed it as the noblest demonstration of loyalty to the late Emperor. To a British officer in Tokyo, it showed that the cultural difference between the Japanese military and his own was not to be underestimated, despite all his admiration for "this wonderful army."

Before he left to resume his sentence in Burma, Masa gave Arthur some strands of her hair, which he tied round the inside of his signet ring and secured with cotton. His mind was briefly diverted from the separation from Masa and the prospect of the awful Shwebo, and his military curiosity was rearoused, when his ship made a stop at Tsingtao, on the northeast coast of China. He already knew British China, and now he saw German China. German-held Kiaochow was a showplace concession, much talked about in both Tokyo and Hong Kong. Starting later than the British, the Portuguese, the French, and the Japanese, the Germans also wanted a place in the Chinese sun to call their own and a Pacific base for their navy. At the time of the German takeover in 1898, Baron von Bülow explained in Berlin, "All that we have done is provide that, come what may, we ourselves shall not go empty handed."[38] In Kiaochow the Germans were opening factories, improving agriculture, planting millions of trees on bare hillsides, and a new railway linked the port of Tsingtao with the lines to Peking and Shanghai. Towering mountains enclosed the deep bay, an Imperial Eagle carved from granite was mounted on a high rock, and ships of the Kaiser's navy sheltered behind a three-mile-long concrete breakwater just completed to protect the harbor. Arthur told Masa that Tsingtao, with its brewery and clean wide streets of European houses, was more like a German town than a Chinese one. He hired a carriage and driver and cast a professional eye over the place. He saw the drydock that matched anything at Port Arthur or Hong Kong, and the guns and forts that German military engineers were setting up in the hills.

Reaching Hong Kong, the ship sailed close to the shore of the island and North Point, slowly passing the Japanese house where he had spent so many months with Masa, a few hundred yards across the water. He had written to ask his old servant Konwa, who had helped with the house from the very start, if he would come to work for him in Burma, and Konwa came on board. The two sailed on for Rangoon, Arthur in first class and his loyal retainer well below. Konwa was miserably seasick, and complained that the third-class deck was full of noisy Indians, so Arthur paid for him to move up to second class. Nor was Konwa impressed when they reached Burma. "We arrived at this horrible Shwebo at four in the afternoon. It was unpleasant finding the house in a terrible mess. I cannot tell you how I hate it. There is no wardrobe or furniture. Shwebo is a truly awful place. Konwa was surprised to see this and said, 'This is not a suitable place for Missississi.' I wondered what you would say if you could see the house."[39]

Since Arthur's continuing efforts to find a new position on the staff had come to nothing, he must have assumed a black mark was being held against him, in which case he would be stuck in Burma for an indefinite period, until it was time for the regiment to be transferred or until he left the army. The return to Shwebo brought back the sense of desperation, and the familiar moans. "When I think about you I want to leave the army immediately. It may be the right thing to do. I cannot bear living with the regiment any longer as I hate it so much. I cannot stand it. To tell you the truth I am tired of the army. We could live happily on my pension. When I think about it, I am wasting my time in the army. As I have given 23 years to the country, I think I have done enough. Darling, I feel as though I am in a desert when you are not with me. If I am with you it will be paradise, wherever it is."[40]

"I hate this place, the people in Shwebo, and the work I have to do in Shwebo. I wish I could get away."[41] When his colonel returned to Britain on leave, Arthur acted for him. He used his new powers to make some changes to the slovenly catering arrangements. "I am now in charge of the Officers' Mess. Before, there were four cooks and five dirty Indian boys for five officers, and they also drank. So I have sacked three cooks and all the boys, and put four British soldiers in their places instead."[42] Week after week he repeated the same musings. "If I cannot be made a staff officer, I would like to leave the army straightaway as work with the regiment does not suit me. Let us live together."[43]

His loneliness was slightly reduced by the presence of Konwa, who had shared memories of Hong Kong and Masa. Arthur went fishing with him in the evenings. His health was now suffering. He had several recurrences of fever, and was afflicted for weeks with prickly heat, his body covered with painful blisters that prevented him from attending the regiment's Christmas party. He took quinine regularly, but the fever continued into the new year, 1913. "A doctor came to see me this morning and told me I am all right. I must be careful not to get ill like this. Your hair which I tied in my ring is still there but I have fastened it with new thread. Tomorrow is little Kiyoshi's birthday."[44] Arthur was now more interested in his elder son, even if he could not remember the correct date of his birthday, which had been in the previous month. "I enjoyed the story of Kiyoshi. He is such a funny and good boy. How wonderful it will be for all of us to live together."[45] But he never mentioned Hideo.

Increasingly, he comforted himself with his bucolic vision of the life ahead. "Let's live somewhere in the countryside, growing fruit and keeping bees, when I leave the army. I wish I could do this sooner."[46] It seemed he had at last accepted, in his own mind, that Masa would not be coming back to live in Ballymoyer with him. A month later, he said, "Reading your letter makes me wish I could leave the army soon and live with you in the Japanese countryside, as you do not want to leave Japan."[47]

He was concerned about his mother in Ballymoyer. She had continuing kidney trouble, and the doctor's reports were alarming. His brother Ronald, worried about what would happen if she died, wrote a rare letter to Arthur. "We have got to face the fact that mother might die suddenly, and if you are in the East it will be difficult to act satisfactorily. Meanwhile . . . will you delegate to me full powers to represent your interests? If mother died while you were away and I am not legally empowered to represent you, chaos will result. If you agree please write a formal letter to Messrs Falls and Co, 62 Upper Sackville Street Dublin saying you wish me to hold full powers to represent you in all matters concerned with Ballymoyer and our mother's affairs, until such time as you are able to return to Ireland. I shall see Falls tomorrow and will tell him to expect a letter from you."[48] When Arthur told Masa, and sent her the original of Ronald's letter to keep her fully informed, she encouraged him to go back and see his mother, but he did not want to. "The news from Ballymoyer is the same. She will not recover but fortunately she is not getting worse. I cannot do anything even if I go to Ireland. It is kind of you to suggest I go, but my being there will not be any use so I am not planning to return."[49] Nevertheless, he implied that he would go, only if she would go, too. "My mother's letter arrived at the same time as yours and she wrote to say she will not be here in this world for long. I would like to take you to Ballymoyer to meet her and to show you my father's grave."[50]

In April 1913, he was saying, once again: "I really do not like Burma or the regiment. I cannot tell you how I hate it. I want this to end soon, and I want the day when we are together to come soon, I long for the day when we can be together and never be parted."[51] In his efforts to find a way out, he bought several tickets for a sweepstake organized in Calcutta. "I wish I could win that big lottery. If I win, I could be free."[52] He saved on his food and drink bills, and saw his Burmese lessons as a means to raising his salary. "I am taking a Burmese language test next month. If I pass the exam I will get an extra 380 rupees. Are you surprised how greedy I am about money? By the way the Indian lottery tickets came from Calcutta at last. There are four numbered tickets. The result will be announced on 28 May."[53]

In Tokyo, Masa, who was much more realistic, put little store on the chances of winning the lottery and looked forward to the summer, when she planned to rent a house with the children again. By then, March 1914 would be only nine months away. Nevertheless, she believed Arthur's place was now with his mother. "In your letter you urge me to go and see my mother instead of returning to Japan for my holiday. What a kind person you are, but I am not going back to England. There is nothing I can do back home, and you are the most important person in the world for me. Don't you know how much I want to see you? I will see you in two months' time. Now I must study Burmese."[54]

He passed his Burmese test. Once the colonel had come back from his leave, Arthur left for another three months in Japan with Masa, arriving in the middle of July. He was in Tokyo when he heard that his mother had died, and the Ballymoyer estate was now his, but he did not return. He had put Masa first, and he wrote to his brother and asked him to try to rent out the house.

SEVEN

DOG OR LION?

I wish this war was over and I could live with you.
I am your captured prisoner.
· A.H.-S., March 1917[1] ·

Arthur was among the earliest British officers to go out to learn Japanese and one of the pioneers of the scheme. By 1914, ten years after he arrived in Tokyo, looked for a teacher, and fell in love with Masa, over fifty other officers from the British and Indian Armies had followed in his footsteps. They had varying degrees of success with the language, and none of the others became as emotionally enmeshed with Japan as Arthur, but they all knew why they were there. If the new allies were ever to find themselves on the same side in a war, or had to fight alongside each other in a joint operation, the Japanese speakers would be needed so the two armies could work closely together. Some believed that despite . all the effort involved—the attempts to get officers' minds round the three thousand or more written characters, the charcoal fumes from the hibachis in the winter, the torrid heat of the summers, and the cultural bafflement—the hard-won skills of the language officers would never be needed. By the end of August 1914, the scheme seemed both real and necessary. With the outbreak of the Great

War, Japan had come in on Britain's side, citing the Anglo-Japanese Alliance.

Only a few weeks later, British and Japanese troops were alongside each other, in driving typhoon winds and drenching rain, crossing swollen rivers and moving between flooded sweet-potato fields in northeastern China, pushing on to attack the Germans. The joint Japanese-British landing on the north coast of the Shantung Peninsula was aimed at Germany's concession of Kiaochow and its model city, Tsingtao. After the main army of 23,000 Japanese had gone ashore, with six fragile military airplanes flying experimentally overhead, they were joined by a force of 1,000 Welshmen and 500 Indian troops. The operation was proclaimed as the alliance in action, a partnership working in practice. For the first time ever, British troops were serving under a Japanese commander, and a British officer was needed to liaise with the Japanese headquarters. The man chosen was one of the early language officers who had sailed out in 1904, Everard Calthrop. Arthur had seen himself in competition with Calthrop from the start. Now, to Arthur's chagrin, Calthrop had managed to become military attaché in Tokyo, from where he had been sent to Tsingtao.

Calthrop did not find the job easy. The battalion of the South Wales Borderers, under General Barnardiston, was only a token force, but relations with their Japanese commander-in-chief, General Kamio, were marked by polite bickering. The Japanese thought the British had brought the wrong equipment, since they arrived in shorts and without winter clothing, and snow was falling before the operation was over. The British complained of blocked roads, difficulty moving their supplies up into the hills to the rear of Tsingtao, and a general lack of information as to what they were meant to be doing. The Japanese infantrymen found it hard to tell the difference between one European and another, and between British ally and German enemy, so the troops had to wear identifying tags to avoid being shot at by their own side. The Japanese thought the British too cautious and unwilling to risk lives. On Port Arthur principles, Tsingtao's defenses consisted of concrete forts linked by deep trenches filled with barbed wire and metal stakes. Before the final attack, to be launched from saps that had been chipped into the rocky hillside until they were only a few yards from the Germans, General Kamio confided to the British general that he was prepared to lose a regiment of men in this last stage. Barnardiston was horrified. Anxious to avoid the loss of his entire battalion in the type of suicidal assaults Nogi had specialized in, he would have preferred a more drawn-out siege with fewer casualties.

The bloodletting General Kamio envisaged was not required. After putting up a spirited fight for a few hours of the final attack, the Germans surrendered, hopelessly outnumbered. The British lost 13 killed and 61 wounded, compared with 415 Japanese dead and 1,450 wounded. More than 4,000 Germans were shipped off to be prisoners in Japan, the granite Imperial Eagle was removed, and the Japanese took over Tsingtao, complete with brewery, solidly built banks and public buildings, and the fine bathing beach with curving promenade and comfortable hotels that justified its reputation as "the Brighton of China." The Japanese maintained they were doing all this for the highest of motives. They would keep Kiaochow in trust and return it to China after the war.

By now Calthrop was impatient to get to the real war, and managed to get himself released to join the British Expeditionary Force in France. Any grievances General Barnardiston may have felt during the short campaign were eased by the way the Japanese played on his vanity afterwards. He was brought back to Tokyo and fêted as a conquering hero. Children waved Union Jacks once again, and the menu at a grand dinner with the war minister began with *saumon à l'alliance* and ended with *bombe Tsingtao*. He made a warm speech about the distinction and honor of serving with the Japanese forces and was given the Order of the Rising Sun, Second Class, by the Emperor. Seen from Europe, Tsingtao was a remote sideshow, but for the Japanese it was a heaven-sent opportunity to seize the German concession and the port that went with it for themselves, as well as German islands they coveted in the Pacific. Tsingtao—along with Port Arthur, which they had gained ten years before—allowed them to control the sea approaches to Peking and northern China. The alliance had given them a justification and an excuse to do something that would have been impossible in normal times. Skeptics believed that General Barnardiston and his British force had been used as window dressing, to disguise a well-executed Japanese land-grab.

If the opening of the war brought a national gain for Japan, it brought a personal setback to Masa Suzuki, still in Kashiwagi with two small Anglo-Japanese children and her mother. The fighting might be over by the end of the year, or it might last as long as the Russo-Japanese War, which had dragged on for sixteen months. Until it was finished, Arthur's plan to leave the army, which they talked about when they were together at the seaside house on the Boso Peninsula in 1913, would not be possible, and he would not be able to get to Japan during his leave. Only one thing made her less worried. Arthur was not fighting in France or Belgium and was still in the East, but had been rescued from Burma, and his military career had suddenly been rehabilitated. General Broadwood, his friend and Hong Kong commanding officer, had put in a word with the chief of the Imperial General Staff Sir John French, suggesting that Major Hart-Synnot's talents were wasted on Shwebo. French already knew Arthur, from South Africa. Memoranda had passed down the corridors of the War Office, and Department M2, which dealt with staff movements, had offered him a new posting with the General Staff, still in India. At the end of 1913, he had said farewell to the 2nd Battalion of the East Surreys, the rough golf course, and the corrugated iron mess, and put the Irrawaddy River behind him. When the war started, he was in the safety of northern India, working as a staff officer at an army headquarters.

. . .

As the war went on through the winter, and on the Western front the two sides dug in for a struggle that looked as though it would last for some time, Masa was preoccupied with the care of their two sons. Hideo was four and still prone to infections, and his elder brother was having trouble at school. Kiyoshi, now eight, had just moved up to a local elementary school, but the term did not start well. The Suzuki boy, with his Western features and unusual height, looked different from other children. Boys in his class picked on him, and his teacher was unsympathetic. In June 1915, Masa's worries were compounded when Hideo became ill with stomach trouble. She continued to write to Arthur each week, sending news of the boys and her family, and asking about fellow officers she had known in Tokyo who she assumed were fighting. Was Major Toke all right? Unable to care for Arthur in person, she packed up parcels and sent them to Lahore, with comforts that would remind him of Japan. She made several more cotton *yukata*s and posted a supply of the hand-carved wooden picks Japanese used to scoop the wax decorously from their ears, about which Arthur could truly say that nothing similar was available from Britain. She dispatched still more pairs of tightly woven straw *zori* sandals for the summer heat. "I received a parcel this morning and found six pairs of *zori, makigami* paper, envelopes, and silk yarns. You are always kind. I still have three pairs of the *zori* you gave before, so now I have plenty."[2]

Masa had grown used to being patient, and her faith in Arthur was undiminished, but in the meantime she was paying a price. She told him about difficulties with unpleasant neighbors, who were shunning her or gossiping. As a single woman with two Western-looking children, an income that came from abroad, and experience of travel and the wider world that went beyond that of her neighbors, she stood out in a Tokyo street where conformity was valued above all else.

. . .

After the steamy jungles of Burma, Arthur was back in the harsh light and bright colors of the Punjab, with the 3rd Division of the Northern Army in Lahore. With the British Empire at war, the high command in London saw India as a vast pool of manpower. Grimy troop trains loaded with Indian and British soldiers were making slow journeys across the subcontinent towards Bombay or Calcutta, on the first stage of the long voyage that would take them to fight for the King in Europe. The East Surreys, whom Arthur had left behind in Burma, were among the battalions to receive the call, and sailed for France in the autumn of 1914.

For the officers and troops who remained behind, the daily routines continued unchanged. Lahore was the provincial capital, and the military cantonment, three miles beyond the walled native town and the European quarter, was a busy military center. Long rows of cheaply built barracks, and rows of identical white-painted officers' bungalows, were separated by dusty avenues and parade grounds. The infantry and artillery lines still ran to the same schedules and the same drills. Colonels led their officers into dinner every evening in strict order of rank, in mess kit, their shirts stiffly starched. Subalterns still played polo and cricket in the afternoons and drank chotapegs. More British females were present than in the 1890s, and most senior officers now had their wives in India, though the influx of British girls who came out each winter for a broadening experience and the chance to meet eligible men had halted with the war. Servants were plentiful, and social life still revolved round the Punjab Club, with its shade awnings and cane furniture, where the memsahibs could while away their time. Differences of class were even more finely studied than they were in England, careful social distinctions being drawn between officers and officials of different grades, and the "boxwallahs" in business.

In his earlier Indian posting, Arthur had spent much of his time on active service. He was now behind a staff officer's desk, for an army whose historic mission had been to defend the most vital flank of the British Empire, stretching along the northern frontier of India from Afghanistan to East Bengal, from the Russians on the other side of the Himalaya Mountains. The need to be on guard against Russian incursions was now reduced. The alliance with Japan had strengthened the British position, and after 1914, Russia was on the same side as Britain in the Great War, and fully occupied with a German and Austrian onslaught from the east. Instead, the army was increasingly occupied with its other, less heroic, task of maintaining order within India itself.

Arthur was made officer in charge of internal security for the 3rd Division at a time when nationalist clamor was rising and the old British nightmare, of another Indian mutiny, was renewed. Fear of local rebellions rose after an incident in February 1915 when over eight hundred Sikh soldiers, serving in Singapore as part of the garrison, mutinied and turned on their British officers. Breaking out of their barracks, the Punjabi soldiers killed Europeans and besieged their commanding officer in his house. So exposed was the British community in Singapore, and so depleted were the British forces in the area, that the authorities called on their trusty ally to help put the mutiny down. Two cruisers of the Japanese Navy sailed in, and a detachment of Japanese marines went ashore to round up the rebellious Sikhs, as one imperial force helping out another. In the following week, the leaders of the mutiny were shot by British firing squads, and German spies were blamed for provoking the incident. The lesson of the Singapore mutiny was noted in India, with a new concern that German agents might be fostering trouble in the bazaars of Lahore or Delhi.

Major Hart-Synnot coordinated intelligence from a network of agents and visited the city of Amritsar, which had become a dissident hotbed. He investigated bomb attacks and advised his general on handling riots, but he had not joined the army to be a colonial policeman. He knew that this was not where his father would have wanted him to be, when in northern France the small British Expeditionary Force had only just stemmed the first German onslaught and was fighting for its life.

For families like the Harts, who had provided the major part of the British officer corps for generations, the outbreak of the Great War was another call to duty. Once again there were chances of advancement not available since the Boer War, when Arthur, his brother Ronald, and his father, General Fitzroy, had all been able to serve in South Africa at the same time. In the autumn of 1914 the men of the Hart family were trying to get to the fighting. All three sons of Arthur's uncle General Sir Reginald Hart, VC, were already in the regular army. Harold was in France by 23 August 1914, as a major in the Royal Warwickshire Regiment, in the retreat from Mons and the battle of the Marne. Reginald had had the misfortune to be attached to the Camel Corps in Egypt, and his requests for a transfer were refused, but he would get to Gallipoli in 1915. Norman, Arthur's favorite cousin, the only member of the family who knew Masa, was with the Buffs in the trenches near Armentières by November. The twin sons of Uncle Horatio were also in action. Laurence was a captain with the British force about to land in German East Africa, and William was fighting in France.

Only Arthur, the most decorated and most capable of this generation of Hart officers, was out of all this, stuck in India. In January 1916, when the Gallipolli landings had just failed and the Germans were attacking around Arras, he was tending his garden. "Darling, There is nothing interesting here and everything is the same. The English sweet peas have grown well. One of the varieties has grown to eight feet high and we had lots of peas, though we have a problem with mice eating them. The chrysanthemums are almost over. The violets, stocks, wallflowers, and carnations will start to flower from now on. They will all be pretty, and the tomatoes will be ready soon. I really enjoy gardening. Let us garden together when this horrible war is over. It will be wonderful for us to live together."[3]

The pattern of the imperial calendar was unchanged. At the end of every April, as the heat rose on the plains and Lahore gardens shriveled up, the government and the army headquarters moved up to the hills. Arthur sent his own entourage, consisting of his Indian groom, his two army horses, his Indian bearer, and the two Chinese servants who had come with him from Burma and Hong Kong, on ahead to prepare his summer bungalow. His office closed down for six days so that the files and papers could be packed and moved to the railway station by bullock cart. Arthur left Lahore a few days later, and changed to the narrow-gauge mountain railway at Kalka Junction. The small train climbed slowly away from the plain, and ground up through a succession of reverse curves and switchbacks, through tunnels and across mountain streams, until it reached Simla sixty miles and seven hours later, and the cooler air was filled with the scent of resinous pine needles. In the hill station, Arthur was even more cut off from the war that his friends and contemporaries were fighting in Europe.

The letters he wrote to Masa from his division's summer head-quarters at Jutogh, one of the military cantonments on the slopes around Simla, described the slow pace of hill-station life. "On Sunday I went to the general's house for lunch and in the afternoon we played cricket. Every day is the same. At 9 a.m. I go to the office and work till 2 p.m. After coming home I have tea and read a book. From around 5 p.m. I go out for a ride or a walk, return for a bath and dinner around 7 p.m., and read the newspaper or a book before going to bed at 10 p.m. This is my daily routine."[4] His letters were not as obsessively focused on Masa the woman as they had been from Burma and Hong Kong, and he sounded less sorry for himself. Simla might be isolated, but it was a marvelous relief after Shwebo, and he had friends there. He told her about walks he took in the forests, a rickshaw journey in the moonlight returning late from a dinner, cricket matches, and tennis. "I was playing in the tennis tournament all last week, and I won. It was a surprise as I haven't played for ten years. The prize was a beautiful silver cup. I was with you last night in my dreams and we were riding in a carriage together when I woke up, which was a pity. Let us meet in our dreams."[5] He said he had been picking walnuts and making jam from the wild apricots on Mount Jakko, and sent her a picture of the house.

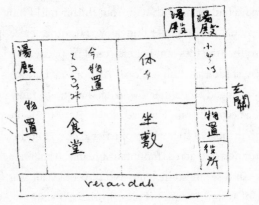

If it were peacetime, Masa might have been able to come to Simla, and it was the sort of place she could have stayed in comfortably, unlike Shwebo. But the uncertainties of the war made this impossible. Even if she had been willing to try to make the long journey, more difficult because of wartime shipping restrictions, Arthur could not ask her, because he did not know how long he would be in India. He could only look forward to better times ahead. "I hope I will be able to take a long holiday with my darling sweetheart when this war ends. You must visit my home at Ballymoyer. It would have been better if we had gone to Ballymoyer from Hong Kong at that time. I wish I could show it to you."[6] He still had not completely ruled out her coming to live in Ireland, and it was his younger brother Ronald, interested because he would have liked to take over Ballymoyer himself, who reopened the question. "My brother wrote asking what my plan is once the war ends. He wanted to know if I am going to live at Ballymoyer or in the Far East. It will be good if you can come with me to Ballymoyer. It is a difficult question. I think it will be best for me to leave the army after the war but I cannot decide now."[7] At other times, Arthur grew despondent about the burden and responsibility of the house. The estate agents had still not found a tenant. "Ballymoyer is all right but it is difficult to find anyone to rent it. The house is very big, so it needs to be someone who is well off. I wish Ballymoyer was not mine, it is a white elephant."[8] He blithely translated vernacular English expressions straight into literal Japanese, so when he wrote the Japanese words for white, *shiroi,* and elephant, *zo,* Masa may have wondered what he meant: the expression made no sense in Japanese.

Arthur wrote to Masa about the humdrum daily round, but he could not articulate his deeper feelings about the war, or any guilt he felt for not being there. Several times a week, he rode the three miles to Simla, along a narrow bridle track with wild roses growing along the banks, to call at the block of offices south of the mall, which housed the chief of the General Staff for the summer months. Army Headquarters, India, was connected to the War Office signals system, and it was possible to get the latest war news from the official telegrams and the daily casualty lists. With a growing sense of gloom, he saw how the war was snatching the lives of so many of his friends and contemporaries. Major Charles Yate, who had arrived in Tokyo in the same group of language officers as Arthur, died in September 1914 after winning the Victoria Cross for bravery at Le Cateau. The first casualty among the Hart cousins was William, one of the twins, killed on the first day of the landing at Tanga, in German East Africa. Arthur's old Burma regiment, the 2nd Battalion of the East Surreys, reached France in January 1915 and moved up to the front in the Ypres sector almost immediately. A and C companies, which Arthur knew well, were almost annihilated within a couple of days of arriving, and after five days only two hundred survived of the thousand men who had just disembarked at the end of the long journey from Shwebo. Then he learnt that his other twin cousin, Laurence, had been killed in Flanders. Over the summer,

Cousin Norman was wounded in the knee in France and Reginald was hit in the shoulder at the Dardanelles. "This war is terrible. Many of my regiment have been killed. The Germans are worse than savages. They are inhuman to use poison gas. I wish I could go to the front but I have not been called for."[9]

Arthur asked to be sent back to Europe, but the army maintained he was doing too important a job in India to be released. "Last night I received your letter number 52. You were worried about the war, and said a lot about it, and when you wrote you did not know if I was going to be called to the fighting or not. Now I have to tell you. I very much want to go, but the government has so far refused my application. I don't know if I will be called later or not. If I am, I will let you know as soon I hear."[10] He did not try to justify or defend his feelings. "You say you are glad that I am not at the front fighting, but as I am a military man I wish I could go."[11] "I would be so happy if the war was over. It is worse for me, because I cannot even take part in it, though I know you don't agree with me on this."[12]

His uncle General Sir Reginald, who had been trapped in India himself during the Boer War, undoubtedly sympathized with him, as did the other Hart men. But his spirited sister-in-law, Violet, took an independent line. "I am still so glad you have not gone to the war, although I am very sorry you are disappointed. And I am sure Peachblossom is delighted too and I really do hope they will keep you in India and you must be doing lots of splendid work there."[13]

The nearest Arthur came to being a casualty came when he fell off a motorcycle and damaged his hand. "Don't worry, it was caused by a dog jumping out in front."[14] He tried to be as philosophical as he could. "More of my fellow officers have died. I have just read the telegrams and found four have been killed and three are casualties. One of the dead was my friend Major Patterson. I feel very sad. I don't know how many of my friends have died in this terrible war. If I had gone to the front I could have died, too. So I must not complain even if I want to join the fighting. There is a Persian proverb:

'A live dog is better than a dead lion.' I often think about this saying when I feel sorry not to be fighting."[15]

In Tokyo, Masa was now less concerned about Arthur's military agonizing than she was about their younger son, Hideo, whose stomach pains and fevers continued through the summer months. Arthur tried to allay her worries. "I am sure he will be better soon. Peritonitis is not a common illness for a child. I feel very sorry for him."[16] In August he was still asking, "How is little Hideo? I pray for his quick recovery."[17] At Arthur's encouragement she took the boy to the Tokyo University Hospital, where X-rays were available. He was a little better in September, by which time Arthur was back in Lahore, but then had a relapse. Hideo was now pale and feverish, and in great pain. His stomach was inflamed, and his liver and other functions were soon affected by the infection. He died in the middle of December. Masa wrote to India to break the news, and heard back from Arthur in February 1916. He had seen Hideo only three times, and the child was not a fully formed character in his mind, as Kiyoshi had become. There was little he could really say. "I received your number 126. It was a very upsetting letter, with the news of the death of Hideo. I am very, very sad. You had been nursing him so carefully and he was getting better. Why did he suddenly take a turn for the worse? I feel so sorry for you. I was not able to help because I am so far away and that makes me even sadder. I wish I could be near you. I cannot write anymore as I am so upset. To you, darling, darling Dolly, from sad Arthur."[18] It was at moments like this that the limits of Arthur's Japanese must have added to his feeling of inadequacy. He could not do justice to the seriousness of the moment for Masa, who was putting up with so much for him, or really address the unequal nature of the relationship. A few weeks later, he hinted at this. "I am so grateful for your kindness in writing when you were so distressed. Kiyoshi must feel the loss, too. I wish I could

tell you how I feel, but it is too difficult to explain."[19] Once more
Masa had to rely on her mother and brothers for support. Her family dealt with the cremation arrangements, just as they had helped
when the children were born. Arthur was sorry about Hideo because Masa was upset. He did not appear to mourn the child for
himself. He never mentioned him in his letters again.

I n the summer of 1916, Arthur was at the small hill station at Dalhousie, 6,600 feet above sea level, having ridden the last fifty
miles up from the nearest railway on his motorcycle. If Simla had
been away from the center of things, Dalhousie was even more
remote, a small settlement of bungalows and houses with fretted
wooden eaves and verandas, a little bit of suburban England perched
on the edge of the Himalayan range. After six days of work at the
summer headquarters, it was possible to get even farther away.
"Last Sunday, very early, I went across the hills with an Indian
guide. We walked for three hours and came to a beautiful valley.
There were many water mills in the valley and the going was quite
hard. We did some fishing and caught forty fish with a net. The
place was wonderful, full of figs and strawberries."[20] As he looked
out over the snowy peaks, which stretched to the west towards Ti-
bet, the feeling that he was on the sidelines, an uninvolved specta-
tor, while the world he had known was being torn apart thousands
of miles away, must have been even sharper, and brought a continuing sense that he was not serving his country as he should be.

The news from Europe was increasingly grim. Even Ireland was
in turmoil, after the Easter rising in Dublin, when armed nationalists seized the post office, and the army had to fight in the city center for five days to reestablish control. In June came news of the
greatest modern sea battle fought until then, entailing the loss of
6,000 British sailors in a few hours at Jutland. With the relentless
German assault on the French at Verdun, the charnel fields of the

Western front had reached a new level of horror. Then, at the end of July, when Arthur was walking in the valleys and cedar woods around Dalhousie, the British Army launched its own long-expected offensive on the Somme, and 20,000 British soldiers were killed on the first day alone. Arthur again told Masa that he wished he could be sent to the war, but knew he should be grateful he was alive.

By this time, British officers were being killed so quickly that those who managed to survive soon found themselves rapidly promoted. Arthur heard that Roundell Toke, who had been with him in Tokyo and had spent so much time at their house in Juniso with Oharu-san, was already a lieutenant colonel. "My colleagues are being promoted quickly while I remain here. I would have been promoted to major general by now if I was at the front and had not been killed."[21] As a professional soldier, he was impatient to be with the lions. In October, shortly after coming down to Lahore from the hills, he at last received the order he was hoping for, to return to Europe. After the safety of India, the war became more real once his ship passed through Suez, and passengers were told to wear their life belts at all times and sleep in their clothes in case of a torpedo attack. "Darling, darling, a destroyer has been escorting us for the past three days and at about 4:30 her guns fired. I was having tea but went to look. A German submarine had fired a torpedo at a cargo ship close to us. The cargo ship was sinking and the crew took to the lifeboats and were rescued by the destroyer. I don't know why our ship was not hit. It was very close. Tomorrow we will be arriving in Marseilles and I can post this letter."[22] Had Arthur come back a few months later, he would have had the experience, which nearly 700,000 British and empire troops shared, of being accompanied through the Mediterranean by the Japanese Navy. With German and Austrian submarines taking a high toll, London asked its Japanese ally to help. The Imperial Navy had already taken over patrols in the Indian Ocean east of Colombo, and was accompanying troopships from New Zealand and Australia across the Pacific. From

early 1917, Japanese warships were based in Malta, and took over
Mediterranean escort duties from the British. The squadron eventually rose to seventeen destroyers and cruisers, and when the destroyer *Sakaki* was torpedoed by an Austrian U-boat, sixty-eight
Japanese sailors lost their lives off Crete.

W hen Arthur reached London he found a worn city, enduring food shortages and restrictions quite different from the
comfortable life that continued for the British in wartime India. In
their own effort to play their part, his two sisters had gone to work
in a car factory. The parks were dug up for allotments, and German
zeppelins had made the first bombing raids over South London. He
stayed at the Army and Navy Club, close to the hub of buildings
around Whitehall and Trafalgar Square, from which the war effort
was being run. The Admiralty, the army, and the huge new Ministry
of Munitions had all expanded rapidly, drafting in thousands of new
staff and taking over hotels, clubs, and nearby offices to make room
for them. Rows of temporary huts filled the embankment gardens
along the River Thames.

Arthur reported to the new War Office, which he had first
known in its hushed grandeur just after it opened, when he had
made several visits to the Asian section to try to get sent back to
Japan. The bustle of officers and visitors in the central hall, under the
great dome, now gave the feeling of a busy railway station. Older
men had come back from the reserve list to allow younger staff officers to leave for the front, and Boy Scouts acted as messengers.
Women typists and telegraph operators were packed into parti-
tioned offices. Up on the flat roof, behind the sculptures symbolizing
Peace and War, Fame and Victory, more officials were accommo-
dated in a row of wooden sheds known as Zeppelin Terrace. In a
vain attempt to provide reassurance, a cat's cradle of netting had
been strung above the roof, to catch any bombs tossed from Ger-

man airships. Arthur reported to the military secretary's department and was told he could have two weeks' leave and would then be sent to France, though the detailed order had not come through yet. "I don't know for certain but I think I will be a staff officer. I will let you know when I find out more. Please send your letters to this address and they will forward them."[23]

Major a. Hart-Synnot
c/o
Messr. Cox & Co.
16. Charing Cross
London
England

Arthur had no time to go back to Ballymoyer. He spent his last few days getting himself equipped and seeing his family in London. He bought warm boots, and a new khaki overcoat, which he told Masa had cost forty-seven yen. He assured her the financial arrangements would continue. "I went to the Chartered Bank and told them to send the money to the Specie Bank in Yokohama. When the transfer comes, your bank will notify you. . . . I think this way is better as it will be very difficult to send money from the front. I am going to write my will before I leave for France. If I die in action I will leave you 10,000 yen. I have already told my brother. When the will is finished I will send you one copy, the other will be left at my bank. It is hard for me to write about this sort of thing but it has to be done in this situation."[24] He had not seen his family for five years, and by now they accepted his commitment to Masa. Beatrice agreed to forward his letters on to Tokyo. He saw his brother Ronald, and his sister-in-law, Violet, who had probably brought Ronald round to the idea of the Japanese girl she was so fascinated by. "They asked many questions about you. They said, 'Why didn't you get married? If you had, you could have spent three years in India together.' They thought it was a pity, and I agreed."[25] He saw his cousin Norman, who sent messages to Masa. Though his situation was better understood than on his visits in 1906 and 1911, Arthur still had not told them about Kiyoshi.

He waited for the movement order to come through, and wrote letters every day in his club. On 28 December, he learnt that he would be leaving on 1 January. "I cannot tell you how much I have been thinking about you. You will be very worried as I am going to the front. But, darling, I will be all right. I will be very careful for your sake. If I am injured my brother will write to you. But I am sure everything will be fine. Goodbye, from Arthur, to my darling, darling Dolly."[26]

EIGHT

FORGET-ME-NOT
FROM ARRAS

When we get together again I will never let you go,
even if you beg and cry. My darling is my prisoner
and you will never be able to escape from me.
· A.H.-S., March 1917[1] ·

The letters Arthur wrote from January 1917 onwards became a kind of war diary, an account of the horrors of mechanized war, written from the trenches on handmade *makigami* paper that would have been familiar to samurai in the seventeenth century, in the many-stroked Japanese characters he could now write so beautifully. He had not seen Masa for over three years, but she was still at the center of his life, the person around whom all his future plans would turn. He joined the 17th Division on the Picardy plateau, the undulating chalk land north of the Somme River, where the front-line trenches came down from Flanders to cross the Somme Valley, and where the British sector ended and the French carried on to the south towards Verdun. Before the war this had been an open countryside of wide horizons, immense fields of corn and sugar beet broken by patches of ancient woodland, and compact villages with orchards and red-tiled houses clustered around a church. By the time Arthur reached it, most of the villages were heaps of debris, the fields were pitted by shell fire and seamed by half-obliterated trench lines, and the ground was so broken and disturbed that the topsoil was gone and the limestone substratum exposed. Huge mine craters added to the sense of a lunar landscape. The Manchurian battlefields had never looked like this. At the cost of hundreds of thousands of lives shed in the previous summer and autumn, the British line had edged forward a few miles to the east. The division Arthur was joining was made up of regiments from Lancashire, Yorkshire, and Northumberland, and was at the most advanced point of the previous year's battlefield, on the crest looking towards the German strongpoint of Bapaume.

In his first letters, Arthur was conscious of the strict censorship rules, and gave Masa little detail. On 5 January, he wrote from his bunker in Arrowhead Copse. "Darling, darling, I am sending you my first letter from the war. I left on New Year's Day and received your first letter of the year. I found many lovely things inside your packet. Thank you for the beautiful handkerchiefs and the Japanese textbook. I brought it with me and will use it. I left London on New Year's Day and reached this place on the night of the 3rd. I cannot tell you where I am but it is inside the fighting zone. It is extremely noisy with the sound of the artillery firing day and night but I will get used to it in a few days. As I cannot write about the war this will not be very long, but I will send you a short letter whenever I can. It will set your mind at rest. It is cold here, and has been raining heavily. I am thinking about you all the time. I will be with you when this horrible war is over. Please give my greetings to your mother and little Kiyoshi. With love to my own little darling, goodbye from lonely Arthur."[2] After a few days, they were pulled back ten miles and others took over their section.

Divisional headquarters were now in the small town of Corbie, at the fork of the Somme and its tributary the Ancre, and lines of trucks and horse-drawn wagons passed up the battered main street taking food and supplies to the front. Arthur was able to buy a paraffin stove to try and keep warm, in the most severe winter of the war. "It is terrible to come suddenly to such a cold place from a hot country but I will manage as I am fit. I had some photographs taken before I left England. Three were good so I have asked Beatrice to send them to you. Your old photographs have traveled with me for hundreds of thousands of miles. They are getting frail, so I would like another small picture."[3] Because the army postal service would not accept mail for Japan, his sister Beatrice acted as go-between and forwarded his letters to Masa. For all his time in France, he sent his letters first to Woodbridge in Suffolk, where Beatrice was now working as a driver, and she sent them on to Japan by registered mail. "I am billeted in the upstairs of a little shop. I can sleep well because there is a good bed and the people are very polite. I am speaking French a lot. I have not used it for a long time but it has improved. I am glad you and the others are well. I wish this terrible war would be over soon. Everywhere you go at the front there are graveyards for the dead. It is a terrible sight. Last night snow started to fall and now it is six inches deep. The roads are all frozen hard and it is very cold, but please don't worry, I am well. I cannot write about the war. I think about my darling every day and I have my darling's photographs with me all the time."[4]

The prewar regular-army officers of Arthur's generation who had managed to survive to 1917 were by now experienced veterans of the type of fighting imposed by the Western front. The tactics and equipment of the South African war, or even the British Expeditionary Force of 1914, had long since been superseded. Arthur was coming in two and a half years late, joining men who had survived the worst days of 1914, the first battle of Ypres, and the Somme, and younger officers who had never known the prewar army at all. He had to learn about the planning of night attacks, the use of poison gas, trench mortars, and the fine timing of artillery barrages. He told Masa, "So far everything is new and interesting to me,"[5] and a week later, "I don't know what I shall be asked to do but I will be here about a month. I am new to this war, but I will pick everything up in a month."[6]

At the beginning of February, the division was conducting a series of small operations north of the River Ancre. Just as in Hong Kong and Burma, Arthur added to his weekly letter to Masa each day. "3rd. Here it is very cold and there has been frost for the past seventeen days. Everything is stone hard. It looks like the North Pole, covered in snow. Last night was a beautiful moonlit night so I went out to visit the front line. The enemy was only 140 feet away, very close, so it is very dangerous. We can only move at night, and we wear steel helmets and take a gas mask. 4th. One of our aircraft crashed close by, but luckily the pilots were saved. It was hit by enemy gunfire and is lying on the snow. There is nothing interesting to write, but as I have time I will write every day. 7th. Last night the temperature went down to minus 5 or 6 and it is incredibly cold because of the north wind. Now I am writing in a bunker 35 feet below the ground. Even though we are so far below the surface we still feel the whole earth shaking when the shells come in. 8th. Today is Thursday so I shall send this letter off to you. We were in a battle early this morning and we won. We captured over 70 Germans. It is not over yet and the shooting is still going on."[7] Soon after reaching France, he was promoted to lieutenant colonel. "You must write Colonel instead of Major from now on. Do not laugh. As it has taken such a long time to be a colonel, it may not be long before I am a general."[8] As a staff officer, Arthur was seldom in the front line, but he was going forward to visit the brigade and battalion headquarters and was well within range of the German guns. "Yesterday I was lucky. An enemy shell fell right beside me. We all throw ourselves down on the ground when that happens. It exploded twelve feet from where I was. It took me by surprise. I was half buried in earth and my ear felt blocked from the pressure of the sound but fortunately I was not hurt at all."[9]

For a few weeks in March, Arthur and the British Third Army

had a new and rare experience for the Great War. By now it was generally assumed that every yard would have to be fought for, in a war of attrition, but suddenly they found themselves moving forward, unopposed. The enemy were withdrawing, leaving a devastated countryside behind them, burnt barns, destroyed orchards, poisoned wells, torn-up railway tracks, flattened villages, blown bridges. "The Germans are completely inhuman, they are devils. I saw horrible scenes in the places they had abandoned."[10] In four days the Germans pulled back about twenty miles, in a brilliantly executed retreat to the better-constructed and fortified trenches they had been preparing over the winter known as the Hindenburg Line. By eliminating a D-shaped bulge, they now had a shorter length of front to defend, and more guns and men to deploy along it. "The enemy is withdrawing and we are advancing but the road and railways are all destroyed, so it is slow progress repairing them as we go. I went up to the front. It was terrible. Whole villages were demolished. The place looked like a desert, and there were piles of dead soldiers' bodies. It was a truly horrible scene. War is stupid, isn't it? It is very sad to see the loss of so many lives."[11]

At least there was movement, though on German terms, and for the first time since the disasters of 1916 there seemed some cause for Allied optimism. The United States was expected to enter the war at any moment, provoked by a German decision to lift restrictions that had held their submarines back from attacking "neutral" shipping. On 6 April, President Wilson finally announced the American entry, bringing an immediate lift to Allied morale. There now seemed a better chance that the war might end sooner rather than later. Arthur also knew, though he could not write it to Masa, that a bold new offensive was about to start, which he and his fellow staff officers were busy planning. "It will be so good if this war is over soon. When we get together again I will never let you go, even if you beg and cry. My darling is my prisoner and you will never be able to escape from me."[12]

. . .

Masa received these letters in a Tokyo that was hearing little about the war in Europe. Her own ignorance of the geography of northern France and Belgium, and the vagueness of Arthur's letters as he followed the censor's rules, meant she had little sense of where he was or the context of the fighting he described. Since Hideo's death her mother had been living with her. Masa continued with her sewing and embroidery, making small presents for Arthur and sending off a cushion, small Japanese towels, and an embroidered pouch, along with the wooden ear-picks he liked. She queued to buy special commemorative postage stamps for his sister Beatrice, and sent new photographs of herself. Arthur asked for an English-Japanese dictionary. "I did not bring mine with me as it is so big and I sent it to Ballymoyer. I only brought our Japanese-English dictionary with me. I would like to write something about the fighting sometimes, but because the words are not everyday words I forget them. There are lots of new things in this war and I would like to tell you about them, but it is very difficult for me."

Masa had one major worry. Her money was running low, because the arrangements for Arthur's regular transfers did not work. The quarterly payment of 150 yen, or $75, due at the beginning of December 1916 did not arrive, nor did the payment for March 1917. She made trips to Yokohama to question the bank and wrote to Arthur, but the letters were taking so long to reach him that it was only in March he found out about the problem. During the German withdrawal, as he rode forward across the devastated countryside, it was Masa's money that was on his mind. "I have had a letter from my bank and will enclose it. It says they sent the money to your Yokohama Specie Bank, but the Yokohama branch was told that you did not have an account. I don't understand why your bank does not know your name. I wrote to my bank in London and asked them to send the money and wrote your name in Japanese."[13] To explain the difficulty, Arthur sent her the letter from London.

DAL

All letters to be addressed to the
CHARTERED BANK OF INDIA AUSTRALIA & CHINA
TELEGRAPHIC ADDRESS
PIGTAIL-LED LONDON
TELEPHONE N° LONDON WALL
4925 (4 LINES)

Chartered Bank of India, Australia & China.

38. Bishopsgate.

London, E.C. **2nd March** *19*17

Major A. Hart-Synnot,

    Headquarters,

        17th Division, B.E.F.

Dear Sir,

    On 6th December last we remitted Yen 150. at your request to our Yokohama Office for payment to the Yokohama Specie Bank, Ltd, Tokio on account of M. Suzuki.

    We are now informed by our Yokohama Manager that the Yokohama Specie Bank Ltd, are unable to trace Mr. M. Suzuki We shall be glad if you can let us have his address so that the money may be paid over to him.

        Yours faithfully,

        p. Manager.

The problem had occurred before, from Lahore, when the banking system had found it hard to acknowledge that a single woman might be receiving international transfers. Arthur was full of remorse. "I thought I had done everything possible to make things easy for you before I left. I am sorry if I did not do well and I apologize. It is not my fault. You will have a problem with the delay, but it must reach you in the end. Everything is difficult because of this war."[14] By June, Masa's money was finally sorted out, and Arthur wrote to her, "Yesterday I received the receipt for 300 yen which you signed at the bank in Tokyo. You signed it in English letters. Looking at it, I thought how happy I would have been if your signature was Masa Hart-Synnot."[15] Masa had another concern. Kiyoshi was being teased in school again, and she and her brother Yokichi decided to move him to the elementary section of a private school in Kojimachi, near the Officers' Club and close to her brother's barbershop. The Gyosei School was used by better-off families in western Tokyo, and had some foreign children, so Kiyoshi would be less of a curiosity. When he was told, Arthur agreed to pay the fees. Masa encouraged Kiyoshi to write regular letters to his father, which she enclosed with her own. He gave Arthur news of his new school and said he now needed a watch.

Since they had parted in September 1913, Arthur had written Masa more than 200 letters and Masa had sent 180 in the other direction. With German submarines hunting in the Atlantic and the Mediterranean, and the loss of many ships carrying mail, Japanese post was now being sent by a slightly safer route, round South Africa and the Cape, which meant Masa's narrow white envelopes could take eighty days to get from Kashiwagi to Picardy. Arthur still logged the numbers meticulously and realized that some of the letters that were so precious to him had been lost to enemy action. "Darling, darling, I received your number 199 and 200 today. How happy I am to have them after eighteen days with no letters. Thank you for checking your notebook. Out of the letters you have sent since 29 October last year, I have not received 175, 178, 180, 182, 183, and 192. The rest have all arrived safely up to 200."[16] Arthur was saving money. In the brown Army Field Service notebook he used for his jottings and accounts, he listed his expenditure on haircuts, pipe tobacco, and chocolate, and his winnings and losses at bridge in the mess. He told

Masa that he had spent less than ten pounds since arriving in France, and everything else had been put aside, which would help them after the war. "Now I am a colonel my pension will be twice as big. This is good, don't you think?"[17] He looked at the prospect of further promotion with the same eye to the future. "If I become a general my salary will be 1,000 yen a month and I will be very well off."[18]

Arthur wrote a rather stiff letter to his son, trying to limit himself to the simple characters a ten-year-old would have learnt. "The other day I received a letter from you. Thank you very much. I was very pleased to have it. I am now fighting in the war. It is very different from India. It is cold here. I cannot go to Japan because of this horrible war but I will return when the war is over. You must take care of your mother for me as your father is away. Shall I bring you some souvenirs of the fighting when I come? Goodbye, to Kiyoshi, from Father."[19] His son persisted over the watch and suggested how it might be acquired. "Thank you for the letter from Kiyoshi. I shall reply to it. I will buy him a watch when I go to England again. I cannot take a watch from a German soldier."[20] Kiyoshi, who must have drawn some prestige at school from having a father fighting in France, kept on about the watch, and made another request. "I also received a letter from Kiyoshi. Thank you. When I return to England I will buy him a watch. I cannot take it from a prisoner."[21] Later in the year, Kiyoshi was still asking, and Arthur's hard line on looting almost wavered. "On my leave I will buy Kiyoshi a watch. We confiscated many watches from the German prisoners but I did not see any good ones. In any case, I cannot take prisoners' possessions."[22]

With an offensive planned for April, Arthur was not able to take leave that was due to him. "I still don't know if I can have my ten days next month or not. I do not care, as I have no one waiting for me. If you were in England I would go back as fast as I could. To be honest, I don't mind whether I can or not, as you are not there."[23] In May, he finally managed to get back to Armagh for the first time since his mother's death. "I took the train and the boat and went up to Ballymoyer in our carriage. The Irish countryside is very beautiful at this time of the year. It looked wonderful and I am also pleased that everything was all right in the house."[24] The gardener and his wife were acting as caretakers, but it was not worth opening up the house, so Arthur collected his summer clothes and stayed with an aunt. He saw the steward about the farm, which was doing a little better with the higher wartime prices for corn and potatoes.

Fresh from his brief home leave, and with better weather, Arthur seemed more optimistic. "I don't know when the war is going to end but there is good news from all sides. The enemy are losing everywhere."[25] He had asked to be released from being a staff officer, and to get a command of his own. "I am well and I am glad you and the others are well too. I am still with the division, but I am going to be a colonel in charge of a battalion soon, and after a month or two I will be a general. We are fighting well, and the Germans always lose. If this war ends, it will be good for the whole world. When we get together after the war I will never let you go again. I will take you with me everywhere I go. I cannot tell you how much I miss you. Please give my greetings to your mother and little Kiyoshi. With love to my own little darling. Goodbye, from lonely Arthur."[26] "My guess is that the war may be over by the end of the year."[27] He sent her more summer flowers, pressed between pieces of the silver paper from his chocolate wrappers. "Goodbye from lonely Arthur, to my darling Dolly. P.S. Do you know the name of this flower? It is called a forget-me-not. Please listen to the flower."[28]

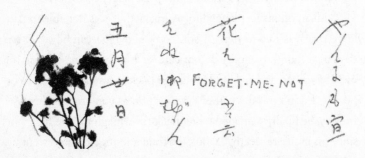

At the end of June, Arthur was transferred to the 42nd Division and given command of the 1/4th Battalion of the East Lancashire Regiment, part of a brigade from Manchester and the mill towns of Lancashire. When he took over, they were in Havrincourt Wood, facing the massive barbed-wire entanglements of the Hindenburg Line southwest of Cambrai, and he was now more exposed to danger. "From the night of the 3rd to the 8th we were in the front trenches. As I had to be on duty day and night, I did not have much sleep, just one or two hours. It was exhausting. We were in a large forest, and there was continuous noise from shells coming in day and night. But I am fine. The enemy used poison gas on us twice."[29] With many of his men suffering from the cloud of mixed tear gas and phosgene that the Germans had released on them, the brigade then went back to a training area to the west. Arthur confided to Masa that the general thought his battalion were no good at maneuvering. "He is right. Both the officers and the soldiers are new and they do not know anything, but they are all good people. So I shall work hard to make them into a fine battalion. They have already improved, in just a week."[30]

Arthur was now more professionally fulfilled, doing the work he had been trained to do. In his letters to Masa he was as cheerful as he could be in the circumstances, but the war was continuing to take its toll, and he knew the risks and the dangers. Most of his contemporaries from Sandhurst, and from the East Surreys, and many he had fought beside in South Africa, had been killed. In the middle of June, Arthur had heard that his old commanding officer and golf partner from Hong Kong, General Robert Broadwood, had been a casualty north of Armentières. The charming and approachable bachelor general, who knew about Masa and had helped rescue Arthur from Burma, had left the army in 1913. He had come back from retirement in 1916 to command a division, at the age of fifty-five, but his voluntary return to action was soured when his corps commander criticized him for declining to launch his troops in attacks that had no chance of success and for showing "a lack of fighting spirit." He felt the imputation deeply, and was so distressed that he may have taken an unnecessary risk. Making an inspection of his division's gun positions, he was crossing an exposed railway bridge two thousand yards behind the front line when the Germans started to shell it. The colonel who was beside him was killed immediately. Broadwood was severely wounded and was left on the bridge while the shelling continued, losing blood rapidly, both his thighs broken. He died in a casualty clearing station three hours later.

The pattern of months of defensive fighting punctuated by carefully prepared offensives continued, each new offensive failing to bring the gains expected of it. The April assault on Arras and the Hindenburg Line, which Arthur had helped plan, began with great hopes but incurred mounting casualties. In the House of Commons, MPs led by Winston Churchill argued it was better to wait for the arrival of American troops than to squander the remaining armies of Britain and France in the meantime, but the attacks were renewed. Later that summer, the British commander, Field Marshal Sir Douglas Haig, launched another major operation, to the north in Flanders. The plan was for the Fifth Army to break through where the line looped east in what was known as the Ypres salient, strike up to the Belgian coast, and clear the German U-boat bases, which were still wreaking havoc with shipping in the English Channel. The main offensive opened at the end of July, with an artillery barrage greater than that of the previous year on the Somme, but the planned schedule and targets for each day were soon seen to be hopelessly unrealistic. Instead of a bold breakout, the campaign became a struggle for control of low-lying land that had been fought over several times since 1914, and included several villages rising up to Passchendaele. Rain started to fall, turning the ground, already pockmarked with shell craters, into a wasteland of muddy pools. The initial artillery bombardment had broken what remained of the natural drainage system, and as torrential rain continued to fall, the whole Ypres battlefield became an oozing swamp, spreading in area with each day.

In the same summer downpours, but in a rear area fifty miles to the south, Arthur worked up his battalion with classes in the rapid laying of barbed wire, bayonet fighting, and throwing the Mills hand grenade, which had to be hurled as great a distance as possible so the bursting iron fragments did not hit the user. They rehearsed trench-to-trench attacks and held a realistic exercise in which troops advanced close to a creeping barrage with live shells. The weather was hot and humid when it was not raining. Arthur knew where they were headed, and the sound of the continuing battle in Flanders could be heard during the pauses in their own training. Arthur had fallen out with his brigadier general and again confided in Masa. "The men are much improved but I do not like the work I am doing now. The battalion is fine but the brigadier general is very unpleasant. I cannot stand him for long. Now I wish I was still a staff officer. It was unfortunate that I had to join the brigade of such an awful man. I have lots of work to do, I work from morning till night, there is no time to do anything else, it's the life of a slave."[31]

Long before Arthur and the battalion were ordered north to Flanders, the Ypres offensive had failed. The commander of the Fifth Army, General Gough, told Haig in the middle of August that success was out of the question and the attack should be abandoned, but Haig insisted that it carry on. The campaign officially referred to as the "third battle of Ypres" would be known simply as "Passchendaele," the village on the ridge which was the objective for so many months. Passchendaele came to symbolize all the worst horrors of the Great War, and trench warfare at its most grotesque. With the exceptionally wet weather, roads and paths disappeared, and troops could not move except across wooden duckboards. Guns had no solid base to fire from. Horses, mules, and men were sucked into the mud. It could take sixteen men to bring back the wounded on stretchers. The offensive was continued only because it was believed to be wearing down the Germans more than the British and French.

At the end of August, Arthur's brigade was once again loaded into railway wagons, each one designated for forty men or eight horses, and taken up on a slow, jolting journey to join the battle in the swamp. They left the train at Proven, and stayed in a tented camp in the support area just behind the front, an industrial hinterland of ammunition dumps, military light railways, artillery repair shops, and Royal Flying Corps airfields. Arthur knew he was about to face his greatest ordeal so far, and tried to stop Masa from worrying, but the fact that she would not receive his reassurances for another two months, by which time he might be dead, made the effort unrealistic.

"26 August. Now I am in Belgium. We came north but we will be moving up to the front in a few days. Don't worry, I am all right. I think of you when I go to bed, hoping to see you in my dreams. 27th. It started to rain again last night and everywhere is a sea of mud. It is horrible, and a little colder. We are about twenty miles from the coast here. 28th. There was a storm last night and it rained heavily and it is still raining. This morning we received the order to go forward so we will be leaving here. It may be difficult to have time to write even a short letter, but I will if it is at all possible. Darling, do not worry. I carry my darling's photographs in my breast pocket, next to my heart, always. They are with me when I am fighting." On 30 August, they reached the remains of the medieval cloth town of Ypres, long since evacuated by civilians. As they marched into the ruins, every building flattened by the incessant shell fire, they passed the rectangles of rough ground fenced off as temporary graveyards. One of them contained the remains of Colonel Everard Calthrop, the former language officer and military attaché in Tokyo. After the joint Anglo-Japanese operation at Tsingtao, Calthrop, whose career had run in parallel to Arthur's but who had always seemed to be one step ahead, had managed to get himself released to go to the war in Europe. He had made the long journey back to rejoin the Royal Field Artillery in Flanders in 1915. When he arrived at Ypres, he carried a Japanese sword into action with him. Within a few days he was killed by a shell. In his memory, his mother gave his sword to the Japanese officers' training school in Tokyo.

On the night of 10 September 1917, Colonel Hart-Synnot and the 1/4th East Lancashires made their way out along the cratered road towards Menin, past Hellfire Corner. They moved on to perilous duckboard tracks, crossing the ooze where Belgian cows had once grazed on lush fields, and took over a section of devastated woodland from a battalion that was going to the rear. They were next to a railway line. The deafening roar from heavy German and British shelling carried on twenty-four hours a day, flares fizzled into the wet sky, and on days when there was a slight improvement in the weather air battles raged overhead. They stayed in the railway wood, among the charred and splintered trees, as working parties tried to shore up the underground shelters dug among the tangle of tree roots. Arthur's battalion managed to advance a short distance, consolidated their position by building a new trench, and captured a point known as Sans Souci. Because of the intensity of the shelling it became hard to get supplies up to them, and they ran short of food and ammunition. After enduring five days of this nightmare, with mud clogging their clothing, packs, and rifles, they were relieved and returned to the camp at Brandhoek, which offered baths, a cinema, and football grounds. It was, by the standards of Passchendaele, an easy turn, with only a few casualties sustained. Arthur wrote, "Darling, darling, I came back from the front line yesterday. I am fine, but I am exhausted. I went through hell on the nights of 6th and 7th and I am worn out. The continuous roar of the guns gets on your nerves. I wanted to tell you I am all right."[32]

Arthur could now have expected a few weeks in the reserve lines, but he was moved at short notice to another command. "The day before yesterday I received a telegram and I have to join another division, so I left and came here yesterday. It is a very good battalion, but I have to go back to the front with them without a rest. That is a pity, isn't it?"[33] He was now with the 29th Division, as commanding officer of the 1st Battalion of the Lancashire Fusiliers, a battle-hardened unit who were to play an important role in the next phase, a renewed series of attacks along an extended section of the front towards the village of Passchendaele. This was to be Arthur's first coordinated attack, with men he trusted, and part of an offensive that became known as the battle of Poelcapelle. Between meetings with his officers, and with orders streaming in from the brigade, he found time to write to Masa on 6 October from his headquarters. "A major battle is starting. The enemy is losing everywhere. My battalion is fighting so I shall not have time to write once I get to the front. Please do not worry as I am fine."[34] Though he had no idea what would happen over the next forty-eight hours, he looked ahead to the days after the war. "I want to do the best thing when the war ends. I don't know when I can quit the army, but if I don't I would like to go back to India. But if you want, I will quit. Let us talk about it when the war ends. If I go back to India I will come to fetch you. I cannot bear to be apart anymore."[35]

Having written to Masa in Japanese, the colonel changed back to English and completed the operational orders for the attack that was about to begin, setting out the plan crisply. "The attack will be made in three bounds. First bound to the GREEN DOTTED LINE, second bound to the BLUE DOTTED LINE, third bound to the GREEN LINE." In well-rehearsed and familiar tactics, the different companies would leapfrog their way forward. "At ZERO hour the whole battalion will move as close to the Barrage as possible, maintaining the interval between lines and waves. . . . The Barrage will rest in front of the first objective from ZERO and 40 minutes to ZERO plus 1 hour and 46 minutes, and C and D companies will pass through A and B companies as soon as possible after the Barrage halts. When the Barrage begins to creep, C and D companies will advance and will capture and consolidate the second objective."[36]

Similar sets of detailed orders were being issued to troops all along the six-mile breadth of the attack, and as ever the textbook clarity of the plan lost much in the execution. Their sector was northeast of Langemarck, where the German and British lines made a sharp bend. Rain had continued during the day, and by the evening the ground was wet and slippery. Once night fell, the battalion's intelligence officer laid out white tapes to show the positions on which the four companies were to form up. Work was slow because of the mud underfoot. There was no moon, and several platoons became lost while looking for the tapes on the churned-up ground, in the pitch-darkness. German shelling continued throughout the night, lighting up the base of the low cloud with flashes.

Just before dawn the division's own artillery began firing, and the 1st Battalion moved forward at five-twenty a.m., making their way around water-filled shell holes and over the sticky clay behind the acrid smoke and blast of the creeping barrage. For nearly four hours, Arthur followed the attack from his headquarters in a ruined farm building, as ground was gained and prisoners and wounded were brought back. Confused reports came in from his four companies as the enemy attempted counterattacks. With a stream of lethal machine-gun fire coming from one pillbox, Sergeant Joseph Lister rushed it ahead of his men, shouting to the Germans inside to surrender. Only one refused, and Lister shot him dead. Within a few moments, about a hundred Germans emerged and gave themselves up. The companies drifted away from their original objectives, and the battalions on each side became intermingled. The regiment's official history described the confusion. "From now on the operations were continued by the individual initiative and leadership of junior officers and N.C.O.s who gathered round them small groups of soldiers, regardless of their regiment, and did their best to push on."[37] They reached their target successfully, Arthur recommended five of his officers for the Military Cross, and Sergeant Lister won the Victoria Cross.

As soon as they had been relieved, and were back at Elverdinghe Camp, Arthur wrote to Masa with a proud account of the fighting. "Darling, I wrote to you on the 6th and I went to the front on the night of the 7th and fought a major battle till the 10th. My battalion was the first to reach the enemy line. It was very hard. I had orders to capture a first and second objective. We moved off from the front line at 5:20 a.m. and captured the first target within 46 minutes and the second after two hours. We killed many of the enemy and took more than 500 prisoners. It was hard fighting. I will not be able to forget the date 9 October for as long as I live. My battalion fought very well but, sadly, over half died or were injured. Over 70% of my officers were casualties. I am really lucky, I am thankful I was not hurt at all. On the 11th the commander of the Second Army, the general in charge of the division, and the brigadier general all came to see me separately to congratulate me on the way the battalion fought. I am sure you will be pleased to hear this as this will be very good for me. I think I will be promoted to brigadier general soon. It is raining every day. It is truly awful. I don't know when this will all stop but I hope it will be before the winter. From lonely Arthur, to my darling Dolly. P.S. This is a ration coupon I took from a German on 9 October. I took two or three as a souvenir."[38] The slow progress towards the pulverized heaps of rubble that had been Passchendaele continued till November, when the Canadians finally reached the ridge. By the time the third battle of Ypres was over, it had taken 66,000 British lives, many of them drowned in the mire.

Apart from the letters Arthur was getting from Masa, his brother's wife, Violet, remembered to write to him. "We were so pleased to hear you had come out of that last awful battle and that your regiment has done so well. You must have had an awful time but you must feel very proud of having got on so splendidly. . . . I hope Peachblossom is very well. Does she know what an awful time you are having or don't you tell her? I am sure she must be very anxious."[39] His sister-in-law was affectionate, and he appreciated her letters and sent them on to Masa, but the truth was that, with his parents dead, he felt increasingly distant from his own relatives, and after his years away he was out of tune with his own country. Since first joining the army in 1890, he had been abroad for a total of twenty-five out of the past twenty-eight years, in South Africa, Japan, Hong Kong, Burma, India and now France. When he came back to England from Lahore he had written, "I did not want to come back if I had not been summoned. There is no one I love here now, and I do not like the weather or the people. If it was not for the war, I had no wish to return."[40] As a commanding officer he was impressing his superiors, but he kept himself to himself. He always complained to Masa about the dinners with the corps commander and the top brass that he sometimes had to attend, just as he had disliked the flummery of the Viceroy's Simla, or the governor's receptions in Hong Kong. He played cards with other officers and tried writing poetry. In his Field Service notebook he wrote some creaky verses, which appeared between his monthly accounts. He was a better soldier than he was a poet, but they showed his state of mind. One of them was about a fortified concrete pillbox known as "Kit and Kat" that had served as a battalion headquarters at Ypres that autumn.

A CORNER OF HELL

No moment of the night or of the day
Passes in silence or in peace away.
Man to slay man, in thousands, ever tries
By hurling tons of metal through the skies.
A very hell of noise and filth and stench.
Dismembered corpses rotting in the trench
Outside my den . . . Remember Kit and Kat!
Who could forget who stayed there? Or I that
Friend of my youth, and comrade old and tired,

In this foul spot was blown to bits and died.
There at the very entrance hole his head
Was parted from his body, and instead
Of gaining Glory, now in mud he lies.[41]

Arthur was fighting again in November, at Cambrai, where the British launched the first mass tank attack and stormed across the Hindenburg Line. The 29th Division was to exploit the breakthrough, and capture woods overlooking the village of Marcoing. Early in the attack, Arthur had to take over command of the Royal Guernsey Light Infantry, newly trained and untried troops whose own colonel had been wounded. In fierce fighting around Marcoing and Masnières he was hit in the arm, and gassed again, but carried on after being treated at an aid post. When the Germans counterattacked, Arthur and the surviving Channel Islanders were caught in Masnières, in a quarter of the town known as Les Rues Vertes. For three days at the end of November, Arthur was in his most terrifying and exhausting battle yet, with close hand-to-hand fighting through narrow streets obstructed by fallen masonry and through ruined houses. For much of the time his headquarters were in a cellar by a canal. He managed to get off a brief note to Masa: "We have been fighting since the 20th. Luckily I am all right. I am absolutely exhausted, as we are fighting day and night and cannot sleep. I carry my darling's photographs in my breast pocket all the time. I am writing this as I think I can get this letter taken tonight"[42] They lost the position twice and retook it, and held it for two days against seven German attacks with superior forces and artillery. Their gallant fight proved a waste of effort and lives. Despite their own stand, the Germans had advanced to the right and left of them, and they were surrounded on three sides. They were told to abandon the ground.

"Darling, I am lucky to be alive. Apart from a small injury to my arm, I am fine. The injury is nothing, it may have been a flying shard of brick. Darling, darling, it was a terrible battle, with fierce fighting

Ballymoyer House, County Armagh, Ireland, in a late-nineteenth-century watercolor. Visitors coming down the drive saw the eighteen-bedroom house across a fast-running trout stream. The older and lower Georgian section projects from the back.

The Matsuchiyama hill on the east bank of the Sumida River in Tokyo, around 1900. The temple is among the trees at the top; Arthur and Masa rented a house to the right of it, by the bridge over the Sanya Canal.

Arthur's father, Major General Arthur Fitzroy Hart-Synnot, CB, CMG. Born Arthur Fitzroy Hart, he added Synnot to his surname after his wife inherited Ballymoyer in 1901.

Arthur's mother, Mary, daughter of Mark Synnot of Ballymoyer, whose family had owned the Armagh estate since the seventeenth century. Her younger sister married her husband's brother, Reginald.

The Hart military spirit in action. Lieutenant Reginald Hart, Arthur's uncle, wins the Victoria Cross for gallantry in the Bazar Valley, Afghanistan, after the British had invaded the country at the start of the Second Afghan War. (Engraving from *The Pictorial World,* London, 1879.)

Arthur Hart-Synnot as a captain, around 1903. He is wearing the Distinguished Service Order he had just won in South Africa, with a crown on a white enameled cross. He gave this picture to Masa.

Masa Suzuki in 1905 or 1906, after Arthur's return to Tokyo from Manchuria. She had three brothers and three sisters.

The Kaikosha, the club built in Tokyo for the use of officers of the Japanese Imperial Army, where Masa was working in early 1904.

The centrally situated Imperial Hotel, close to the Emperor's palace. Arthur stayed at the hotel when he first arrived in Tokyo.

Dead bodies strewn over a Russo-Japanese War battlefield, in a photograph taken by Arthur Hart-Synnot on the first day of the battle of Mukden, in March 1905.

Arthur dressed for the Manchurian winter, when temperatures fell to five below zero Fahrenheit, during his time as a British military observer.

Triumphal arch erected outside the Shimbashi railway station in Tokyo to celebrate Admiral Heihachiro Togo's victory over the Russian Navy at Tsushima.

Teahouses along the bank of the Juniso pond, on the western edge of Tokyo beyond Shinjuku, around 1900. The Kumano Shrine lay behind the trees.

Both places where Arthur and Masa lived in Tokyo were famous beauty spots, and both were included by the woodblock master Hiroshige Ando in his *ukiyo-e* series *One Hundred Views of Edo* in 1857. *Left:* Hiroshige's print showing the pond and the Kumano Shrine at Juniso. *Right:* His moonlit view of the Matsuchiyama hill and the entrance to the Sanya Canal, from the opposite bank of the river at Mukojima.

During the summer of 1905, Arthur and Masa spent time on the coast at Matsushima, with its bays and islets, two hundred miles north of Tokyo.

At Mukojima an avenue of cherry trees stretched beside the bank of the Sumida River for more than a mile, and crowds flocked to see the blossoms every April.

Kyoto's Kiyomizu Temple, with its great balcony built out from the hillside on the eastern edge of the city. The Matsunoya inn was a few minutes' walk away.

Masa and Kiyoshi in a photograph taken for Arthur in 1907, when he had moved to Hong Kong and she had rented a smaller house in Kashiwagi.

Arthur's letters were written in Japanese on handmade *makigami* paper. They could unroll to more than six feet in length, and many carried a delicate background pattern of morning glories, bamboo, or cranes.

Letters were sealed with Arthur's crest and often sent by registered mail.

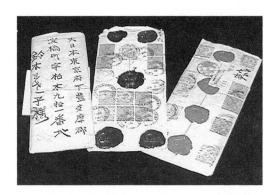

Arthur and Masa together in a Hong Kong photographer's studio in 1911, when he was about to return to Europe. He was forty and she was thirty-two.

North Point, Hong Kong Island, two and a half miles from central Victoria, and the beach where Arthur took his horse swimming. In 1908 he found a site for his ideal house on the heavily wooded hillside, looking across the water to Kowloon.

The completed house designed by Arthur, with Masa approving the plans. It was prefabricated by carpenters in Japan under the supervision of Masa's brother Haru and brought to Hong Kong by ship for assembly.

The portico of Ballymoyer House in a 1911 photograph, with the family coachman and the black landau carriage that the family used to get to and from Newry.

Left: Arthur's sister Beatrice. Born in 1872, two years after Arthur, she helped run the house for her mother while Arthur was abroad. She never married.

Right: Violet, the clergyman's daughter who married Arthur's younger brother, Ronald. Always intrigued by "Peach-blossom," she wrote to Arthur in India and France.

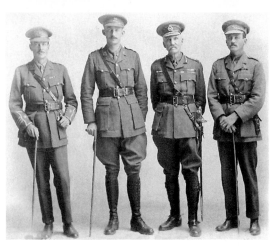

Military cousins. *From left to right:* Harold Hart (Royal West Surrey Regiment); Norman Hart (East Kent Regiment); their father, Major General Sir Reginald Hart, VC; and his other son, Reginald Hart (Notts and Derby Regiment).

Masa's mother. Hatsu Suzuki with her grandson Hideo in 1914, when she was seventy and living with Masa.

Kiyoshi in Tokyo, aged around seven, before his move to the private Gyosei School.

Main street of a small town in central Burma, close to Mandalay and Shwebo, the remote military post to which Arthur was sent in 1911.

The horse Arthur acquired when he returned to India as a staff officer and was based in Lahore.

Major Arthur Hart-Synnot at the end of 1916, just before he left for France to join the 17th Division in Picardy.

Letter with pressed sweetbriar, sweet pea, shamrock, and forget-me-not Arthur had gathered at Ballymoyer. He sent more forget-me-not and other pressed flowers from the Western front.

Men of the Lancashire Fusiliers, under Arthur Hart-Synnot's command, carrying duck-boards over the battlefield near the wrecked village of Poelcapelle during the third battle of Ypres, in October 1917.

Courtyard of the mansion in Bois de Guillaume, Rouen, that was taken over for the British 8th General Hospital during the Great War.

VAD Sister Drower, holding a rabbit in Cannes, 1919, with the Hôtel de la Californie in the background.

CALIFORNIE PALACE -- CANNES

Postcard Arthur sent to Masa from Cannes in 1919. Arthur's room is at first-floor level, with a balcony, six bays to the left of the main entrance, and marked with an inked square.

Brigadier General Arthur Hart-Synnot in 1919, with his uncle, Major General Sir Reginald Hart, VC, his mentor after his father's death. Sir Reginald had just retired, having been lieutenant governor of Guernsey during the war.

Arthur and Violet Drower on the terrace in Juan-les-Pins around 1922. The Mediterranean Sea was just across the road behind them.

Masa Suzuki and Kiyoshi by the Tama River, in the countryside west of Tokyo, in 1925.

The collapsed Etai Bridge over the Sumida River after the Tokyo earthquake of September 1, 1923. Masa's parents' house and barbershop were on the far side of the river, to the right of the bridge, in Fukagawa ward, which was 85 percent destroyed.

The Villa du Golfe, the nineteenth-century house at Juan-les-Pins, between Cannes and Nice, that Arthur bought in 1922.

Arthur Hart-Synnot at the wheel of "Little David," the car he started to drive in 1928, using it for journeys along the Côte d'Azur.

Kiyoshi while at the elite Third Higher School, which prepared boys for the Imperial University in Kyoto, around 1926.

Masa and Kiyoshi in Kyoto, after Masa had moved there and rented a house to be near him.

Arthur in the garden of St. John's College, Oxford, where his brother, Ronald, was bursar, around 1941.

Masa in Tokyo after the war, when she was sharing a house in Nakano with her daughter-in-law.

Kiyoshi and his fiancée, Tetsuko Katsuda, after his return to Tokyo from Paris in 1939.

from 20 November to 4 December. Sometimes I thought I would never get out alive, but luckily I survived. I did not change my clothes from the 18th to 7th December, and only took my boots off twice. I cannot tell you how filthy I was."[43]

Arthur was decorated for bravery after the fighting at Marcoing and Masnières, and given a bar to his Distinguished Service Order, to mark another action that would have merited the DSO, if he had not won it already.

The standard rotation—of weeks of resting and training, and then short periods of intense and dangerous fighting—continued, and Arthur's letters became more depressed. After a short spell of leave, he was back at Ypres in January 1918. Whereas his descriptions of the offensive the previous autumn had stressed how well his men were fighting, and his own achievements, he now wrote mainly about his physical and mental weariness. "I cannot tell you how horrible that place was. The mud was awful and I cannot describe it. Some of the soldiers were up to their necks in the swamp and then it is impossible to rescue them. This is the most ghastly place of all. We were there for nine days and nights and came back here and at last had some rest. I detest this war."[44] All attention now focused on when the Germans would launch their own offensive, which would need to be soon if they were to do it before the arrival of the Americans really changed the balance of strength. Arthur had another turn at Ypres in early February. "I returned from the front about 3 a.m. on the morning of the 11th. We are billeted in a small village now, and the day after tomorrow we will go farther back and stay there for two weeks. The other night I went out on duty and suddenly sank into the mud up to my waist. It was very difficult to pull myself out. I almost gave up, but managed to get myself out, though I was covered in mud all over. There can be no other place in the world as horrible as this."[45]

He was no longer responding to news Masa was including in her own letters, and the correspondence had ceased to be a dialogue.

There were no inquiries about Kiyoshi. "I wish this horrible war would end soon. I am tired of it. We have been apart for four years because of this fighting. It makes me angry when I think about it. It is awful to waste our lives like this. We have had enough, haven't we?"[46] Sometimes he still allowed himself to look forward to their life when peace came. "When we get together after the war's end I shall never let you go. I will take you with me wherever I go."[47]

He had still not received the promotion to brigadier general that was so important to him, not just because of the difference it would make to his pension and their future plans, but because he knew his family and his uncle expected it of him. He was physically and mentally exhausted. "Everyone is tired of this war. Even though I am fit, I am beginning to feel the effect. My hair is getting grayer and I shall be completely gray by the end of it. You will not like that, will you?"[48] In March, he collapsed, taken sick with pneumonia that went back to his gassing at Marcoing. For three days and nights, his condition was critical, and he was kept in a military hospital on the Channel coast. Army doctors insisted he go back home on sick leave, and by early April he was at Ballymoyer recuperating. Though he wanted to return to his brigade, the chances of his surviving the war were rising all the time.

NINE

BROKEN SWORD

O Shades, were you about me when I fell
Beside your broken sword?
· A.H.-S., 1921[1] ·

In the middle of April 1918, Arthur left the house at Ballymoyer, where the Japanese garden he had planted before the war was now overgrown and the irises he had bought with Masa had been eaten by the rabbits, and headed back to the war. By the time he reached Folkestone, the soft silence of the Irish countryside had already been replaced by the distant rumble of the front, thirty miles away. The quays were noisy with troops coming in from the embarkation camp on the cliffs and filing onto the transports, which had been shuttling men across to the battlefields every day for nearly four years.

Most of those crossing that afternoon were new drafts, going out to replace the tens of thousands of British casualties from the great offensive the Germans had launched in March. With Russia out of the war, the Germans had brought additional troops across from the Eastern front. After an intense and violent artillery bombardment, over sixty German divisions had moved forward against the twenty-nine British divisions then in the line. They came out of the cover of a morning fog, onto trenches that had been battered with

high explosives and gas shells for six hours, annihilating whole battalions, and leaving the survivors stunned and disoriented. Breaking
through at point after point, the Germans soon had the British Army
in a full-scale retreat.

Colonel Hart-Synnot, when he was still on sick leave and recovering from pneumonia, had followed these grim events from the distance of the morning room at Ballymoyer, studying the maps of the
front in each day's newspapers, as the dotted line and hatched area
of the German gains moved forward.

Arthur knew what his friends in the 25th Division were enduring. After three weeks, many more of them had been killed, and the
rout made the sacrifices of the previous year, and all they had been
through together, appear an even greater waste. They had fought for
strips of devastated Belgian and French farmland yard by yard, at
enormous cost in lives. Now the vast swamp at Ypres, the splintered
woods and broken roads, the wrecked villages of Langemarck, Poelcapelle, and Passchendaele, were all back in enemy hands again,
and farther south the Germans had advanced across the old Somme
battlefield until Amiens was under threat. On 12 April, Arthur read
Haig's defiant order to his troops: "There is no other course open to
us but to fight it out! Every position must be held to the last man:
there must be no retirement. . . . Each one of us must fight on to the
end." When Arthur left Ireland a few days later, he was expecting to
rejoin that fight. Though the German offensive was running out of
steam by mid-April, the front had been shifted back to the trench
lines the British Expeditionary Force had held nearly four years
earlier, in the autumn of 1914.

It was thirteen years since Arthur had sailed in another troopship packed with conscript soldiers through a December snowstorm, from the north coast of Japan, when he had to part from Masa
for the first time. At least the Manchuria battles, though equally ferocious, had been short and brought a conclusive victory. This war
had dragged on, keeping him five thousand miles away from his son

and the woman he wanted to spend the rest of his life with. They had not seen each other for nearly five years, though their correspondence was as intense as ever. In his letters to Tokyo in January and February he had sounded depressed and exhausted, increasingly impatient at the continuation of the war, though he always put the principal blame on German aggression and a national trait identified as "beastliness." General Ludendorff's offensive, and the reverses of the last month, might have added to his desperation. However, by the afternoon of 19 April his mood must have changed completely. He can only have been elated, because of what had been put to him earlier that day. As the troopship churned out of Folkestone on a dull afternoon, zigzagged through the lanes marked in the minefields, and was joined by the navy destroyers escorting it across the Channel, Arthur had good reason to believe that for him the fighting in France was already over, and he would be going to Japan.

Most officers on the ship were continuing that evening to their units in northern France, to St.-Omer, Abbeville, or the base at Amiens, where the Germans were now only a few miles away. Arthur had changed his plans and would be staying in Boulogne. From the docks he went straight to a hotel to wait for new orders from London. Within a few days, he expected a telegram telling him to return to England and head for Tokyo via the fastest possible route. This meant a crossing from Liverpool to New York, a transcontinental rail journey to Portland or Vancouver, and then another sea passage on to Japan, which he could reach by early June. There he looked forward to a joyful reunion with Masa and Kiyoshi, and to joining a daring if controversial expedition alongside the Japanese Army he so admired.

The sudden change in his prospects had come amid the clinging wartime farewells on the continental-departures platform of a London station that morning. While other officers going to France were being seen off by wives or girlfriends, Arthur had to be content with a sisterly embrace from Beatrice, who had managed to take a few hours away from her war work as a volunteer driver. Five minutes before his train was due to depart from Charing Cross, at noon, a staff officer hurried up to them. He had come from the War Office, nearby in Whitehall, with instructions to catch Colonel Hart-Synnot before he left and give him a message that needed an immediate reply. The Japanese job that he had inquired about earlier in the week was now extremely likely. Could he confirm that he definitely wanted it and would take it? If so, it was too late to stop the journey to France, but he should go to Boulogne and await a firm telegraphed order. Then he was to turn round and head for Japan.

The belated recognition that Arthur might have something special to contribute because of his Japanese knowledge and training had been brought about by the turmoil that followed the Russian Revolution in 1917, as the Bolshevik "Reds" tried to take control across the whole of Russia, and the anti-Bolshevik "White" forces tried to reverse the revolution. The Japanese government, seeing the ease with which one great emperor had been brought down, were alarmed by the possible future threat to their own. More immediately, they worried that their commercial interests in northern China and the Russian Far East might be threatened. A senior Japanese officer made a secret visit to London in February, sounding out the British attitude if a Japanese expedition were to be sent to Siberia to support the anti-Bolsheviks and secure the Trans-Siberian Railway. Meanwhile Britain and France were keen to reopen an Eastern front against the Germans, following Russia's withdrawal.

Partly for fear of what the Japanese might get up to if they intervened on their own, the other Allies insisted that any Siberian expedition should be an international one, and the British War Office was preparing for it. An officer was needed as liaison between the British troops that would be sent to Vladivostok and the much larger Japanese main force. Quite how the expedition would fare once it reached Siberia, where Bolshevik bands would be able to harass it from the forests and cut the few railways, remained to be seen. For

Arthur this was the opportunity to work with the Japanese Army he
had missed at Tsingtao, and a period in Tokyo would be required beforehand. Once he was back from Siberia, he could reasonably expect the war in Europe to have ended, and he would be demobilized
and free to settle in Japan with his family at last.

Arthur waited for the order in Boulogne, checked the sailings
and timetables, and tried to organize his equipment for the journey,
in which the steamy heat of Japan in midsummer would be followed
by a Siberian winter. He wrote an excited letter to Masa: "I have
been waiting for the past five days so the order should come soon. It
is like a dream, and incredible. I think I will be in Japan by the time
this letter arrives. Darling, what do you think of this news? Do not
cry, but I am half crying with joy myself. If I have time I will go to
Ballymoyer to get my things, but if not I shall leave from here without them. I have not written you a letter as I have been waiting for
the order every day. You will be surprised by this news. I will send
you a telegram when I arrive in Yokohama. I will have to go to the
embassy first. I cannot think of anything else apart from being with
you. From happy Arthur."[2] He took the letter to the Boulogne post
office himself, to make sure it was safely dispatched. When he returned, he found a telegram waiting for him.

The message from the War Office was brief and crushing. All the
optimistic plans he had allowed himself to make in the previous few
days were swept aside. The army did not, after all, require his services in Japan or Siberia. As ever, the posting decisions had moved in
a mysterious way, and it had been decided to send someone else.
Later, he learnt that Major John Hulton, an officer ten years younger
than he who had completed the Japanese language training in 1911,
would be going to act as the liaison with the Siberia expedition,
which eventually fizzled out amid much squabbling between the
British, American, French, and Japanese contingents, and a suspicion that the Japanese had an agenda all their own.

Arthur now had to reconcile himself to the fact that there was no way he would see Masa and Kiyoshi till after the war ended. He had little time for moping or introspection, because a few hours later a second official telegram reached Boulogne, giving him his own brigade and promoting him to the rank of brigadier general. Arthur's professional satisfaction at having at last gained his promotion seemed to push the personal disappointment to the side, and he plunged into his new command. His 6th Brigade belonged to the 2nd Division, in turn part of the VI Corps, whose corps commander was now Lieutenant General Aylmer Haldane, with whom Arthur had shared much of the icy winter of 1905, roughing it in a Manchurian village. Haldane may have asked for Arthur's services. Another Manchuria veteran, and one of the German attachés they had both known in Mukden, General von Stetten, was commanding the II Bavarian Corps opposite them. After getting his instructions at the divisional headquarters, Arthur went on to take over the 6th Brigade, and found them near Boyelles, holding a length of old trenches across exposed, slightly rolling farmland, in front of three German-held villages.

The men were exhausted after the fighting of the previous weeks, and were in desperate need of time in the reserve to recover and take in replacements. Meanwhile, the whole sector was so dangerous and open to enemy shell fire that movement behind the front line was impossible during daylight. The ragged and decrepit trenches, dug hastily in 1914, needed to be shored up to make them more habitable and secure, and new barbed wire had to be laid. In his first few days, Arthur pressed tired men into endless work parties, digging new communication trenches between the support and front positions. There was still intermittent shelling, and his new batman was injured and sent back to England soon after his arrival. For the moment, his brigade was too weak and short of men to be capable of any attack, but was maintaining what the military called an "active defense."

It took a while for the mail, forwarded first from London and then on again from his old division, to catch up with him. On 2 May, he received a backlog of five letters from Japan, including three from Masa, one from his son, and another from Masa's niece Ohatsu. Masa gave him the news that her mother, who had lived in the house with her and helped bring up both Kiyoshi and Hideo, had died at the age of seventy-four. Once he had time, after the first four days of visiting the lines, ordering the new trench work, and getting to know his officers, Arthur took out his *makigami* paper. His own mother had died five years before, and he tried to comfort Masa. "I was very distressed at the news about your mother. You must be very sad and lonely now, because she was always there in the house with you. I know she was getting old, but I had hoped to see her again."[3] In fact, Hatsu Suzuki had been one of the main obstacles in his way, discouraging Masa from going to England when Arthur put on the pressure in 1911, but they had liked each other. When he was first in Tokyo, she had helped initiate him into the workings of a Japanese household, and the small but important rituals that went with daily life. It was only because she had been willing to look after the children that he had been able to travel with Masa, and he always remembered to send her messages at the end of his letters.

After trying to console Masa, he told her about a medal he had been given by the French government, and his new rank. As always after his promotions, he was looking on to the next stage. "I may become a lieutenant general soon. I like the 6th Brigade and this division. We are very close to the Germans now."[4] Nevertheless, his brigade headquarters were nearly a mile back, and he should no longer be in the midst of the fighting, as he had been when he was leading the Guernseys at Cambrai or the Lancashire Fusiliers at Ypres, with the rank of colonel. The weather was much better, and after several days of blue skies and drying sunshine, dust rather than mud became a problem, with the danger that marching troops gave their positions away. Farther back from the front, the dust clouds were increasingly likely to be raised by the American soldiers now arriving in France in mounting numbers. With the German offensive stalled, it still looked possible that the war could be over by the end of the year.

Arthur's friend General Haldane, making a tour of the units in his corps, stopped to see how he was settling in. They discussed German activity in the trenches opposite them which had been observed by British pilots. Though he was desperately busy, Arthur started his first long letter to Masa since reaching Boyelles, and continued to add to it over several days. "7 May. You say you read my letters whenever you feel lonely. I am so sorry you are on your own. I would like to be with you immediately, when I know you are missing me so much. The other day I thought I could come to Japan, but sadly I could not. Maybe I can go later. 11th. If the enemy does not attack us, we will pull back tomorrow evening for a rest for a while. I am writing today as we will be busy tomorrow. I am fine though we are very close to the enemy. I don't know when this awful war will end but I think it will be over by the autumn. Before I left England I asked Beatrice and my brother to write you a letter if I were to be injured or die. They promised to do it. Also I left a will with the Chartered Bank in London. The address is 38 Bishopsgate, London. If you want to ask about me, write to B, or D, or my brother.

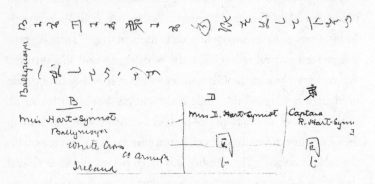

I am sure everything will be fine. I am thinking about you all the time. I miss you very much. I am working very hard here, without much rest. By the way when you write to me please write General instead of Colonel. Please give my regards to Ohatsu-chan and Kiyoshi. From lonely, lonely Arthur."[5] He finished that letter on the morning of Saturday, 11 May, and saw that it was in the post. Later that day, he and his brigade major were due to go out and visit his three battalions.

The mail was still unreliable and taking two months to get to Japan from France or Britain. In Tokyo, Masa was only just receiving the letters Arthur had sent from the hospital after his collapse from a lung infection back in March, during the week when Arthur was writing from his headquarters bunker at Boyelles. The already out-of-date news that he was on his way to Japan would not reach her till June.

Though Japan was a fellow belligerent, and an ally of Britain, France, and the United States, the conflict seemed to be someone else's. The perspective Masa was getting from Arthur's letters from the front, of a vicious war that was all the fault of "those horrible Germans," whom he called "demons," using the word *oni,* which usually described the ogres of Japanese folktales, was not shared by Masa's neighbors. The Germans had done the Japanese no wrong, and the common perception was that Japan had been drawn in only because of her formal alliance with Britain. At Tsingtao, senior Japanese officers had been friends with some of the Germans they were besieging, since the Germans had provided instructors and been the model for the Japanese Army during its rise, just as the British had helped the navy.

With their great respect for their former teachers, many Japanese military experts dismissed the British Army as badly led, and lacking fighting spirit. The Japanese criticism was most widespread in 1916, the year of so many reverses. When a British force in Mesopotamia had to surrender to the Turks, the popular *Hochi Shimbun* newspaper wrote, "The Japanese nation cannot understand why a great army of nearly 10,000 troops should have surrendered. . . . Was there not a way of taking a more soldier-like stand . . . ?" The writer thought it might be "the difference between the moral conception of the Japanese and the Western people which makes the position different." Another paper, the *Kokumin Shimbun,* took a broader swipe at Japan's ally. "England on the whole pays too much attention to economic and financial matters and too little to military matters. This has led to the defeat in the Dardanelles, the surrender of General Townshend, and the lack of any remarkable success along the French and Belgian front."[6] Many expected that the Germans would eventually win, and that the Anglo-Japanese Alliance was therefore a liability. The Japanese government tried to counter this, and one of the fathers of the alliance spoke out against "certain weak-kneed Japanese."[7]

British Embassy efforts to stir up enthusiasm for the Allied cause met with little success. When photographs were distributed to newspapers showing British troops shooting rats in their trenches, to illustrate the privations of life at the front and the sporting resilience of the Tommies, they were misinterpreted. Captain Malcolm Kennedy, a language officer then studying in Japan, found that the reaction of a naturally thrifty people was to ask why soldiers wasted ammunition on harmless wildlife, not the enemy. In November 1917, he stopped in villages to ask peasants about the war. "They were frankly incredulous when I assured them that not only was there a war, but Japan was taking part in it. If Japan really was at war, they argued, surely all the male youth of the country would be summoned to the colours."[8] They did not know that Japanese sailors had already lost their lives in the Mediterranean.

To raise awareness, the Emperor of Japan was given the rank of a field marshal in the British Army, and George V was awarded a similar rank in the Japanese armed forces. In the salons of Tokyo, wealthy families contributed to a special relief fund that sent £5,000 to buy comforts for the British wounded, and a benefactor shipped tins of Japanese marmalade to troops on the Western front. The Foreign Ministry backed a pamphlet about the alliance, giving new life to the idea that there were natural similarities between the two peoples. "Behind our mutual interest and aspirations there is the great moral and sympathetic tie of national characteristics. . . . The English gentleman is a peaceful Samurai, and the Japanese Samurai is an armed gentleman. The basic ideals and the aspirations of the two are identically the same. Thus, the best of England and the best of Japan constitute a gentleman's brotherhood for East and West."[9]

For urban Japanese who did know about the war, there was no sense of a struggle shared between brothers, and the horrors of European trench warfare made no special impact. At the time when Arthur was fighting at Passchendaele, a popular opera company in Tokyo's Asakusa district put on a highly successful production called *The Women's Army Is Off to the Front.* The lighthearted revue was based on the conceit that, with the loss of so many men, it was necessary to dispatch an army of women to help the fighting. The spirited song-and-dance numbers included a hornpipe, a Highland fling, and a chorus of Tokyo girls singing "Tipperary."

Nevertheless, by the start of 1918 the Great War was becoming more familiar to the Japanese, and closer to home with talk of the joint Allied expedition to Siberia. More space was given to the news from Europe after the big German offensive. Masa must have worried when she saw the "Great Battle on the Western Front" headlines at the end of March. According to the *Asahi* newspaper, which was printing stories from both Allied and German news agencies, "British reports said the German artillery bombardment had been greater than any before. There are mountains of corpses. . . ."[10] A German dispatch described a breakthrough south of the Somme, and the capture of 25,000 British prisoners and four hundred heavy guns. Though the papers started to carry maps, with tiny graphics showing Bapaume and St.-Quentin, the names meant little to Masa.

She had no idea where Arthur was, and she knew that if he were captured or killed it would be weeks before she heard.

Masa must have been overjoyed, as well as taken completely by surprise, when, in the middle of June, she received Arthur's letter saying he expected to be coming back to Japan. She understood the context, for by then the papers were full of news of the intervention in Siberia. The elation lasted only a few days, before she heard that he was not on his way after all. She had grown accustomed to these reversals, was used to Arthur's wishful thinking about future appointments, and could only resume her patient and passive wait for the end of the war. Like Arthur, she was in a state of emotional suspension, living for the day of his return, but wondering if the ever-receding prospect of a normal family life was just a chimera.

Daily existence in Tokyo was becoming harder, and Arthur's allowance of 150 yen every quarter did not go as far as it had done with the additional expenses of a growing child. In early 1917, the price of rice rose to 15 yen a *koku,* the standard measure of five bushels. By June 1918, the price had doubled to 30 yen, as speculators held back supplies. As the summer went on, popular unrest grew at the way prices were rising far faster than wages. In the working-class eastern districts of Tokyo, crowds rioted outside government offices and attacked the rice stores. A nervous government ordered a news blackout. The temperature and humidity increased.

At the end of June, a letter arrived at house number 371 in Kashiwagi, addressed in an unfamiliar hand. It contained a short note in English from Beatrice Hart-Synnot, telling Masa that Arthur had been gravely injured in France, but that he had survived and was in a military hospital. Masa's worst fears now began to play out as she felt the helplessness of her position. She had no idea what had happened to him in the weeks since the letter was written. Arthur might already be dead, or might need her desperately, but there was nothing she could do. In the following days, as she waited for more news, her anguish was hard to bear.

. . .

Six weeks earlier, around dusk on the evening of Saturday, 11 May, Arthur had been returning to his own lines after visiting the general in command of the brigade next to him. He left the village of Blairville, with a small château and several acres of sand quarries where bunkers had been tunneled into the steep sides, in the direction of his own headquarters. He knew the area well, from months spent fighting south of Arras in 1917. The fields were crossed by a number of deeply cut old tracks that ran between stone pits, now filled with the metal scrap, packing cases, empty cable reels, and detritus that the fighting generated in such quantity, with some of them being used by the artillery. Arthur was walking beside his brigade major, Captain Wright, when a single German shell scored an almost direct hit on them. It was not clear whether the shelling that started was aimed at the divisional gun positions, or whether a spotter had seen the two officers. As the explosive charge broke the shell into hundreds of metal fragments and sent them flying out at 400 meters per second, Captain Wright was killed instantly, cut in two by the shrapnel. Arthur was left slumped over the edge of the shell crater, still conscious. He was losing blood rapidly. Both his legs were in tatters.

Gunners from nearby carried the general to a field hospital in Blairville, where a doctor injected pints of salt and water into a vein in his elbow, to give his heart something to pump after the loss of so much blood. He drank some tea from the spout of a proffered pot, and later that night a military ambulance took him fifteen miles down the bumpy cobbles of the main Arras-to-Amiens road to a Canadian military hospital in Doullens. In the early hours of 12 May, surgeons cut away the remains of both his legs and amputated above the knees. For the next few days, he stayed in a coma. Aylmer Haldane heard the news late on the 12th, and came across to Doullens to visit him next morning. He wrote in his diary: "Hart-Synnot was asleep after the operation. He looked alright. Both legs were amputated at 3 am. Doctors are satisfied that he will pull through and if pluck will help him, he, like his father and uncle, has a good deal more than his share. They gave him a transfusion of blood. Left a message to be given him when he wakes."[11]

Arthur just pulled through, but the Doullens hospital was taking in new casualties all the time and could not provide the care and further surgery he now needed. After six days, when his condition had stabilized, it was decided to move him. The new era of warfare, producing so much human wreckage every day, required medical operations to be run on an equally industrial scale, to evacuate and sort the wounded. During the recent German offensive, the Royal Army Medical Corps had shipped 93,000 casualties back to England in April alone. Arthur was loaded onto one of more than seventy ambulance trains that were running backwards and forwards between the front and the base areas, the ward carriages lined with three levels of stretchers on each side of a central corridor. He was taken eighty miles back to the city of Rouen, a major supply center, where medical orderlies and doctors waited for each train, and long lines of ambulances queued up outside the station.

The British Army had established six hospitals in Rouen by 1918. Others were being run by the Red Cross, the Australians, the Canadians, and the French. In the aftermath of the recent heavy fighting, all were packed. Arthur was driven past the cathedral and up the steep hill out of the city to the Bois de Guillaume, a wealthy residential district where the British 8th General Hospital had taken over a nineteenth-century mansion. From the original building, with turrets and steep slate roofs, the hospital had expanded rapidly into rows of wooden huts in the grounds, and now had six hundred beds. At forty-seven, Arthur was one of the oldest patients in a place where most men were in their teens or early twenties. The severed nerves around his stumps were excruciatingly painful. The wounds still had to be drained regularly to prevent sepsis, and the flaps of skin that surgeons had sewn around the newly cut thighbone ends had yet to heal, but doctors could now start to tackle some of the other damage. His right eardrum was burst, and he had almost lost his right eye. He had shrapnel in his arm and chest, and a slice of flesh had been torn from his back and buttocks. On his second day he persuaded the nurses to prop him up in bed a little, and bring him pencil and paper, so he could try and write his first letter since the injuries.

His Japanese characters were very shaky, but he gave Masa as much reassurance as he could, with the basic information that Beatrice had not been able to include in her brief note. "Darling, darling, on the night of 11 May, unfortunately, I was injured very badly. Both my legs were shattered by an enemy shell. So both my legs have been amputated just above the knees. I am sorry I have not been able to write for ten days. I survived the most critical period because I was in good health. I am better now and I will recover soon. I am still in France, but will be going back to England as soon as possible. Within two or three months the stumps will be harder and then they can make me a pair of artificial legs. It is difficult to write in bed, and I am sure it is hard to read, but I hope it is better than no letter at all. Did B write to you as she promised? I will send you a short letter every two or three days. I am all right, and will get better with each day that passes. Goodbye, from Arthur with half a body, to darling Dolly." [12]

Still heavily sedated, and torsioned to slings over his bed, he managed to write again a week later. "This is a very large hospital, and well equipped. I am recovering day by day and my strength is coming back little by little. I have been very weak from the loss of so much blood from the injury. Surprisingly the right leg has got better and the pain has gone, but the left leg is still painful. It will get better soon. I realize you must be very worried about me but there is nothing that can be done. I still find it hard to understand why I was not killed. The officer beside me was blown to pieces by the shell. I shall be able to walk with artificial limbs later on. Greetings to Kiyoshi, from lonely Arthur."[13]

Despite their later depiction as "château generals," living in comfort way behind the lines, injuries to senior British commanders were not unusual. A total of 146 generals were wounded and 78 killed during the Great War, in contrast to the Second World War, when only 3 lost their lives in action. At Rouen, General Hart-Synnot was the highest-ranking patient, and they made a fuss over him. The brigade sent his personal possessions on to him, and he soon had a photograph of Masa by his bed. Letters from Tokyo reached Rouen, though they were still written without any knowledge of his injury. "I received your 247 and 248 yesterday. I am glad you are well. Darling, darling, I am getting better gradually but I am still weak. Please forgive me for not writing a long letter but it is very difficult writing in bed."[14] He thought constantly about Masa and Japan, but his first priority was to be sent back to England, and the doctors would not let him travel until his stumps had healed.

It seemed he might need a further operation on his left thigh, to improve on the original amputation. "I am writing this early in the morning. I am still in the same hospital. My left leg is better than before and less painful, but the bone is too long so this is going to have to be trimmed off. They haven't decided whether the operation will be done here or in England. At present my bed is brought outside, and I spend all day there. It is nice because many people come up and talk to me. On the 18th it will be your birthday and I will be thinking about you on that day. We should have been together, if things had turned out differently, but unfortunately it wasn't to be. You have probably found out about my injuries by now, and are worried about me. The first news must have been from B. I was in a coma for two or three days and didn't know what was happening. Today there may be a letter from you, from the Club in London, so I shall stop for now. There will be a post going out at nine o'clock this morning."[15]

He sent Masa a money order for twenty yen well in advance of her birthday, and some photographs of the hospital. With his bed pushed out into the garden, he began to write at greater length, once again adding a section each day before posting it. He resumed his punctilious checking of the flow of mail in each direction. "12 July. I received your numbers 246, 249, 250, 251, and 252 and the post-card arrived on the 9th, with a letter from Kiyoshi at the same time. So I have received all the letters between 223 and 252 except for 236 and 237. I no longer have pain like before, but I could not tell you in words how awful it was. I am getting my strength back slowly but I did not have strength then. It was difficult even to talk. Now I am so much better and have a good appetite."[16]

As Arthur slowly recovered, he could start to take stock of his changed situation. His military career was over, and he was not go-ing to take part in the Allied victories, which were beginning at last, as the American forces went into the trenches. He could expect to be retired early and so would never reach the rank of major general that his father, grandfather, and uncle had all achieved. Perhaps conscious of breaking this family tradition, he would later write a poem, "Broken Sword," in which he tried to assuage the martial spirit of the Hart-Synnots.

> *O Shades, did you look down that dreadful day*
> *Upon the battle, swaying here and there,*
> *Watching with jealous eye to note the way*
> *Your scion should acquit himself, and bear*
> *That honoured brand of yours? If so, you saw*
> *It shattered: and you know it is no more.*
>
> *O Shades, were you about me when I fell*
> *Beside your broken sword? If so, you know*
> *And saw and understood that awful hell*
> *And purgatory of mind that I passed through.*"[17]

The upkeep of the house at Ballymoyer, where the shades of his military ancestors were most concentrated, and where their pictures looked down from the walls, would become a worry to him. But the most crucial question was what would happen to Masa and Kiyoshi and whether he would be able to return to Japan. He did not raise this with Masa until nine weeks after his injury, but on 14 July made it clear he was still intending to come back. "Darling, it is going to be difficult to go to Japan without legs, and you are also going to find me ugly. But it is not my doing, and I must put up with this."[18]

Masa's letters brought him news of daily life in Kashiwagi that he began to respond to again. When she said that her niece Ohatsu-chan, who had agreed to move in after the death of her mother, was going to leave to get married, he urged her to find someone else quickly. She was having trouble with the chickens. "12 July. I am sorry to hear you have had a terrible time with your cockerel. I am glad you went to see a doctor straightaway. I hate cockerels. What a terrible bird to damage your beautiful face. I hope it will heal without leaving any scars."[19]

Arthur was entitled to visits from his family, who could have traveled out and stayed in a Red Cross hotel in Rouen, but when Beatrice wanted to come and see him he asked her not to. His cousin Norman, who had met Masa in Hong Kong and Tokyo, wrote to him in July. "Poor old boy, what cruel and terrible luck you have had; it is quite hopeless to explain how one feels for you. I am particularly anxious to hear from you as I have not liked to write to Missississi till I hear from you. I want to be absolutely sure you have told her first. The grief of the poor little girl must be awful."[20]

The poor little girl was now forty, and Arthur wrote to her again on the day of her birthday, saying he hoped next year would be better. "18 July. Happy Birthday. I woke up before the sun rose and have been thinking about you all day. We thought we would be able to celebrate together this year, but unfortunately we could not. I hope next year we can be together."[21] He kept up his interest in

botany, and sent more pressed flowers: "I am writing this letter under a chestnut tree. In front of me there is a paulownia. It is very unusual here, so I enclose a flower from it. Whenever I see anything to
do with Japan I am cheered up. I miss Japan and you know why. Although I am not in Japan my heart is there."[22]

Masa's reaction to his injury finally reached him. She had received the news in late June, and her first letter, written in great distress, arrived on 18 August together with a sympathetic note from
Kiyoshi. Arthur thanked her. "How you must have suffered hearing
my bad news. It was more painful for me to think of your suffering
than my own injury. I was agonizing over whether to tell you what
had happened or not but I had to tell you. I didn't know if I was going to recover or not. If I had not, you would have blamed me for
not having told you before. So I had to tell you, however painful it
was. Darling, darling, I have been thinking about you every day, looking at your photographs. Since the 13th I have been staying out-
doors all day, and all night as well. Maybe because of that I will get
better more quickly. The left leg has healed at last and I have started
to use a wheelchair. It is quite comfortable. It would make such a
difference if you were with me now."[23] Arthur's time outside was
part of the "open-air treatment" prescribed in military hospitals with
increasing zeal from 1915 onwards, to get as much oxygen as possible to infections and dressings, to reduce potential infections from
the air in muggy wards, and to toughen up the army's invalids. It
was to be practiced not just in summer but throughout the year, and
in some British war hospitals canvas awnings were all that protected
patients from the rain.

Writing to Kiyoshi a week later, Arthur appealed to him on a
man-to-man basis: "I was pleased to get your letter. It is bad luck
that I was injured, but it cannot be helped. To tell you the truth, in
a war like this it was inevitable that I was going to be hit sooner or
later. I did not tell your mother this because I knew she would have
worried so much. I am much better now and my wounds are almost

healed. From Father, to Kiyoshi."[24] Any early doubts that he would
be able to get to Japan seemed to have been overcome by now, and
he repeated his intention to return to them once he had mastered
walking. "When my left leg is healed I will return to England and be
fitted with artificial legs. I shall be able to walk within two months.
Once I can walk with them I would like to go to Ballymoyer. It will
be difficult to travel long distances until I am used to them, but I
will come to Japan as soon as I can."[25]

After over three months in the Rouen hospital, Arthur thought
he was making progress. The further operation on his left thigh did
prove necessary. "If you could see the top half of me, you would think
there was nothing wrong with me. I have been in my wheelchair every
day."[26] He was becoming a little more mobile. "A matron at this hospital is very kind. I have been in my wheelchair to have tea with her
two or three times. There is a French marchioness living near the hospital and her garden is wonderful and I sometimes visit her. I can go
anytime I want."[27] He was taken down to the center of the old city to
see Rouen Cathedral. Colonel Roundell Toke came to visit him, sent
his regards to Masa, and asked if she ever saw Oharu-san.

He was impatient to be sent back to England, so he could be fitted with legs and start to learn to use them, but the skin on his left
stump would not heal completely, and still had to be dressed and
bandaged.

Where possible, he still wrote to Masa on the rolls of white,
wafer-thin handmade paper that she had been sending him for so
long, but dealing with this in blustery weather was difficult: "As the
wind is strong I am using this small writing paper. My injuries are
healing every day, little by little. Although it is getting cooler, being
outside is better for me. I can now get out of bed and sit on a chair.
In fact I am writing this letter sitting."[28] "I hope I can come to you
as soon as I can manage my artificial legs well. Even if the war is still
on, I am sure I can go."[29]

Arthur heard his sister Dilly was finally getting married. "She is now in London and is very happy. I am jealous of her. When will my turn come? And will it come to a man with no legs? I don't know how my darling thinks about a man with no legs. I think I shall be going back to England soon to be fitted with artificial legs. Then I will practice hard and be able to walk in a month. Nowadays artificial legs are well made, and look like the real thing."[30] He was encouraged when another officer, who had had a similar double amputation, came in to see him. "He was walking very well with his artificial legs. It is impressive."[31] He was still spending almost all his time with his bed pushed out in the garden. "It is getting colder and there was some frost. It is a pity to see all the leaves falling. My chestnut tree is now almost bare. I don't like the autumn because it makes me sad. I am enclosing a maple leaf. Let's enjoy the autumn leaves together next year."[32] He wrote some mournful poetry.

The twilight falls, the colours from the sky
Fade and disperse. The green leaves of the trees
As winter comes droop, wither and die
So with our lives—our ever moving tent
Impermanent[33]

The principal goal now driving his recovery was the prospect of life in Japan after the war, and settling down in the countryside he remembered from his journeys with Masa, which had acquired an almost mythical quality in his mind. He started to study Japanese again, using new books and writing exercises Masa sent him. Late in October, he said: "Let us travel next summer and stay somewhere quiet and peaceful for a long period. I cannot tell you how wonderful it will be to be together again after five years. It will feel like going to heaven. I am now only half the man you know, but my heart is the same. The newspapers say the war is going to end very soon. I must stop now, the nurse is coming to change my bandage."[34]

A few days later, Arthur was judged well enough to make the

journey back to England. The trip was exhausting, starting at three-thirty a.m. with a train to Le Havre, then a fourteen-hour Channel crossing by hospital ship to Southampton, and on to London, where the ambulance trains were diverted around the city and unloaded onto platforms set aside at Paddington. Though the armistice was expected at any time, lighting restrictions were still in force, with the street lamps masked. Arthur was driven through the darkened streets to the King Edward VII Hospital for Officers in a converted private house on Grosvenor Crescent in Victoria. In the following days, his sisters Dilly and Beatrice came to see him for the first time since April. He wrote to Masa to describe the new surroundings and seemed optimistic. "I am very lucky to have been brought to such a good hospital. Normally most of the limbless people get taken to Roehampton, but Sister Agnes will not allow me to go there and she gets the best doctors, masseurs, and artificial-limb makers to come here. I will be starting to practice with artificial legs in five or six days' time. I imagine it will be quite difficult. The doctor tells me it may take six months to be able to learn to walk. But I think I can do it more quickly, if I try very hard."[35] In the meantime, taking advantage of a special concession granted to the hospital, he was wheeled across the road and through a rear gate into the gardens of Buckingham Palace, where the officer patients were allowed to exercise on the gravel pathways.

On 11 November, Arthur heard the roar of the crowds in Whitehall and the Mall, and the church bells of London ringing out, as peace was declared. He wrote to Masa, "At last this terrible conflict is over. Congratulations. The whole of the world must be rejoicing, even those detestable Germans must be glad. If this war had ended six months earlier I would not have been injured. It can't be helped."[36] In Tokyo, the news of the Armistice came the following day, on 12 November. The *hinomaru,* the Union Jack, and the Stars and Stripes were flown together, and in Osaka they managed a torch-light procession, but there were no mass celebrations.

Masa had sent Arthur a stream of letters, postcards, and small presents since learning of his injury. With the coming of peace, it seemed that the blocks that had stood in the way of their living together—the need for him to stay in the army for his full service to get his pension, and then the overriding exigencies of wartime— had finally been removed, if at great cost. The only obstacle that now had to be surmounted was for Arthur to learn to walk again.

His first steps on the journey back to Masa were taken five days after the Armistice, when temporary legs were brought to him at the hospital to try. He wrote to tell her about them, with a drawing to show the system of straps and cups with which they were fitted.

"I tried the artificial legs for the first time. They are very light and straight and have no kneecaps. At first I could not manage them. I am still weak and I cannot tell you how hard it was. I tried for three days, sweating all over, and finally managed to walk. This morning I was much better at it, with the help of two sticks, so I am very pleased. It is very difficult but I must try hard. In two or three weeks, if I make progress, they will make me wooden legs with kneecaps. It is hard to believe one can walk with legs like this, but I think if one has the will, and works at it, one can." For the moment Arthur was confident he had the pluck, stamina, and determination to reach his goal, but he was already starting to realize how hard it was going to be. "I wish I could learn to walk soon in order to be able to come and live with you. I cannot plan anything until I can walk properly."[37]

TEN

FALLING ON
THE HILL

I want to be with you soon. Maybe it will be
possible in January, February, or March.
· A.H.-S., November 1918[1] ·

After long months spent worrying about Arthur's health and recovery, Masa became ill herself in early November, and lay huddled under thin quilts on her futon mattress in Kashiwagi. The first signs seemed like the winter flu of previous years: a high temperature, a stuffy nose, and a cough. Soon the fever grew worse, with a severe headache and discomfort behind the eyes, and the pain moved to the muscles of her back and legs until every joint ached. The diagnosis was untaxing. Masa was one among millions suffering from the same symptoms, another victim of the virulent influenza that had now reached Japan. Wartime troop movements had helped carry the bacilli rapidly between Europe and the United States, across the British Empire to India and Australia, and on to China and the East.

After a brief outbreak earlier in the year, the flu reappeared in the western port city of Nagasaki and spread along the railway routes.

The Tokyo authorities tried to prepare for it, spraying gallons of disinfectant in trams and public places, recommending frequent gargles, and setting schoolgirls to work making gauze masks. Lurid posters pointed up the danger of coughing in a train, with a shower of exaggerated, insect-sized germs spraying over other passengers. A British visitor saw a regiment of troops marching through the Tokyo streets wearing their black rubber antigas respirators to hold back the bacteria.[2] The measures were only partly effective. Before the flu had run its course, over a third of the Japanese population had caught it, and the outbreak overshadowed the end of the war.

Masa was well aware that if sufferers did not start to recover after five or six days, the danger increased, as the flu developed into a severe bronchial pneumonia. Bedrest, and careful nursing with ice and a cold water sponge to keep the temperature down, were essential. If patients tried to get up, or their temperature rose above 104 degrees Fahrenheit, the lungs filled with a sticky, blood-tinged liquid, and breathing became increasingly labored. Thousands choked on their own phlegm and died. Doctors were puzzled by the predilections of this particular 1918 bacillus, which posed most danger to those between twenty-five and forty-five, whereas earlier germs had found most of their victims among the very old and the very young. Tens of thousands were off work. Factories and offices shut down, trains were canceled because of the shortage of drivers, and police stations were left unmanned. Kiyoshi did not catch the flu, though many schools closed because there were no teachers. By early November, the hospital at Okubo, the closest to Masa, was overwhelmed with gray-faced victims for whom little could be done. Inoculations and drugs were ineffective, and ice supplies ran out. The city crematoriums could not burn fast enough, so distraught families were told to send their dead to relatives in the provinces, where the ovens were less pressed. A Tokyo newspaper reported piles of corpses at the railway stations awaiting shipment.

The influenza outbreak was known as *la grippe* in France, and

most generally as "Spanish flu," since it had only been recognized as
the pandemic it was when eight million Spaniards went down with it
in the summer. No one knew where the germ had emerged from.
Some traced it back to a U.S. Army camp in Kansas, or to the filthy,
rat-infested trenches of the Western front. Others, including Arthur
Hart-Synnot, believed it had been brewed up by German scientists—
though biological warfare seemed the least likely, since the effects
were as severe in Germany as elsewhere. The Germans called the flu
Blitzkatarr, putting it down to the fumes and poison gas drifting from
the battlefields. With wartime censorship, and confused record-
keeping, the true scale of the 1918–19 pandemic did not emerge till
later, but the final toll was calculated at 25 million deaths around the
world. Masa's illness was a frightening time for Kiyoshi, already without his father and now fearing he might be left without a mother, but
she recovered. At the end of November, after being unable to write
for several weeks, she told Arthur of her escape, and he replied saying
how many lives the flu was taking in England, and giving his opinion
that the Germans had planted the bacteria.

The horrors of the Spanish flu were one of the few wartime experiences that Japanese civilians shared with ordinary people in
Britain, where 228,000 died, fewer than in Japan. Masa was still too
sick to take in the news of the end of the Great War when reports of
the ceasefire were published in Tokyo on the morning of 12 November. Even if she had been able to go out into the streets, she would
have found no general rejoicing, partly because people were more
concerned about the flu epidemic, and also because the newspapers
were bemused by the idea of an armistice and could not judge whether
this was really the end of it all or just a temporary halt. Even the
British Embassy found it hard to interpret the cables, and dithered
about whether or not to run up the flag. The biggest festivities came
in Yokohama, with its far larger European community, where Western residents drove through the streets in an impromptu cavalcade
and set off fireworks. Over the next few days it became clear that

the last shot really had been fired, and reports came in of the delirious celebrations in London, Paris, Rome, and New York. Belatedly, the mayor of Tokyo organized a victory rally in Hibiya Park, and a lantern procession. It was a perfunctory affair, led by schoolchildren carrying out their teachers' instructions, and bearing no relation to the excited, torch-carrying throngs Arthur and Masa had seen thirteen years before.

Technically, Japan was as much a victor as the other Allies. She had joined the war in August 1914 and seen it through to its conclusion. Japanese delegates were already on their way to the peace conference about to open in Paris. When the squadron of seventeen ships that had performed escort duties in the Mediterranean finally left to return to the Far East, the governor of Malta thanked them fulsomely. "God grant our alliance, cemented in blood, may long endure."[3] Similar tributes to Japan's efforts were paid in Washington. When the United States vice president received the peripatetic Prince Higashi-Fushimi, a member of the imperial family who had been visiting the Western front when the guns stopped firing, he gave Japan generous credit. "In welcoming you we acknowledge that splendid part which you took in the winning of the war for civilization."[4]

In fact, the Japanese had not seen it as a crusade for civilization at all, and had stayed emotionally uninvolved, because for them it was never a war for survival. Japan's sacrifice had been on a very different scale. In Britain every family had been touched in some way, losing sons, brothers, or friends. All together, the countries of the British Empire saw more than 900,000 killed, and the United States lost 53,000 in only twenty months. The final number for Japan's war dead amounted to around 500.[5] By contrast, 90,000 had lost their lives in the Russo-Japanese War, and 250,000 Japanese were to die from the 1918 influenza. The Japanese had watched the war, as a former prime minister wrote, "like a fire on the far bank of the river,"[6] turning a deaf ear to the more demanding requests for military assistance. In the early days, the British and French wartime leaders imagined it might be possible to get a Japanese expeditionary force sent all the way to the Western front. Britain's ambassador in Tokyo warned the foreign secretary that this was completely unrealistic from the very start. "Ninety percent of the population have no idea where Europe is and care less."[7] The pipe dream was never entirely doused, and at later stages it was suggested the Japanese might like to help in the East, on the Russian-German front, at the Dardanelles, at Salonika, even against the Turks in Iraq. The Japanese always rebuffed the proposals on the grounds of practicality, explaining that there were not enough ships to carry their soldiers, or that they needed special food, until the intervention in Siberia was proposed and they could see something to play for.

The social impact on the two home populations was also very different. If London was worn out and exhausted in 1918, then Tokyo, the city that Arthur was planning to return to as soon as he could master his new legs, had gone through a very different experience. The streetlights had never been darkened. There had been no zeppelins, and no trainloads of wounded pulling into the stations. In Britain life had become grimmer and meaner, with power cuts and food rationing. Personal income tax had risen by 20 percent. In Japan the war brought a great wave of prosperity, new factories, and rising profits. The Japanese sold rifles and ammunition to the Russians, and copper, zinc, and chemicals to the other Allies. As German submarines picked off British merchant ships, Japanese shipyards won orders to replace them. With British and German exports at a standstill, the Japanese could sell saucepans and bicycles, oil lamps and matches to India, China, and South America. Osaka cotton mills took over from Lancashire. As the money poured in from overseas, Japan's trading position improved rapidly, and her gold reserves quadrupled. Britain's reserves evaporated, and her huge debts at the end of the war included 35 million pounds loaned by Japan. By the end of 1918, Japan was a great financial and manufacturing power.

Masa could see the new prosperity in her own neighborhood, where plots of land were being taken out of the rice paddies as the city continued to extend westwards. A new class of rich, whose money had come from the war, were building larger houses and villas in brick and stucco, not just traditional wood, with European rooms and furniture. The so-called *narikin* made windfall profits from cement and lumber, construction and transport. In a society where no one liked to stick out and modest behavior had been the norm, they spent more ostentatiously, provoking envy from working people, whose own wages had not kept up. In the rice riots earlier in the year, the *narikin* were blamed for the price rises, and a Profiteering Law tried to stop speculation.

If Masa was pleased the war was over, then the newly rich, as well as long-established Japanese businessmen, viewed the news as something approaching a disaster. If the war had continued for another year, even more money could have been made. At the Bankers Club, where Japan's most senior capitalists still arrived for meetings in top hats but the black-lacquered coaches waiting on the curb outside had been replaced by imported limousines and chauffeurs, they feared an imminent slump. With the war orders gone, shipyards and factories would face closure. German and British competition would return in force, and companies to whom they had lent money might go bankrupt.

The Japanese establishment feared political change as well. At the august Tokyo Club, opened during the Meiji era on the hushed model of a London gentlemen's club, Japanese noblemen, who wore frock coats all day and liked to relax by changing into kimonos and playing a few games of billiards in the evening, fretted about the advance of socialism. The war, and the Bolshevik Revolution in Russia, had brought strikes, political agitation, and a ferment of new ideas, with demands for trade unions, universal suffrage, and even the emancipation of women. Conservative Japanese believed that the hierarchical and family system, on which the whole society had been

based, was now in danger. Some of Japan's most fervent foreign ad-
mirers, who had praised the values and discipline of Nippon so un-
critically, thought the same.

With all these changes, a considerable gap now existed between
the Japan in Arthur Hart-Synnot's mind, which went back to 1904,
and the real face of the city Masa expected him to come back to in
1919. Tokyo now had a population of three and a half million and
was uglier, noisier, and dirtier. The streets were clogged with bicycles as well as rickshaws, and a growing number of motor buses
and trucks filled the air with blue exhaust smoke and the smell of
badly refined petrol. Rapid electric trains whirred over busy level-
crossings, and the line that passed Kashiwagi almost encircled the
city in a great loop. Many roads were blocked by excavations and
stacked sewer pipes as the program to put in drains continued; in
the meantime the nauseous night-soil wagons still creaked through
the streets. The original Imperial Hotel, with its tall iron railings and
graveled courtyard, where Arthur had stayed when he first arrived,
had been pulled down and a striking modernist building by the
American architect Frank Lloyd Wright was rising in its place.

Masa must have wondered how Arthur was going to react to all
this. She knew that the older, slower Japan they had seen together
still existed outside Tokyo, for the countryside had changed far less.
Arthur had talked of settling on the Boso Peninsula, to the east of
Tokyo, becoming an English teacher, and keeping bees. In the new
circumstances, that vision was difficult for Masa to share. She saw
his small drawing of the harness and straps by which his new legs
were attached to his torso. Beekeeping was out of the question. If
Arthur needed to be near doctors he would have to be in Tokyo,
and Kiyoshi's school was another reason for staying in the city. Masa
wanted the best for him, his teachers found him to be an intelligent
boy, and in April 1919 he was due to move up to the middle level at
the Gyosei School. With the school fees, and the higher prices,
Masa was finding it hard to pay the bills and told Arthur about her

difficulties. "I am glad you wrote to me about the money. I have asked you sometimes in my letters but you have never asked me for more. If you are finding the money is not enough, I will write to the bank and increase it. So long as I have money, I am happy to give it to you."[8] She could at last see an end to the days of money orders and bank transfers. Arthur was back in London, he had started to learn to walk, and at the end of November 1918 he was putting a timetable on it, saying he hoped to come out to Japan sometime in the first three months of the new year.

At the first Christmas after the war, when the Hart-Synnot family might have hoped to be reunited, Ballymoyer was shut and the glen was silent, except for the sound of water pouring over the cobbled weirs. The gardener who had acted as caretaker had left, and the furniture was covered with dust sheets. The attempt to rent the property had never succeeded, though an estate agent had produced a prospectus. The house lacked electricity and was damp, musty, and in urgent need of repairs. In Arthur's absence, his brother Ronald had helped with the running of the estate, but he was still in uniform, waiting for his demobilization papers in Portsmouth. Arthur himself spent the holiday in a much grander setting in the countryside thirty miles north of London, the next port of call on his prolonged journey back to normal life.

Sister Agnes and her hospital had taken over Luton Hoo, a millionaire's mansion in Bedfordshire, as an annex for senior patients recovering from their wounds. Pushed in his wheelchair down the marble-floored corridors, past Beauvais tapestries and Dutch and Italian paintings, Arthur and other maimed officers had a rare insight into the taste and lifestyle of the European rich. The house, originally designed by Robert Adam, had been bought by the diamond magnate Sir Julius Wernher in 1903 and extensively altered. The architect responsible for the Ritz Hotel redecorated the interiors with ornate paneling and fireplaces, gilded ribbons and festoons, to provide a setting for Sir Julius's art collection. The house, and the treasures it contained, were compared to the Rothschild banking family's opulent château at Waddesdon, in Buckinghamshire. Wernher died in 1912, leaving an immense fortune, and his widow made her contribution to the war effort by lending the house as a convalescent home.

Arthur was happy with his transfer to the country, and his spirits continued to revive. After seven months confined to hospitals in Rouen and London, he was regaining a little independence. His batman Frederick Tansley, who had served him in France just before he was wounded, returned to look after his clothes and run errands. Lady Wernher, a society beauty known as Birdie who had lost her youngest son as a nineteen-year-old lieutenant during the Somme, took a personal interest in her convalescents and came to visit him. "The house is six or eight times larger than Ballymoyer and is splendid. It is very quiet countryside, and I like it. The house stands in a large park and there are several gardens with fruit trees and flowers."[9] From his spacious, almost circular room on the second floor, he could look out over the park and fields beyond. He had a large bed, two armchairs on either side of a coal fire, and his own bathroom and dressing room, and was so pleased that he drew Masa a sketch of the layout.

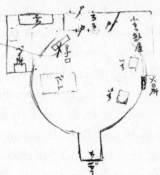

"I like this place very much. If you were with me, I would want nothing else."[10] Now able to sit at a desk again, the general worked at his poetry, as he had done during the terrible months at Ypres and in the hospital at Rouen. He wrote a rhyming tribute to the land-scape of Japan he so missed:

DAI NIPPON

Gem studded seas, where the sun's first ray
Heralds the dawn of the new born day,
Realm of the Isles of the Eastern sea,
Where is a country fair as thee?

Royal and lovely crowned with snow,
Fuji looks down on the scene below,
Down where the noisy torrent brawls
And the jewels flash from the waterfalls. . . .[11]

Arthur's poem ran on for several more verses, taking in the sleepy bays and inland seas, and the drowsy sound of the morning breeze. Though his poems were never strictly autobiographical, there was a recurring theme, of yearning love across great expanses of ocean, and a woman waiting on the other side of the world, though for the purpose of the verses she was on tropical beaches.

VOICES OF THE SEA

Thousands of miles of ocean lie between you, dear,
*   and me,*
Its language is the same, dear, the language of the sea.
So come and stand beside it, and perhaps you'll understand
What the waves are saying, sweetheart, when they curl upon
*   the sand.*

Go, in the summer twilight, to the edges of the sea
And the softly whispering wavelets my messengers shall be.
To tell you how I love you. Ah! Will you understand
The voice of the ancient Ocean, whispering against the
   strand?[12]

Arthur continued to think about his own journey back to Dai Nippon. That autumn he had written, "Let us travel next summer and stay somewhere quiet and peaceful for a long period."[13] At Luton Hoo he was still working towards that goal, with a steely determination and a rigorous timetable. He listed the daily targets he was setting himself. "I have been practicing very hard and can walk surprisingly well. I came here on Monday and am walking as you can see by the chart: Tuesday—600 yards. Wednesday—1,000 yards. Thursday—1,200 yards. Friday—1,800 yards. Normally I walk three times a day, but today I shall only walk twice. I walk part of the day's distance on each try. I feel almost dead from exhaustion when I finish the last one but it will get easier."[14] With the letter on his desk, he came back and added to it over several hours. "Now I have just had my second walk, and I have done a mile. After the walk I had a bath and it helped me recover. I don't know when I will be able to walk better, but I am sure I can be much faster than the others. I want to be with you soon. Maybe it will be possible in January, February, or March. Give my regards to Kiyoshi. He is such a good boy. To my darling, darling, best wishes, from lonely Arthur."[15]

Determined to build up his stamina despite the pain that came from sores and aching muscles, he spent as much time as he could

outside, in the gardens originally landscaped by Capability Brown. Wearing his greatcoat against the east winds, he hobbled up and down past severely trimmed topiary and hard-pruned rose beds, and around the ornamental ponds, with his batman Tansley or a nurse walking beside him.

By the end of the year, the length of each outing was still increasing. "I can walk much better. Now I can do an hour and a half. The doctor and everyone else are surprised at how quickly I am managing. They told me no one had learnt to walk as quickly as I. I don't know if that is true or not. On the 13th I went to London to see a doctor. They took a mold for new artificial legs with kneecaps. They will take about two weeks, so I should have real artificial legs by the end of the year."[16]

Arthur's experience of trying to overcome a severe disability was common enough in the immediate postwar months. Two hundred forty thousand British servicemen had legs or arms amputated because of war wounds. Like all the amputees, he soon found that the fitting and adjustment of the artificial limbs was crucial. Calculating the correct weight for the prosthesis, and getting the least uncomfortable fit for the suede-leather cup into which the stumps of his upper thighs had to slot, were just as important as his own efforts to learn to use them. Ex-servicemen, most of them much younger than Arthur, were entirely dependent on the skill of the staff at the special clinics set up in each region of the country and the private limb-companies who supplied them. Tiny adjustments could make the difference between constant pain and discomfort, and tolerable if awkward mobility. In early 1919, wooden legs came and went between London and Luton Hoo, as the fitters tried to come up with the best shape, and Arthur made a series of trips himself. "On Wednesday I went to London to try out the new legs. I tried walking in them for two and a half hours with two people helping me. It was very hard. It was unbearably painful as the sockets did not fit well. They will have to readjust the sockets and I will have to go back to London when they are ready."[17]

Arthur's letters were as affectionate as ever, with frequent messages to Kiyoshi, and he passed on the small details of life in and around Luton Hoo. He sent Masa a picture of the house. A heavy snowfall broke the branches off many of the trees, and when Arthur tried to go out and walk in the snow he slipped and fell down twice. "On Tuesday a man brought my legs from London but they did not fit again so he took them back. They are strange. They look real. If I am standing still no one can tell they are artificial. They have kneecaps and feet. Yesterday my batman went to London to pick them up, and I tried walking but they did not fit well. The right leg was still painful, so they have to be sent back to London again. It is a nuisance, but I have to be patient. Darling, I now know what it is to be patient."[18] Even when Tansley had returned with the cups reshaped, the problems continued. "My new artificial legs still do not fit. The left stump has started to bleed when I walk, so I shall return them again."[19] Nevertheless, by the middle of February he could walk for two hours at a stretch. Descending slopes was still hard, and even with articulated knees he found stairs a challenge, because the joint, made from a combination of elastic and leather, was jerky and unpredictable. "On Friday I walked three miles but I think I did too much and was exhausted. . . . The weight of both legs is about 16 pounds, so it is not surprising I get tired, but I will be fine once I get used to them."[20]

Though the weather was not as cold as his terrible first French winter in 1917, Arthur found the gray overcast days depressing. It was twelve years since he had spent more than a few weeks in England. His long series of overseas postings meant he knew very few people in London, and many of his contemporaries had been killed. From the Tokyo days he had been in correspondence with Roundell Toke and Aylmer Haldane, and John Gubbins and his wife, but had lost touch with Colin Davidson. Members of his family came out to Bedfordshire to see him, including his sister Beatrice, and they must have talked about the situation in Ireland, now sliding into a guerrilla war. The nationalist Sinn Féin party had just won an overwhelming majority of Irish votes in the general election in December, and had declared Ireland a republic and set up an independent government in Dublin, to the fury of London and the Protestants in the north. Ballymoyer, on the Protestant-Catholic fault line, was likely to be in the middle of any future trouble.

In February, the King Edward VII Hospital for Officers announced it would be closing the annex at Luton Hoo, and Arthur had the choice of being discharged or moving to another hospital. He doubted anywhere else could be as comfortable as Lady Werner's, and sounded slightly despairing. "I am worried about where I can go. I don't like London, and I will be so lonely on my own in Ireland. And yet I cannot come to Japan on my own by ship just yet. Everything has become so difficult without legs."[21] He had not managed to keep to his timetable for his return to Japan, and his letters kept coming back to familiar phrases. "It is so inconvenient not to have legs. I think about you a lot. Those horrible Germans have done a terrible thing to us, haven't they?"[22]

Arthur's rank came to his aid, and army doctors gave him preferential treatment again. Arrangements were made for him to go out to a home for convalescent officers that had been opened by the Red Cross in the south of France. He set off at the beginning of March, with Private Tansley to help him on the journey. They passed through Paris, which was packed with delegations attending the peace talks, all with their own ideas of what they wanted from the settlement, and where the Japanese were installed at the Hôtel Bristol. The following day, Arthur took the Riviera express down the Rhône Valley towards the Mediterranean and the spring, arriving in the warm air of Cannes at ten o'clock at night.

M asa and Arthur had spent some of their happiest times together by the sea. In their last summer before Kiyoshi was born, they had stayed for several weeks at Matsushima, sleeping in a small inn and swimming in clear water off rocky coves. They made shorter trips to the Izu Peninsula, which jutted into the Pacific south of Mount Fuji, and took the train that wound along the coast to Atami. The sheltered resort offered an irresistible combination for the Japanese, with spectacular scenery and sea-bathing along-side hot springs and bubbling geysers. A high range of tree-covered hills rose up behind the town, protecting it from the prevailing northwesterly winds, and the balmy air, the orange groves, and the deep blue of the bay had made it a popular place to come in the win-ter. In the evening, visitors strolled through the streets in their *yukata* bathrobes with clogs on their feet. When the first letters and cards arrived from the south of France, Arthur told Masa several times that Cannes was very like Atami. "Now I am in the garden. There are many flowers and trees and it's so beautiful. I think my strength will come back quickly in a place like this."[23]

As Masa looked at the postcard of the Hôtel de la Californie, with an inked cross showing Arthur's balcony, trying to visualize his life in France, it was clear that he had made rapid progress. Even if his hopes of coming out to them in February or March had shifted a little, she could reasonably assume it was only a matter of weeks before he would be able to set off for Japan. Kiyoshi's only memo-ries of Arthur dated from their summers in rented houses, when he had come back from Hong Kong and Burma for his leave. Since then he had known his father only through letters and photographs. Now that this mysterious figure was coming back, the twelve-year-old Kiyoshi sent him a new list of requests for things to bring. At the end of March, Arthur wrote back encouragingly, "I enjoyed Kiyoshi's letter. If my large shoes fit, then I have plenty of them if he wants them. If there is a magic lantern at Ballymoyer I will happily bring it with me, too. I will bring anything you need when I come back to Japan."[24] A few weeks later Kiyoshi made an additional re-quest, for Arthur to bring some swimming trunks.

Kiyoshi left the house every morning in his black Prussian-cadet uniform and cap and took the tram into central Tokyo to the Gyosei School, not far from the Officers' Club by the Kudan park where Arthur and Masa had first met. He was still with the same children—from well-off families, with homes very different from his own—and that April they moved up to the middle school together. Gyosei expected its boys to take the competitive entrance exams for higher school, the critical stage before university, and the academic pressure began to increase. Though Kiyoshi still stood out as different because of his size and his European eyes, he met less racial prejudice than in the public school he had attended previously, and the Gyosei was more international-minded. The school had been founded by French missionaries and was run on Catholic lines, though few of the children were Christian. The second language of the school was French, several of the teachers came from France, and the boys learnt to sing the "Marseillaise" and studied French writers.

While Masa and Kiyoshi waited for news from Cannes, the rest of Japan had their eyes on what was happening in Paris, where it was Japan's delegates to the peace conference who were meeting prejudice. Japan wanted a "racial equality" clause included in the covenant of the new League of Nations, to prevent other countries from discriminating against her emigrants on the grounds of race. The United States voted against Japan's proposal, because of the old and continuing fear of "Yellow Peril" immigration in the Western states. The British opposed it on behalf of the Australians, as exercised about the "Yellow Peril" as the Californians. In blocking Japan's proposal, which seemed to be entirely in the spirit of Woodrow Wilson's new order, the two great powers seemed to be insulting the ally whose help they had needed so recently. To nationalist Japanese, this was another instance of Western trickery and racism. To a generation of British, who were used to making subtle ethnic and racial distinctions, it was another reminder of the difficulty Rudyard Kipling had noted forty years earlier: that whereas the Chinese could be regarded as a "native," "the Japanese isn't a native, and he isn't a sahib either."[25] Hostility to foreigners started to grow again in Japan, and the Americans, who had also tried to stop the Japanese from holding on to Tsingtao, were particularly unpopular.

The first letters that Masa received from Arthur on the Riviera showed he was clearly enjoying himself. "The place is warm and has a wonderful view of the sea, and the flowers are beautiful. The weather in England is bad in March and April, so it is good for me to be here. My legs are fine."[26] From his own account, he was leading a more sociable life than had been possible at Luton Hoo. "There are lots of visitors here. I have met five or six people I know. It would have been wonderful if you were here with me."[27] Masa heard about a trip he had taken along the coast to Sanremo in an open car, and picnic trips to the mountains behind the Côte d'Azur. She read about people who had been to see him, including the matron of the Rouen hospital, who had looked after him the previous summer. "I went to a friend's house to meet Aylmer Haldane. Do you remember Haldane-san? He was in Manchuria with me and now he is a lieutenant general. He has been here for six days' holiday. He is getting old."[28]

Social notes apart, Masa was most anxious to hear about Arthur's walking. "I am getting better day by day. Yesterday an excellent doctor came to see my legs. He said I will improve, and will eventually be able to walk without sticks like before. That is good news, isn't it?"[29] He seemed positive, despite the problems. "This place is very nice and similar to Atami. The hotel is good, too, but it is situated on a hill, so I have to go down the hill to get to the sea. It is very hard for me but I am sure I will get better at it. This morning I went down by car and walked for two hours on the flat by the beach. It was wonderful."[30] Three weeks later, he told her, "I can walk quite well on the flat. I can also climb the hill, but going down is still troublesome. When I am going down it is still difficult, and I sometimes fall because my knee bends suddenly. I will be able to manage better soon."[31]

Masa wrote at least once a week, and since she kept all of Arthur's letters carefully she must have been able to chart the state of his morale. By the middle of April he seemed to have reached a plateau, talking about the difficulties more than his progress. "I don't know when I will be able to walk properly. I cannot tell you how inconvenient it is without legs. I cannot go anywhere on my own."[32] "I have been practicing every day, but I still cannot walk fast however hard I try. It is a nuisance not to have legs."[33] Back in November, six months earlier, he had said he hoped to rejoin her and Kiyoshi in January, February, or March, but it was already April, and his last mention of the journey to Japan had been on 23 March.

Masa may also have begun to sense a change in Arthur's tone after he reached Cannes, though it was more a matter of omission than anything he said in particular. He seemed to become less effusively affectionate. When he first arrived at the Hôtel de la Californie, he was writing, "It would have been wonderful if you were here with me!"[34] A couple of months later he was sounding more formal. "I am pleased to hear you and Kiyoshi are well."[35] His letters grew shorter and rather negative. "There is nothing new to tell you."[36] "I shall stop now as there is nothing interesting to tell you."[37] He stopped enclosing the small pressed flowers and leaves he had always sent her, even from the trenches, even though Cannes had more flowers than anywhere he had been before.

Towards the end of May, he told her he was returning from Cannes. "Today is 20 May. I was busy on Sunday, and out all day on Monday, so I am two days behind in writing to you. Your number 298 arrived on the 13th. I am soaked with sweat after an hour of walking. It is so troublesome without legs. I cannot go anywhere on my own and always have to have someone with me. I wouldn't be able to get up if I fell down. I am going back to England at the end of this month. I will stay in London for a bit and then travel to Ireland."[38] This was the first Masa had heard of any plan to go back to Ireland, and there was still no mention of a date for Japan.

Masa received his next letter a fortnight later. Arthur started by describing how difficult the journey home had been. "Though we took a day to rest in Paris, I cannot tell you how exhausted I was. I am in London now, but I am not in too good shape. I have received your number 301 and 302, thank you. I am glad you are keeping well."[39] As she read on, it looked as though her suspicions were going to be borne out. Despite his determination, the practical difficulties were in the end going to prove too great, and she and Kiyoshi would have either to continue on their own, enduring the silent disapproval of their neighbors, or to uproot and move to England, as he had asked them to in 1911.

"Now I have to tell you something that is very hard to say, but I have to do it. I knew for some time that I had to tell you, but have been dreading having to tell you this. The truth is that I would not be able to travel very far in this condition. So I could not possibly go back to Japan." There was more to come, and as Masa continued to unroll the fragile white paper, and her eyes skimmed down Arthur's neat columns of Japanese characters, all the assumptions that had underpinned her life for fourteen years started to tear away. "Maybe it would have been better if I had died when I was injured. I am no longer able to leave England, and as I cannot live on my own, I am going to marry an Englishwoman."[40]

Having delivered the blow, he pleaded. "I am sure you will forgive me. If I had not had this injury I was coming back to you. But now I am in this condition I cannot live alone. You are a very kind woman, and if you think about my loneliness, I think you will forgive me marrying. Please tell me so. I will not forget my darling for the rest of my life, but we will never be able to see each other again. I cannot express in words how difficult this is, and with what a heavy heart I write, but I had to write sooner or later. Please forgive me. Please forgive me. Sad Arthur."[41]

The extraordinary relationship, which had survived so many tests since their last parting at Yokohama in September 1913, and which had given Arthur his reason for surviving the war and inspired him through his slow recovery, appeared to be over. The reserved Englishman who had so often promised that he wanted to be with her till he died, and had told her that their souls were as one, was going back on his word. Masa's immediate reaction, in her despair, was to take the step she had refused to take in the past, and travel to London as he had once implored her. With her mother gone, and Kiyoshi old enough to stay with relatives, taking a ship on the long voyage to Europe seemed practical, and at this stage perhaps the only thing to do.

ELEVEN

ON THE CROISETTE

The place is warm and has a wonderful view of the sea,
and the flowers are beautiful.
· A.H.-S., March 1919[1] ·

The bride's parents wanted a traditional ceremony, to be followed by a reception. The church had to be booked, the banns had to be read, dresses for the bridesmaids had to be made, and the planning for the London wedding started well before 3 June, which was when Arthur Hart-Synnot and Violet Drower announced their engagement in the "Forthcoming Marriages" column of *The Times*. Arthur did not fire off his shell to Masa in Japan until 8 June, so for some weeks his letters had been a lie, as he held back from telling her that he was abandoning her. With the admission finally off his chest, he wrote again a few days later, still trying to explain himself. "I thought hard about how you would take the news. I don't know if I have hurt you or not. But I am disabled, and I could not tell you how lonely it is to be on my own. All my family have encouraged me to get married and are pleased about it. Please don't get angry with me. I have told my future wife about you and she fully understands. She is called Violet. I would like to be kind to you as before. I have thought about you a lot. . . . Please forgive me. The marriage will be on 3 July. Sayonara, from Arthur, to darling Dolly."[2]

In the early years, Arthur had constantly assured Masa that he was there for the long haul, and she had come to trust him completely. When he left for Manchuria in 1904, and for England in 1906, he had managed to persuade her that he did not see her as "a temporary wife." Pointing out the difference between Major Toke's affair with Oharu-san, and their own relationship, he had written to Masa, "They are not like us, who will be able to stay close until we die."[3] When Masa received the shocking news in the summer of 1919, and was trying to decide what action to take, she wondered whether he had been deceiving her over a long period, or if this was a recent and sudden betrayal. Had he known Violet for a long time, or was she someone he had met in Cannes? Was he as besotted with the Englishwoman as he had proclaimed himself to be with her? When she tried to work through exactly what had happened, she may have reread his letters between March and May for clues. When Arthur had said, "There are lots of visitors here. I have met five or six people I know,"[4] were these reunions with men or women? Who else had gone on the drive in an open car along the Corniche to Sanremo, just across the Italian frontier? When he went on the all-day picnics he had told her about, had Violet been part of these excursions from the start, setting the rugs out on the beach? Who was the woman sitting beside him near the Cannes port in the photograph he had posted her?

The explanation for the great turnabout, and all the questions about Arthur Hart-Synnot's character that arise from it, have to be seen in the context of Arthur's physical state after his injury, his feelings about himself and his predicament as he began to recover, and the special atmosphere of Cannes and the Riviera in the spring of 1919.

A fter all he had been through over the previous two years, Arthur found the move to Cannes encouraging and reviving. The physical hardships of service on the Western front, and the terrors of the Somme, Ypres, and Cambrai, had been followed by an injury that nearly killed him, a double amputation, months of intensive nursing, and the spartan open-air regime of the 8th General Hospital at Rouen. Once he was well enough to be sent back to England, he had set himself a daunting physical test, as he tried to master walking as fast as he could, in the raw chill of the British winter. The newspapers were full of gloomy news of violence in Ireland and postwar coal and rail strikes, and there was no way of resuming a more normal social life while he was isolated in the Bedfordshire countryside. When he moved to the Côte d'Azur, he suddenly found himself in a place that was balmy and beguiling, the air scented with pine needles and mimosa, the sweet peas and carnations in flower, and among a sizable British community that included friends and connections with whom he could relax as he had not been able to since he left India in 1916.

The winter resort, which had drawn the moneyed classes from all over Northern Europe since the 1860s, and which the French guidebooks referred to as a *"station hivernale aristocratique,"* had taken on a drabber and more practical role as a vast hospital for the injured and suffering during the war. Whereas most of the British casualties were sent back to the bases in northern France, to Amiens or Rouen, or to the sprawling hospital encampments on the Channel coast at Boulogne or Wimereux, the French and Belgian army medical services shuttled most of their wounded down to the south. The serving staff and croupiers of Cannes were called up to fight, and the ornate, Belle Époque wedding-cake style hotels, the Beau Séjour and the Beau Rivage, the Windsor and the Grande Bretagne, were commandeered as hospitals and sanatoriums. At the time of the battle of Verdun, even the Municipal Casino was divided into makeshift wards. When the U.S. Army reached France, it added to all this, setting up its own hospitals with beds to accommodate four thousand American wounded in Cannes alone.

Five months after the Armistice, in the spring of 1919, bandaged and disabled servicemen were still to be seen limping along the streets, and sitting out on benches under the palms, but the Allied hospitals were emptying, and leisured visitors were starting to return. American millionaires tied up their steam yachts in the small port to reclaim their corner of Eden after four years away. Russian aristocrats, who had flocked to the Riviera to avoid the long winters at home, were straggling back on the still-disrupted trains, though now permanent exiles after the Bolshevik Revolution. The well-to-do English, by far the largest contingent of foreigners before the war, were booking into the hotels that had managed to reopen and renting villas and apartments. Queen Victoria had helped establish the British presence by her extended winter stays with a huge retinue at the Regina Excelsior in Nice, and during the long years when her eldest son, Edward, was waiting to succeed her on the throne, he had idled away much of his time along the coast in Cannes. Some of the more peripheral members of the British royal family were among the first to reestablish their sybaritic rights at the war's end.

As Arthur arrived in March 1919, Cannes was coming to life again. The temporary partitions that converted the gaming rooms into wards for the wounded were torn down, and the casino re-

opened, still looking rather shabby. The first postwar tennis tournament was under way, under cloudless blue skies, and delegates were
arriving from around the world for a meeting of the International
Red Cross. Cannes seemed all the more wonderful because of the
contrast with the rest of Europe that spring. In Germany they faced
severe food shortages. In northern France and Belgium vast swaths
of country were left as a desolate, war-scarred wilderness, littered
with rusting barbed wire and munitions. Civilians were returning to
homes that were in rubble, fields that were untillable, and a blood-
ied landscape that would take years to recover. On the Riviera, at
least superficially, the pre-1914 world seemed to have survived intact, and Cannes was unmarked.

Arthur's injury had been reported in the London newspapers
the previous summer, and his rank and record made him something
of a celebrity in the reassembling British colony. He was asked to
lunches and tea parties and found he could venture out by car or
taxi with Tansley to help him. The elderly Duke of Connaught, Queen
Victoria's third son, a retired soldier who had been commander-in-
chief in Ireland and knew Arthur's father and uncle, asked him to
call. At the villa of Sir Ralph and Lady Paget he met Aylmer Haldane, the officer who had led his group of observers during the
Russo-Japanese War, and whose room he had inadvertently set on
fire in the Chinese temple at Mukden. General Haldane had last
seen him just after his surgery at Doullens, when he lay hooked up
to tubes and transfusion bottles and was desperately weak. Eleven
months later, Haldane noted in his holiday diary, "Hart-Synnot
came for tea. He gets around wonderfully in spite of having no
legs."[5] Arthur's own military service was over, but Haldane remained as ambitious as ever. Now a lieutenant general, he would
soon leave for Baghdad to take charge of the British force that was
occupying Iraq, facing a violent and hard-to-put-down revolt by nationalist insurgents. Haldane's continuing upwards trajectory must

have reminded General Hart-Synnot of the career path he was now leaving, and his uncertainty about the future.

In the first few weeks, Japan was still at the center of Arthur's mind, and he continued to make comparisons between the south of France and Atami and the Izu Peninsula in his letters to Masa. As the benign atmosphère of Cannes took its effect, it started to undermine the concentration on a distant land that had kept him going since his parting from Masa. For six years he had got through his most difficult challenges by denying or discounting the present, always projecting forward, focusing his thoughts on life after the army or the end of the war, on how wonderful the return to Japan and Masa would be, on the Boso Peninsula, on a future idyll. In Cannes, as his body and his spirits warmed up, he saw that the immediate present could have a lot to recommend it.

Cut into the steep hillside at the eastern end of the town, the Hôtel de la Californie occupied one of the finest positions in Cannes, looking out over the shimmering arc of the Bay of Napoule, the small Îles des Lerins clearly visible a mile out beyond the point, and the green Esterel hills rising up from the sea farther to the west, towards Fréjus. It was the sort of grand panorama Arthur always enjoyed, with the same drama as the view from the Peak in Hong Kong. Part of the imposing six-story Californie was still running as a hotel, but the British Red Cross had taken over most of it at the end of 1918. There were only a handful of patients at first, and the Red Cross doctors ran the establishment with such a light hand that the army complained of laxness and took direct control, sending out a colonel to impose more military discipline. When Arthur arrived, there were around 150 officers in residence, with a full medical and nursing staff to look after them.

As in most military hospitals, the nursing sisters of the Army Medical Corps were supported by auxiliaries, middle-class and sometimes well-born young women who had joined the Voluntary Aid

Detachments to do their bit. A certain tension between the volunteers, universally known as VADs, and the professional army nurses,
was traditional. One VAD at the Hôtel de la Californie, in a letter to
her parents in Surrey asking them to send out white skirts and cool
blouses, wrote, "The matron hates V.A.D's and is always on the
prowl. She says beastly things about us in the Mess, and some of the
sisters share her spitefulness too, and so we have to be careful what
we do as they magnify every little thing they see or hear."[6] The VADs
were used to this, and since many had endured years of harrowing
work close to the front, they saw their final posting as a just reward.
Cannes seemed as blissful to them as it did to the patients, and they
knew they were lucky to be there. In their off-duty time they could
play tennis, ride horses, or swim in the sea or at the Cercle Nautique,
as long as they returned to the Californie by seven p.m. Once back,
they were subject to the colonel's rules. "The evenings here are rather
dull . . . ," complained the VAD Phyllis Goodliff, "as the Colonel
does not like us dancing with the men after dinner."[7]

The presence of a contingent of young women, not overbur-
dened with nursing work, only added to the tonic effect that Cannes
had on the convalescing officers. Arthur had been away from female
company in anything approaching ordinary circumstances for a
long time, the gap in his life filled by the *makigami*-paper intimacies
of the correspondence with Masa. At Rouen the army nurses and
VADs had plied him with morphia, peeled back the dressings to the
wounds on his back and side, and painted iodine onto his post-
operative bone ends, at a time when he was still psychologically as
well as physically shattered. He was deeply grateful to the women
who nursed him through this period, but felt he was in a different
world from them. In poems he wrote a little later, he referred to
them as "ministering angels," heavenly beings, kind but remote,
when he was a dependent invalid. At Cannes, though the nurses
were still taught to keep their distance and not have favorites, the
dealings were more normal.

From the point of view of the VADs, the work was far less demanding than it had been while the fighting was still in progress. They were no longer dealing with mutilated men delivered to the hospitals with gaunt faces and hollow eyes, torn bodies still caked with mud, wailing with pain and sometimes dying in their arms, but with the survivors, who were past the worst and regaining their strength and confidence. Nevertheless, because many of those sent to Cannes had suffered severe damage to their lungs, or major wounds that were not yet completely healed, the VADs had to dispense medicines, take blood pressures, help with washing and deal with prostheses. When Arthur was taken down the steep hill, past St. George's English church and the Villa Kazbek, where the Russian Tsar's family had stayed before 1914, so he could walk on the level pavement beside the sea, a nurse always accompanied him. Just as at Luton Hoo, he practiced for hours at a time, using his thighs to shift his awkward and heavy jointed wooden legs along the wide promenade that ran between the Boulevard de la Croisette and the beach, bearing a stick in one hand and holding the nurse with the other.

Getting men ready to face everyday life again was one of the aims of the hospital, and the colonel in charge allowed his patients to make outings. Arthur found others to join him in expeditions along the coast to St.-Raphaël and Fréjus and the forested hills behind them, or inland to Grasse to see the fields of flowers. Nurses went along on these trips to help with steps and stairs, manage the picnics, and make sure nothing set back their recovery. They were dealing with adults who were no longer bedridden, and it was natural that over the weeks the relationships became less formal. Many of the VADs came from families similar to those of their officer patients, and the acute class-antennae, which allowed the British to find their social peers in any situation, worked as effectively as ever. A relaxed mood developed within the hospital that Arthur appreciated as much as he enjoyed the wider atmosphere of Cannes.

Arthur was now getting a clearer idea of what the rest of his life

might be like, and what his disability was going to allow and prevent, based on his own experience rather than the doctors' optimistic early forecasts. He was feeling better than at any time in the
previous ten months, and was out of pain, though he soon developed sores on his stumps if he walked too much. He could sit at a
dining table, play cards, enjoy short car journeys and being in the
open air, but he still needed a very personal kind of help, to get in
and out of the bathtub, dress, and put on his uniform. Shaving was
hard. He could not get up and down the stairs, or into a car or tram
on his own. Though he relied heavily on his military servant, there
was a limit to what Tansley could do, and he was frustrated to find
how much assistance he still needed from the nursing staff.

There was one VAD nurse whose advice and experience he particularly appreciated. She had seen many men trying to deal with the
worry and pain of mastering artificial limbs, and had a realistic sense
of what was possible. She also understood how much help he needed,
and would continue to need in the years ahead. Violet Drower had
spent the war in England, most recently helping convalescent officers at a hospital in the seaside town of Brighton, where many of the
hotels had been taken over by the army. Because of the similarity of
the work she had been doing, and her good French, she was chosen
to accompany the first batch of officers who went out to Cannes by
hospital train in January 1919. Although she was on the books as an
auxiliary, she was more experienced than the other VADs. As a
trained senior nurse who had spent seven years working in hospitals, Violet was able to keep her end up with the fiercest matron. She
was self-confident and at ease with officers, and as she walked beside Arthur he told her about the estate in Ireland and his experience in India and South Africa.

Over the weeks, as the traditional winter season ended and
Cannes began to empty, Arthur learnt something of Violet Drower's
own background. She did not come from a country-gentry or aristo-

cratic family, but was the daughter of a surveyor from a London suburb who had joined the ever-expanding Ministry of Munitions during the war. Her parents, ambitious for their only daughter, had sent
her off to board at the highly regarded Cheltenham Ladies' College
for a year, and then to finishing school in Paris. She made useful connections and attended some of the events of the London social season, and the fashionable artist Philip Streatfield painted her portrait,
but by her mid-twenties she had still not made the match her parents
would have liked for her. At twenty-four she took an unusual step for
a girl of her background and started as a probationer nurse at Guy's
Hospital in London. With the outbreak of war, she volunteered for the
Red Cross. She served as a ward sister in a large military hospital close
to her parents in South London, before being transferred to Brighton.
When a young man to whom she might have become engaged was
killed in France, she immersed herself in her nursing work even more
completely. She was now thirty-three, well beyond the age at which
girls normally married, and must have been worried about her
prospects at a time when so many men had been lost in the war.

Violet soon became aware of Arthur's passion for Japan, and saw
him sitting out on his balcony, writing interminable letters in Japanese. He showed her his album of Japanese photographs, with temples and castles, lakes and waterfalls, and pictures of Masa. Violet's
only slight exposure to Japanese culture had been through her father's set of *netsuke,* the miniature Japanese figures carved from
ivory and wood that he and many others had started to collect during the era when Japanese arts and crafts were the height of fashion.
Arthur's enthusiasm for Japan made him seem all the more intrigu-
ing to her, though to his fellow officers at the Hôtel de la Californie,
most of them from a younger generation, it may by now have appeared rather eccentric. In the years since Arthur first went out to
Tokyo, British perceptions had changed, just as the reality of Japan
had changed itself. The admiration for Japanese patriotism and the

bushido spirit that Arthur had shared during the Russo-Japanese War was now forgotten. Despite all the official tributes to the Japanese role in the Great War, there was a belief that they could have done more, and a growing impression that they were devious and expansionist, in danger of becoming "Yellow Prussians." The Anglo-Japanese Alliance was still in force, but it must have upset Arthur that the respect and admiration with which the Japanese were regarded before 1914 were gone. From the distance of Cannes, the old house that he had shared with Masa, next to the temple at Juniso, seemed more remote than ever.

Though Arthur's senior rank meant Violet deferred to him much of the time, they identified each other's loneliness and found they could talk candidly and freely. As they made their way slowly along the Croisette—Violet in her VAD uniform and cap, holding Arthur's left hand—or sat in the shade of the gnarled pine trees in the Californie garden, they had plenty of time to talk about the future. When the convalescent hospital closed and the Cannes chapter came to an end, Arthur would be on his own and would have to decide whether he could or should set out for Japan, and if not where he was going to live. Violet's future must have seemed equally uncertain. She knew she would be demobilized, given a certificate of good service and a railway ticket to London, and thrown back on her own resources after four years with the Red Cross. She was unsure whether she could maintain her independence as a single woman, or would go back to living with her parents in Mount Ephraim Road, Streatham.

Arthur was still writing to Masa once a week. He had been writing to her for so long that his letters followed a yearly pattern, with a seasonal predictability. In early April he told her, "I expect the cherry blossoms will be opening in ten days' time. It would have been wonderful to go and see them together,"[8] just as he had in many other Aprils since 1906, but he was now holding something back from the woman he had always confided in. His letters grew shorter as he put more stress on the physical difficulties he was encountering, and he told her less about the minutiae of daily life in Cannes. At the end of one letter he sounded distracted. "Now I must stop, as there are many people coming in and out. Goodbye from Arthur."[9] Violet may have been hovering in the room as he wrote.

At some point in the second half of April 1919, the relationship between Arthur and Violet moved on a stage, and became more than that of patient and nurse. Each had grown fond of the other. Both spoke good French and loved France, and they now had friends in common. Though Violet was not as curious or philosophical as he was, and was the more conventional, she found him entertaining, and a man whose war record and efforts to learn to walk again showed his stamina and bravery. He found her charming, competent, kind, and good company. Violet was not regarded as a great beauty, but was personable, with an open-faced smile. Her most remarked-on feature was her brilliant blue eyes, and her nickname among her fellow nurses was "Chi," as in "China blue." In a very short space of time, only six or seven weeks after they had first met, Arthur and Violet decided to get married.

Arthur would later explain that he was "grateful" to Violet for taking on someone as injured as himself, implying that he was the one who had put the proposition and seized the moment of opportunity. At this stage it was hard for others to know if there was a real romantic frisson between them, but at the very least it was a practical alliance. Both knew how much they had to offer each other, even if this was never directly discussed. Violet would gain the security and social position that would come to her as the wife of a distinguished soldier and an Irish landowner, and Arthur would win a companion and helpmate with whom he could share life at Ballymoyer, or wherever they chose in the future. What Arthur could not share, or even start to articulate, was the permanent damage he had now sustained to his own sense of honor and of himself.

In this sad triangle, Arthur had faced a dilemma, and had put himself first. He was asking Masa to understand his loneliness, but ignoring the consequences for her or the loneliness she might feel herself. No one else, apart from Masa, knew the extent of the promises and pledges he had made to her, or the scale of the sacrifices she had made on his behalf. Only he and Masa could know the traumatic effect this breach of faith was likely to have on his surviving son, who had lived without a father for most of his twelve years, and had believed that this brave, trustworthy, almost legendary foreigner whose photographs were in the house and whose letters arrived regularly, was soon coming back.

Arthur's hope was that he could justify his action to Masa, get her to accept that he had no alternative, and rely on her good nature. Even before she had a chance to raise her own doubts and suspicions, he must have realized that he had more options than he was acknowledging. If it was clinically true that he was not in a state to travel to Japan that summer, there was no way of knowing how things might change in six months' time. By acting so quickly, he was throwing away the possibility of coming later, if his walking improved enough for him to make the journey. If it took two to travel, then there was no reason why he should not go out to Japan with a helper. Once in Tokyo, where there were doctors and limb fitters as there were in Europe, Masa would be able to help him in his daily routines as well as Violet. Arthur was also ruling out the possibility that the woman he had once assured, "I will love you and take care of you till I die,"[10] would finally be willing to come to him in England herself, if Arthur could not return to her.

As yet Masa had had no chance to ponder these questions, because she was still waiting expectantly to hear the date when Arthur would be arriving in Yokohama to start their postwar life together. The time it took for letters to get from Britain to Japan had hardly improved since the war, because the Trans-Siberian Railway was still blocked, and it would be another five weeks before she knew that anything had changed for her.

On a cool and showery Thursday afternoon in early July, less than four months after they had met, Arthur and Violet were married in London by Bishop Cecil Hook at St. Paul's Church, just across Knightsbridge from Hyde Park. It was a moving service, with a full choir and a large turnout of Hart-Synnot and Drower relatives, many of the men still in military uniform. Arthur, wearing his decorations, had his brother Ronald to hold his elbow and steady him, and Violet, in a dress of soft ivory georgette, was given away by her father, John Drower. Two bridesmaids, in equally pale georgette, with gold lace hats, carried her train. For the Drower family, the wedding was a moment of some pride, because Violet was marrying up a social notch. When she had left England for Cannes she had been a thirty-three-year-old girl from the suburbs, on a nurse's wage of one pound, fifteen shillings a week. Now she was joining the landed gentry. On the Hart-Synnot side, Arthur's father's brother, General Reginald Hart, VC, now seventy-one, was the senior representative, with cousins and aunts from Armagh. It seemed a cause for genuine celebration that Arthur, unmarried for so long, had been able to recover from his injury so well that he could take this step. Though his sisters and brother knew of his earlier liaison with a woman in Japan, they were probably relieved he had put all that behind him. Of those in the church, only Cousin Norman, who had met Masa in Hong Kong, seen them living together, and knew what sort of a woman she was, can have really sensed what must have been passing through Arthur's mind.

Later Arthur and Violet said goodbye to the wedding guests and set out from the Hans Crescent Hotel on a ten-day motoring holiday that would eventually bring them to Ballymoyer. They headed west towards Wales, sitting behind the chauffeur, seeing churches and castles, border country and mountains that were new to both of them, until they came to Holyhead. They reached Ireland on 13 July, the day after the anniversary of the battle of the Boyne, when members of the Orange Order marched with brass bands and accordions to celebrate the victory that confirmed English and Protestant domination of Ireland over two hundred years earlier, and allowed the Synnot ancestors to establish their considerable fortunes.

In July 1919, the atmosphere was tenser than ever. Sinn Féin had defiantly proclaimed that Ireland was now an independent republic, and dismissed proposals for Home Rule under London. The Irish Volunteers, about to become known as the Irish Republican Army, had begun guerrilla attacks on British government targets. When Arthur and Violet drove through Newry, they saw more British troops on the streets and guards outside the police stations. When they reached the gates of Ballymoyer, there was no reception party waiting for them, and the car bumped down the long avenue, with more potholes in it now, to the dank, shuttered house. Arthur may have tried to suppress the dream he had had so often, about making this return journey with someone else.

They stayed with his aunt at Rostrevor, beside Carlingford Lough, while Ballymoyer was made ready enough for them to move in. Arthur still had no idea how Masa would take the news that he was abandoning them, but she was very much on his mind, and he was confident enough, or insensitive enough, to want to tell her about his wedding. Only two weeks after the ceremony he wrote to her from Ireland. "I am sorry for not writing for some time, please forgive me. I was married on 3 July in London. I wanted it to be a simple service, but the church was filled with lots of people. Many of my relatives came. My wife is called Violet and she is a very good person. She knows all about you. I am very pleased about it and I hope you feel the same. It is terribly hard to write a letter like this but as you are kindhearted, you will understand."[11] More of Masa's regular letters had been forwarded to him during the honeymoon journey, and she had asked for a blanket and some of Arthur's old shoes for Kiyoshi, so he continued as if everything was back to normal. "I received your 305 to 308 on 10 July. I will send the things you have requested from Ballymoyer, and greetings to you and Kiyoshi. Goodbye, from Arthur to Dolly."[12] He was trying to convince himself that what he had done was rational and excusable, and trusted she would understand.

TWELVE

A FURY ROUSED

*You have a kind heart, and will forgive me
when you see my situation.*
· A.H.-S., August 1919[1] ·

With a Japanese sense of order, Arthur and Masa always meticulously numbered the letters they sent to each other, so they could check that everything they had written had arrived at the other end and make sure no piece of news or especially tender endearment had been lost in the post. Their procedure was to start numbering from 1 again every time they parted from each other, so that when Arthur was back in Ireland and Jersey in 1906, the numbers reached as high as 80. After Arthur had returned to see Masa and the infant Kiyoshi in April 1907, they started their numbering from 1 all over again, until he made his first visit back from Hong Kong, and so on. They had now been apart for nearly six years, and the numbers at the top of their letters had been rising all the way through Arthur's time in India, on the Western front during the war, and through the weeks at Rouen, Luton Hoo, and Cannes. By the summer of 1919, Arthur was on his 338, and Masa had reached 316.

Masa's letter number 317 can only be reconstructed from

Arthur's response to it, but it must have been unlike any other. His announcement that he was marrying a nurse from Cannes roused her from the subdued and philosophical calm she had managed to maintain for so many years into an aggrieved fury. Coming from a woman who had been so understanding, accepting, encouraging, and loving for so long, the letter she sent him in the middle of July 1919 was angry and distraught. Her faith in Arthur, with all his romantic words and lifelong pledges, had been exploded away. She accused him of completely misleading her. As recently as December, he had told her he would be back by March, and she and Kiyoshi had waited patiently. Now she had been betrayed. She was coming to London to confront him and marry him. The only thing that might stop this was if he paid her a large sum of money, and she named the figure of 10,000 yen, or $5,000, the amount he had told her she would get if he was killed in action, through his wartime will.

Once she had written her diatribe, and sent it off to him care of the Army and Navy Club in Pall Mall, Masa was left feeling humiliated and isolated. Her neighbors in the street were no comfort, and they would have been as unsympathetic as ever, judging she had got what she deserved for behaving in such a flagrantly unconventional way. In the past there might have been other Westerners she could have turned to confidentially for help, but the little circle of expatriates she had known in Tokyo was long gone. Though Masa was unusually independent for a woman of her class, and the head of a household, she was still a member of the Suzuki family, and sought their advice when faced with any big dilemma. With her mother and her brother Yokichi now dead, her eldest brother, Seijiro, still running the barbershop in Fukagawa, was the natural person for her to turn to. Yet she knew that her family's earlier advice was partly responsible for what had happened. She had listened to them in 1911, when Arthur learnt he was being called home from Hong Kong and begged her to go back with him. He had spent weeks trying to persuade her to become Mrs. Hart-Synnot. "If we are married it will be forever and we will not be separated. . . . I will love you and take care of you till I die."[2] She had refused him, because her family believed she would be unhappy and meet the sort of racial prejudice immigrants to the United States were known to face. Arthur had gone back alone. In the packets of his old letters she had kept so carefully, there was one he sent a few months later when he reached Armagh. "I am always thinking, 'If only you were here with me, I would be so happy.' . . . Had you come back with me you would have come to know Ballymoyer by now and would be loved by all my family."[3] She must have been wracked by all the "if only's" of their long separation.

Though the memory of the lost chance eight years earlier added to her torment, she did not believe it excused Arthur's behavior now, and a series of questions must have run through her mind as she tried to calibrate the degree of his betrayal. Why had he told her that he was mastering walking, with almost yard-by-yard accounts of his progress at Luton Hoo, and then suddenly claimed it was impossible for him to travel? Had he exaggerated his progress just to encourage her, or was it simply that he had fallen for another woman, fair-skinned and seven years younger, who had more in common with him and spoke his language? If his account was true, and he had become involved with Violet only after realizing that he could not get to Japan, then there was another option he was completely ruling out. Why had he not told her the situation and then asked, again, if she and Kiyoshi would come to England themselves?

Arthur would not get her letter 317 for another four or five weeks, and she could not expect to hear back from him till October. Conducting a bitter argument of the heart at this snail-like speed, trying to make her case and persuade him to return to her when each claim and counterclaim took so long, would be debilitating and so drawn out that the exchange might eventually run into the ground. There was much to be said for direct action and traveling to London straightaway to confront him, as she had threatened in her letter. Masa had the funds for the ticket. She had traveled to and from Hong Kong several times on her own without difficulty. The fastest route to England, via Canada with changes of boat and train, might be daunting, but an NYK ship, where Japanese would be spoken, still left Yokohama every fortnight for European ports via Suez. Once arrived, she would have to meet Arthur in London or go over to Ireland, and there her real problems would begin. It would be less a difficulty of language than one of class and position. The unmarried barber's daughter from Fukagawa would have to confront a respected general in the British Army, who would be embarrassed and defensive. Probably on the advice of her brother Seijiro, she decided not to take things so fast.

Masa also saw that her own position was desperately weak. Her claim on Arthur was a moral, not a legal one. Even if the question of paternity arose, the official papers stated Kiyoshi was her brother's son. If Arthur could not be persuaded to take her back, then the row would inevitably come down to money and his financial obligations to them both, after he had strung them along and then broken his promises. At the age of forty-one Masa had no occupation and no income aside from the regular remittances that came to her from London via the Yokohama Specie Bank, which by now amounted to 800 yen, or $400, a year. It was Arthur who did not want her to work, and encouraged her move from working-class eastern Tokyo to the newer, more salubrious, and more expensive area around Shinjuku. Her own standard of living had certainly risen because of the connection with Arthur, and she had left the rest of her family behind in an economic sense, but she had been thrifty, and her own comfort does not appear to have been her main concern. She believed she had to fight for what was due to Kiyoshi.

Masa resigned herself to a long wait, through the hottest time of the year, in the small rented house that smelt of pine and cedar. Kiyoshi was starting his summer holiday and was at home with her. His Gyosei friends, from wealthier families, left Tokyo for the cool hills of Karuizawa, or the seaside resort at Zushi. Kiyoshi had nothing much to do except read and study Japanese and French for his schoolwork, water the vegetables in the garden, or walk down the dusty unsurfaced side streets of Kashiwagi, past the shrine and the large house where Masa and Arthur had lived before he was born, to what remained of the Juniso pond. People still came to Juniso to hire rowing boats on the stretch of open water and catch the breeze, though urban Tokyo had surrounded it.

The torpor of the summer was broken, briefly, by the news that Japan had signed the Treaty of Versailles in Paris with the other great powers. In the covenant of the new League of Nations, the great hope for world peace in the future, there was no clause asserting racial equality. Talk of peace seemed premature in Japan's case, since seventy thousand troops were still away in Siberia as the major force in the international operation launched, without the presence of Colonel Hart-Synnot, in the previous year. The intervention had failed in its original aim of helping the anti-Bolshevik forces and had now turned into an ill-concealed effort by the Japanese military to establish their own control over eastern Siberia, but casualties were mounting. In February, three hundred Japanese soldiers were massacred by the Bolsheviks at Nikolaesvsk, at the mouth of the Amur River.

Modest celebrations of the final Versailles peace settlement were held in Tokyo in early July. Masa and Kiyoshi may have been more interested in the reports of the spectacular ceremonies in London on 20 July 1919. Fifteen thousand servicemen from Britain and the empire, and contingents from all the Allies, took part in a victory parade that lasted over two hours. The Americans came first, three thousand doughboys in steel helmets with bayonets fixed and roses in the muzzles of their rifles, marching behind General Pershing; then the Belgians; and on in alphabetical order to the French led by Marshal Foch on a white horse. The Italian detachment was followed by Japan. As they came under Admiralty Arch and down the Mall, the Japanese passed terraced seating reserved for wounded men and officers, and widows and children of the dead, until they reached the reviewing stand, where Colonel Abe and his small contingent turned their eyes to the left and saluted King George V smartly. High above the crowds, Japanese flags were among those flapping from the upper windows of Buckingham Palace.

Masa's own respect for British honor, and the British Army, was much reduced. Her wait was made more painful because she continued to get further letters from Arthur after his wedding, written when he had not yet heard from her and was unaware of her reaction. He took it for granted that she would still be interested in the progress of his walking and the domestic details of his new life. "Please forgive me for not writing for some time. Your numbers 309 to 312 all came safely. Also the commemorative peace stamps and the book have both arrived. I am staying at Ballymoyer with my wife. The house is in a mess because it has been shut for so long, and it seems to be difficult to find a housekeeper. We are here for a short time, and are then going back to London so I can have new legs fitted."[4] Despite this matter-of-fact manner, his underlying anxiety showed itself. "What did you think when you learnt of my marriage? Did you think of me as a cold and cruel man? I hope you didn't. I was not able to come to Japan because of my injury, and yet I could not live on my own forever. It would have been worse than death. You have a kind heart, and will forgive me when you see my situation. I am very happy living with my wife. I will send Kiyoshi some shoes with the blanket. From Arthur."[5] His news about Violet must have seemed callous, and the answer to his leading question was already on the way to him.

In their first few weeks at Ballymoyer, Arthur and Violet opened up the house, and he took his new wife to see the places he had thought about so often when he was in the Far East and France. He showed her the woods and streams, the walled kitchen garden where the beehives had been, and what remained of the Japanese garden.

They had long talks with the steward, John Muldrew, who had carried on running the home farm, with its herd of dairy cows and rough fields of oats and wheat, while the Hart-Synnots were absent. He took her across to the gray stone church where General Fitzroy and Mary Hart-Synnot were buried, and drove her round the lanes with a pony and trap. They made calls in the village at White Cross, where some of the old retainers who had worked for his parents lived, and where, at the small post office, he was able to send off a parcel of used shoes to the son in Japan he did not expect to see again.

At an earlier stage, before it had become clear that he would need to go and settle in Japan if he was to stay with Masa, Arthur had dreamt of life in Ballymoyer after the army. Now that he was there, the experience was poignantly different from what he had imagined, not just because he was with another woman but because his injury made it impossible to do so many of the things he always most enjoyed. He could no longer chop wood, shoot birds, stand in the river fishing for trout, or ride a horse. Making his way slowly around the dilapidated house with the aid of a single crutch, which he found easier than a stick because the extra support to his lower arm made falls less likely, Arthur held a series of meetings with land agents and builders. Little decoration had been done since the 1880s, and maintenance had been neglected during the years when the house was empty. The roof, gutters, plumbing, kitchen, and bathrooms needed work, and the garden had to be reclaimed. Fallen trees lay in the parkland, and the handsome crescent of eighteenth-century farm buildings behind the house needed repairs.

Violet had brought no money of her own to the marriage, and in joining the Irish gentry she was moving into the world of perilous estate finances and genteel debt. Though the scale and pretensions of the house matched the 7,000 acres that still accompanied it when Arthur's parents took over in 1901, it had become a financial liability, and the land that went with it had been dramatically reduced. Parliament had brought in a scheme by which those who paid rent to Ireland's big estates were able to buy the acres they farmed. The Irish Land Acts were hailed as enlightened reforms, designed to remove long-standing resentment, and the Hart-Synnot tenants took full advantage. In 1905, Ballymoyer had 390 tenant farmers. In the next ten years, they bought 6,700 acres, on highly attractive deferred terms according to which they paid less to buy than was previously due in rent. By the time Arthur arrived to take over his inheritance, Ballymoyer was no longer a grand estate, and only the house and the home farm or "demesne land" of 325 acres remained. Meanwhile, the capital sum from the government that was meant to compensate the family was less than it should have been, slow in coming, and had to be used to repay a historic mortgage. To raise capital for the repairs and improvements, Arthur decided to sell still more land. Only a month after arriving, he put 90 acres of the best remaining fields, sloping towards the Newtonhamilton road, up for sale at a price of £42 per acre.

Violet worried about how the rambling old house, with eighteen bedrooms, was to be looked after once the building work was done. On Arthur's pension they could never afford all the servants the family had kept in the past, though by 1914 the number of staff had been cut back to only nine, including coachman and gardeners, before all were dispensed with during the war. By occupying only part of the house, they thought they could manage with a single married couple living in. After failing to find anyone locally, they persuaded Arthur's former batman Frederick Tansley, now out of the army, to move to Ireland with his wife as butler/valet and cook/housekeeper.

Arthur preferred decisive action to delay, and was impatient to get going again after the long hiatus of 1917 and 1918. In October, the social column of *The Times* carried a small announcement— probably placed by Violet, since it was not Arthur's style. "Brigadier-General Hart-Synnot D.S.O. has taken up his residence at Ballymoyer, Co. Armagh, where he is starting extensive industries on his estate."[6] It was an inauspicious time to be making a major commitment to the

Armagh countryside, and other local landowners of the Protestant ascendancy were thinking of selling up. Arthur knew the religious and political geography of Armagh as well as anyone else. Ballymoyer was on a dividing line, between the parts of the county with a majority of Protestant loyalists intent on retaining the union with London, and the Roman Catholics in the hill country of the south, where villages like Crossmaglen and Creggan were nationalist redoubts. Each small community had a different religious balance, and Ballymyre Civil Parish, in which Ballymoyer stood, was over 70 percent Catholic. If any Irish settlement were reached, involving some sort of Home Rule or even independence for Dublin, one group or the other would be disaffected or resented.

The Irish downpours washed away much of the sense of well-being Arthur had regained in Cannes. He suffered from aches and pains in the damp climate and complained of tiredness. His latest pair of artificial legs was still heavy and awkward, and yet another set was being made for him. Violet was plucky and supportive, but was unused to country life and dismayed at how much needed doing. She started to call herself Violette Hart-Synnot, to distinguish herself from her new brother-in-law Ronald's wife, also a Violet Hart-Synnot. All the time, Arthur was waiting anxiously to hear back from the woman he had always hoped to bring to Ballymoyer. Though he had abandoned her, he still needed her forgiveness, even approval, for what he had done. He knew her letter was probably buried in a sack of mail deep in a ship's hold, being carried across the Indian Ocean at a speed of eighteen knots.

Arthur was in London to have new legs fitted when the narrow white envelope, addressed to General Hart-Synnot in rather shaky roman characters, finally reached the porter's desk at the Army and Navy Club in the middle of September. The strength of Masa's diatribe jolted him. His optimistic assumption, that she would be willing to put aside her own feelings and see what he had done from his own point of view, was misjudged. Arthur was astonished at the idea that she might be coming to London, and wrote back quickly. "Your number 317 arrived. Finding how angry you are at my recent marriage I feel very sad. . . . In my letter of December last year I told you I would be back in Japan by March. But I did not know much about artificial limbs then, and I had not yet met my wife. British and Japanese customs are quite different, and you must know that very well. Even if you come to England it is impossible for me to marry you, now that I am married."[7] To her demand for ten thousand yen, he pleaded straitened circumstances. "You talk about the money in your letter. When I went to the front I left a will saying that you were to receive 10,000 yen if I were to die in action. But because I returned from the war I destroyed the will. In England the situation is the same as in Japan. Prices have risen three times since before the war, so living is not easy. Now I do not have ten thousand yen to give you."

In an earlier letter Arthur had said, rather elliptically, "I would like to be kind to you as before,"[8] but he now gave her specific assurances. "I shall continue to send you money as in the past. The annual amount is more than the interest on ten thousand yen, so why don't you start some business that a woman can do, using the money you have saved and the money I send you. I am now married, and I must follow the English custom. You tell me that if your request is not met you will come to England. But I have a wife now, and I would not even be able to see you. I would like to be kind to you, so please do not write to me making such an impossible request. My wife knows about you and I have read her the content of this letter. I shall continue to send you money."[9] The tone was businesslike, acknowledging his responsibilities and making it clear that he did not intend to leave her in the lurch. What Masa might find extraordinary was his continuing inability to empathize with, or at any rate write about, the difficulties she would be facing on her part. It was as if he did not want to acknowledge the sense of rejection and abandonment she might be feeling, or the effect on their son. It was a small sign of his self-centeredness, and inability to think himself into Masa's position, that he told her he was thinking of taking a winter holiday with Violet in North Africa or the south of France. Masa was now trapped in Kashiwagi. There was no mention of Kiyoshi, or inquiry as to how he might be taking all this. Believing he had dealt with her fairly, Arthur sent her the quarterly two hundred yen due on 1 October, hoped he had persuaded her not to set out for England, and determined to get on with his new married life.

Arthur stopped writing his regular letters in Japanese, and a correspondence that had been going on since 1905 was halted, at least from his end, as he threw his energies into the new start at Ballymoyer. With the repairs and improvements nearly complete and the most desirable farmland sold off, he wanted more of an income from what remained to supplement his pension. Apart from the gardens, all that was left was a few small fields for grazing, and two hundred acres of woods, including old stands of beech and the plantations of spruce and fir put in by his father. Arthur planned to cut and sell the timber. He auctioned off most of the old farm equipment and installed a new sawmill in one of the barns, and the farm laborers became woodmen. As the whine and shriek of the saw cut through the stillness of the glen, the general turned to a new project, raising poultry. The steward bought ducklings and turkey chicks and fed them up in tamped-earth enclosures in the parkland beside the drive. Thousands of chickens were set to laying in the henhouses.

With his military approach to detail, Arthur was impatient when things did not go as planned, and worried about the finances. Feed for the poultry cost more than expected, and the price for eggs and birds in the Belfast markets was disappointingly low. The sawn timber was hard to sell. Arthur's brother Ronald might have been able to warn him about what he was entering into, because he had supervised the Ballymoyer farm for his mother before 1913, but by now he had left the army after his safe wartime service and was ensconced in a salaried position at Reading University, teaching estate management. As farming novices, Arthur and Violet began to see they might have taken on too much. The income was less than expected, and the price of everyday necessities, from coal to candles, was rising.

Furthermore, the Armagh countryside was no longer the peaceful haven Arthur remembered. After IRA attacks on troops and police in the south and west, the British government banned Sinn Féin, seized arms and explosives, and suppressed the Dáil Éireann, the self-declared Irish republican parliament. The violence came nearer. In Lisnadill, a neighboring parish to Ballymoyer, gunmen shot the Protestant rector, and there were killings in Newry. In December 1919, the IRA tried to assassinate Field Marshal Sir John French, now the British lord lieutenant in Dublin, lying in wait at the entrance to Phoenix Park, tossing bombs and raking his car with gunfire, but French was saved by the armored flanks of his Rolls-Royce. Arthur had served under French in the Boer War as a young officer, and he had gone to see him when he came back from India at the end of 1916. The government published a new proposal for the future of Ireland, still trying to satisfy the incompatible views of the unionists in the north and the nationalist majority in the south. Instead of one Home Rule parliament there would be two, one in Dublin and one in Belfast. Sinn Féin, who wanted a completely independent republic, dismissed the proposal out of hand. With all this going on, in addition to their worries about money, Arthur and Violet decided not to travel abroad that winter.

During the long months after the break, Masa had far less to distract her than Arthur. Whereas Arthur's life had altered dramatically, and he was occupied and stimulated by a new challenge, for Masa nothing had changed except for the removal of an ideal but always hazy future. After hearing about the place for so many years, and seeing so many photographs, and meeting Cousin Norman, she had a sense of what Ballymoyer was like and must have tried to visualize Arthur's life in the grand house with his Englishwoman. It was probably a rosier view than the rainy reality, and she was unaware of the deteriorating situation in Ireland. Having sent off her letter 317 in July, with the demand that he marry her or give her money, she could not expect to hear back from him till late October, and would not know if she had to go to England until then.

When Arthur's firm reply reached her, Masa was furious that he was still refusing to send her the 10,000 yen she believed her due, the only way she could end her feeling of dependence and disentangle herself. She made one more effort to persuade him, with a further demand, but knew he held all the cards. Masa finally accepted the logic of what he was saying. He was married, and it was too late to change that. Though she was still seething, some of her anger had inevitably died down in the three months since she had been abruptly presented with the news of Violet. Though it was not what she wanted, Arthur's specific undertaking, "I shall continue to send you money as in the past," came as some relief, provided he kept his word and continued to transfer 800 yen a year to her. She knew that if she carried on too aggressively, or went to London against his wishes, he might stop the payments. In the end, though she had talked boldly, her sense of realism and natural caution made her accept what had happened, however reluctantly. She was concerned most of all for Kiyoshi. He had already suffered because of his Anglo-Japanese parentage, when he was bullied by other children, and had at last found a school in which he could flourish. If Arthur were to cut them off, and his son had to leave the fee-charging Gyosei and be thrown back into a local school, he would be the one who would suffer most. To protect him from an ugly and continuing row and try and secure his education, she put her own inclination second.

During the years when she was waiting for the war to end and for Arthur to sail back, Kiyoshi had been a constant reminder of his father and the time they expected to have together, regardless of what her neighbors or relations thought about her behavior. Now that Arthur was not returning, Masa would again be required to live by Japanese rules, subject to a conformist society's harsh judgment of a single woman with a teenage child by a foreigner. It was almost inconceivable that any man would now agree to marry her. Tall, shy, slightly gangly, with his father's looks, even his feet, Kiyoshi was now the principal object of her affection and the focus of her life.

Arthur had told Masa he had to marry because he feared loneliness. That autumn, Masa herself was lonelier than ever. The twelve-year-old Kiyoshi was still a child, not a companion she could share her inner thoughts with. The ending of her correspondence with Arthur, which had provided a substitute for adult company for so long, had left a void. In spite of what she thought about him, she found herself missing the regular routines of writing, posting, and receiving letters, the chance to express herself, and the sense of a different world that the correspondence always brought to her. After several months had passed, she started to write to him again.

THIRTEEN

PASSIONS
REMEMBERED

Shut tight the door, and lock and lose the key
Of that fair casket
Where your heart should be.
Deny, if any ask it
That you have any heart. . . . They cannot see,
Nor any know it once belonged to me.
· A.H.-S., 1921[1] ·

N ew Year was the most important annual holiday in Japan, when doorways were decorated with green leaves and pine branches, and strung with strands of seaweed and sometimes lobsters, to bring good luck. Arthur and Masa had only ever spent three of them in each other's physical company, in Tokyo and Hong Kong, but over the many years they were apart they made a habit of writing each other special letters, reasserting their commitment to each other. On the first day of 1920, Arthur was at Ballymoyer with Violet and may have preferred to forget what he had written to Masa twelve months earlier, from the hospital at Luton Hoo, though Masa had kept it carefully. "Today is New Year's Day.

Darling, darling, Happy New Year. I shall write you the first letter of the year as I always have done. I woke up early this morning and spoke tender words to you. I hope this year will be happy for you. I know you will be thinking about me this morning and the thought makes me happy, too. Let us hope we can spend the New Year together next year. To my darling, darling, with a thousand good wishes, from lonely Arthur, to darling, darling Dolly."[2]

Matters had worked out very differently, and a year later it seemed they would never spend a New Year together again. Arthur was trying to put Japan out of his mind. Masa was intensely lonely, missing the company the correspondence with her lover had brought. The common link between them remained Kiyoshi, but Arthur had never shown much curiosity about the boy's education or interests even before he abandoned them. After the first bitter exchanges that followed the news of his betrayal, Arthur had acknowledged his responsibility and seemed willing to go on paying for Kiyoshi's education. Money apart, she did not know whether he would continue to treat him as his son or would quietly forget him as he grew up. Ever since Kiyoshi was a baby, Arthur had always been ambivalent about him. He had insisted Kiyoshi be left in Tokyo when she came to Hong Kong, and had once written, "The children are lovely but life would be freer without them."[3]

On a cold January day in early 1920, a letter reached Ballymoyer from Masa that amounted to a peace gesture. He had not been in touch with her since September, but wrote back on the same afternoon, his Japanese a little rusty from disuse. "I thought about you at the New Year. I have not had a letter from you in a long while, and I have not written either, but I received your letter this morning. I am so pleased to hear you are well." Masa made it clear that she was now writing in a platonic and unromantic fashion, and Arthur welcomed this. "You say that you are writing to me as if I was your brother. I like that very much. I would like to be your brother for a long time."[4]

After giving her news about his legs, and some general postwar musings, Arthur told her more about his wife in response to her questions. "I don't like England after the war. Nothing is like it was before. I think you can say the same thing about the whole world. Nothing is like it used to be. You ask whether the nurse who was in the photograph with me was Violet. She is not. Violet was a senior nurse in the hospital. During the war there were many injured soldiers and not enough qualified nurses, so thousands of English-women volunteered to become nurses, including Violet. I met her in Cannes and I cannot tell you how kind she was to me. I told her about you and showed her the photographs taken in Japan. Thank you for sending Violet your greetings. I passed your message on, and she also sends you her regards. If you would like it, shall I send you a picture? I think about you sometimes. I will be happy if you write to me occasionally, and I will write to you, too. My hands are cold now, so I shall stop writing. Greetings, goodbye from Arthur to Dolly." He omitted the "Darling, darling" he had used for so many years, and there was no inquiry after, or message to, Kiyoshi.

With this exchange, Arthur Hart-Synnot received the acquies-cence, if not the approval, of Masa Suzuki that he craved. He had relied on her generous nature to understand his situation, and even if his conscience was still not clear, she had made it easier for him to carry on with his marriage. Nevertheless, for all those in the triangle, major questions still remained at the beginning of 1920. Violet did not know the true depth of Arthur's feelings for her, or whether the old ardor for Masa had really been extinguished, or just damped down. It was unclear how much contact there was going to be be-tween Arthur and Masa in the future, and whether Masa's wish to treat him "like a brother" was realistic, given all they had said to each other in the past. Neither knew if their shared memories would trap them forever, or whether the new challenges they were facing in their separate lives would gradually provide a substitute.

· · ·

A rthur had set himself the task of becoming a landowner and making Ballymoyer viable, despite his disability, at the most difficult time imaginable. Sinn Féin was now referring to a "war of independence" or "the Anglo-Irish war." Republican tricolors flew openly through much of Ireland. Police stopped carts on country roads, rooted about in loads of hay for gelignite and detonators, and searched lonely barns for revolvers and machine guns. The Royal Irish Constabulary, fellow Irishmen but seen by Sinn Féin as collaborators with the British, were themselves the principal targets, and IRA bands attacked isolated police posts. Loyalists began to organize militia for their own defense, and the police were strengthened by a new force recruited from ex-servicemen in England, known as the "Black and Tans" for their improvised and ill-matching uniforms. The government was accused of heavy-handed repression, by an increasingly hostile Catholic population. When Black and Tans or Police Auxiliaries sped through the South Armagh villages in their dark-green Crossley tenders, they were jeered and stoned. In May, a band of three hundred raiders fought a four-hour battle to occupy and then destroy the police barracks in Armagh City, and a few days later the IRA blew up the police station in Newtownhamilton, the nearest small town to Ballymoyer.

Arthur gave Masa a sense of what Ireland was like in the summer of 1920 when he was prompted into another letter. "Time flies so fast. I am sorry not to have written to you for a long time. . . . We are still living at Ballymoyer, but I don't know how long we shall stay. The world has turned upside down here. The police station at White Cross was burnt down recently. It is like a war. Prices are high as well, and it isn't an easy place to live."[5] Masa had tried to show she bore Violet no grievance by sending the mantilla from Tenerife that Arthur had once given her. "I found the lace shawl in the large envelope. Violet was very happy to have it. I am enclosing the letter of thanks she has written."[6] Violet's letter to the woman she had supplanted was generous, and the civil and urbane tone showed how successful Arthur's policy of frank disclosure had been with her. Violet was now sharing the task of dealing with Masa, and acting as if all that had happened was inevitable and God-given.

"Ballymoyer, May 29, 1920. I want to write to you myself to thank you for your charming thought in sending the beautiful lace mantilla, which I wore for dinner the same evening it arrived. I shall value it more than I can tell you, because it came from you. It was indeed a delightfully unselfish thought to let me have it and gave Arthur great pleasure too. We live many miles from any shops, but I am getting you something from London which I hope you will wear sometimes."[7]

from London which I hope you will
wear sometimes. We often talk of
you & I am never tired of hearing
about your life in Tokyo. We are
not leaving Bally moyer this summer
as travelling is getting more and
more difficult and expensive.
I will give this letter to Arthur to
enclose in his -
      Maido Yoroshiku.

          Violette.

Arthur and Violet found the burden of running a timber and poultry business with a guerrilla war sputtering around them too much. They went back to London in October, leaving the Tansleys in charge of the house and the steward to persevere with the chickens and ducks, and arranged to spend the winter in Morocco, which was said to be far cheaper than the Riviera. Arthur was by now finding he could travel more easily, begging the question of whether he could have managed the journey to Japan, and in early 1921 he and Violet took a ship to Tangier. However much of a bargain, the disorder and dirt of North Africa did not suit them, and within a few weeks the fastidious pair crossed the Mediterranean and went back to Cannes. The climate was as beguiling as ever, and the big hotels had reopened and were filled with the British upper classes on their annual migration. The Hart-Synnots did not stay in the Californie, where they had met two years earlier, but found a less expensive hotel in Juan-les-Pins, five miles farther along the coast at the eastern end of the Bay of Juan, where a pine-clad peninsula of opulent villas and gardens ran out to the Cap d'Antibes. In the protected, privileged social world of the Riviera they were able to relax in a way that had not been possible since their marriage.

In the continental editions of the English papers that came down by train, Arthur and Violet read of the IRA's burning of the Customs House and more destruction in the center of Dublin, riots in Belfast, and a wave of killings and atrocities, and decided to sit it out in France for a few more months. They rented a first-floor flat in a villa, with four bedrooms and use of the garden, and stayed on when other British visitors started to go back for the summer. Juan-les-Pins was flatter than Cannes, and easier to get around in a wheelchair, with a good bathing beach sheltered from the east wind by the Cap. Arthur found he was able to swim again. Unstrapping his legs on a steeply shelving section of the shore, he shuffled his scarred body into the sea with Violet's help, and paddled off in the clear water. Though he was still getting regular reports from the steward

and the Tansleys, he was insulated from the postwar world that so
dismayed him. He had said, several times, "Nothing is like it was before," and they were still staying in Juan-les-Pins when two of the
underpinnings that supported his view of the world were pulled
away. In the same week of December 1921, the three-hundred-year
union with Ireland was ended, and the twenty-year-old link between Britain and the Empire of Japan was abandoned.

After a cease-fire and negotiations, republican leaders and British
ministers put their signatures on the Anglo-Irish Treaty in London,
and Ireland was cut in two. Twenty-six southern counties became
the independent Irish Free State, and six northern counties would
choose to remain part of the United Kingdom. Though the signing
was greeted as a historic and hopeful moment, the feeling against
partition was intense in both north and south, and violence continued. The line of the new border was to be settled by a special commission, and Ballymoyer was in the middle of a strip of contested
country that both the Protestant unionists and Catholic nationalists
claimed as their own and were ready to fight for. The wooded glen,
and the sprawling old house that had been so dear to Arthur, his
parents, and generations of Synnots, was becoming a battleground.

Two days later he was jolted by another piece of news. Arthur,
probably the only resident of Antibes who liked to make comparisons between the French Riviera and the Atami coast, heard that
the Anglo-Japanese Alliance was to end. The rhetoric of two sea-
faring nations with so much in common was forgotten, and Britannia and Yamatohime were to be disentwined. From the point of
view of the British, the original reasons for the alliance were long
gone by 1921. With Russian power reduced or disabled, and Germany defeated, Britain no longer needed Japan's help to safeguard
India, or her navy to help protect British interests in Singapore,
Hong Kong, and the Orient. The alliance was shot down by the
Americans, who had always been suspicious of it, the first casualty
of a conference called in Washington to work out new security

agreements for the Pacific and limit the naval arms race. The British foreign secretary wrote to his ambassador in Tokyo, "We must do what we can not to make Japan feel we have abandoned her."[8]

In Japan itself, the loss of the alliance caused no great shock, and was attributed to British feebleness and cravenness towards the Americans. To an older generation, sticklers for the appropriate courtesies, it was the unceremonious manner in which the agreement was tossed aside that was offensive. A former foreign minister wrote, "The Japanese people had no lingering attachment to the Alliance, but they were pained to see this famous if not matchless instrument, which had contributed so much to the peace of the world, treated like an old pair of sandals."[9]

Ten years earlier a lonely Arthur had written to Masa, "I hope the Anglo-Japanese Alliance will last forever,"[10] and the hope had been as unfulfilled as his own promises to her. While in exile from Ireland, he continued to keep his distance from Masa. Though he kept up the regular bank transfers, he wrote only once, just before he left London for Tangier. The single letter was to acknowledge an offer Masa had made, to have her money reduced from 800 to 400 yen per year. Arthur accepted the proposal gratefully, explaining how hard it was to live on his pension. Even in this there was no mention of Kiyoshi, whose school fees were one of the main costs.

M asa was also trying to make a new beginning, and free herself from her dependence on Arthur. In the summer of 1920 she took the brave decision to leave the district where she had lived for fourteen years, and which had so many memories of their times together, and to attempt to start her own business as he had suggested. If Arthur had agreed to pay her the sum of 10,000 yen as she had asked, she would have felt secure for the future. With things left as they were, she could never be certain the quarterly payments would keep coming, and there was always the risk that he would cut them off or that something would happen to him. In offering to reduce her allowance, she may have been trying to disentangle herself, and force herself to develop an income of her own. At a time when tastes were changing, and coffee shops, small cafés, and bakeries were becoming popular in Tokyo, she saw a way in which her own firsthand knowledge of Western tastes could be put to use. Arthur had taught her to make sandwiches to British specifications. She moved back across Tokyo, to the area northeast of the Imperial Palace, and opened a shop selling sandwiches, made with slices of the soft white bread that was still exotic in a country accustomed to rice with everything.

Kashiwagi might not have been ready for this, but Hongo, with its narrow lanes full of university lodging houses, bars, noodle shops, and throngs of peak-capped students, was a promising location. The district thought of itself as Tokyo's Left Bank. Masa rented a house and shop in Hongo-4-Chome, a few hundred yards down the slope from the lacquered Red Gate that led into the grounds of Japan's most respected educational institution, the Tokyo Imperial University. Masa may have had another, if unspoken, reason for the move. She was an example of what was already being called an "education mother," the label applied to women who were driven by ambition for their children. In Hongo they would be close to the First Higher School, the prestigious university-preparatory school she hoped Kiyoshi would move on to from the Gyosei when he was eighteen. If he passed the entrance test, he would have the best chance of proceeding to Tokyo University itself, the route to the best jobs in the country and a secure place in the Japanese elite.

The change in Masa's daily routine was sudden and physically taxing—a return to her working life before Arthur, after years of reclusive domesticity on the outer edges of Tokyo. She had been brought up in shops and around shopkeepers, and found herself once again working long hours, trying to keep customers satisfied.

Her older brother's barbershop was down the slope and across Ueno Park, near the river, and her late brother Yokichi's shop in Kojimachi not far away in the other direction. Just as for Arthur when he returned to Ireland, the sudden change in her circumstances coincided with great changes going on all around her. Arthur had complained to her that "nothing is like it was before," and the postwar shock waves were affecting daily life in Japan as they were in Britain.

In the years immediately after 1918, the streets of Hongo reflected, and sometimes led, a political ferment sweeping the country, as liberals and leftists questioned the authoritarian government of the Meiji years and campaigned for more rights. The era of national unity, when Japanese had obeyed their Emperor and officials so placidly, and fallen into line in the great effort to modernize the country or defeat the Russians, was over. For the first time, in a spirit that carried on from the rice riots of 1918, Japanese were joining political parties and lobbying organizations, in an era that became known as "Taisho Democracy." Farmers, factory workers, and university students joined protests and rallies. On any given day, the police, carrying long wooden staves from the samurai era, broke up crowds demanding universal male suffrage and trade-union rights, or watched over noisy demonstrations by rightists resisting these changes and foaming against the threat of Bolshevism. Outside the U.S. Embassy, the Anti-American Young Men's League decried Washington's efforts to get the Japanese out of Tsingtao and Shantung and to cut back her navy.

In November 1921, a young rightist stepped from behind a pillar in Tokyo Station and stabbed and killed Prime Minister Takashi Hara as he went to board a train. The assassin said it was a protest against plans to bring the troops back from Siberia. Many more political assassinations would follow. Unpolitical as she was, Masa must have sensed that Kiyoshi's future would be affected by all this. He was entering adulthood at a time when right-wing nationalists would become increasingly intolerant with each year that passed, and the tussle for power between civilian politicians and the army would become the principal tension of national life.

The sandwich business lasted only twelve months, about the same as Arthur's attempt to become a poultry farmer. The shop was not a commercial success, but the reasons she gave it up were personal. Moving into Hongo, she encountered familiar prejudices among her new neighbors, who disapproved of an unmarried woman living with a foreign-looking child. Because of the taunts to Kiyoshi on the street, she decided to go back to her old district. Masa almost gave up writing to Arthur, because it was so hard to get any response from him, despite his undertaking to write occasionally "as a brother." His letter agreeing to reduce her allowance was the only one he sent over a seventeen-month period.

I n the rented flat in the south of France, Arthur had little to do apart from reading in the garden and taking a daily swim. He was no longer studying Japanese, or spending hours writing letters to Masa, and he turned to poetry again. He had been brought up to learn and recite verse, and saw poetry as a cultivated activity that went well with soldiering. He had been inspired by the Japanese Army, where generals penned lean haiku almost as a matter of routine during the Russo-Japanese War. On the Western front in the Great War he was just one among thousands of soldiers who found writing their own verse a way of dealing with the horrors of the fighting. Though a spate of war poetry was published, Arthur Hart-Synnot was not a Wilfred Owen or a Siegfried Sassoon, and his efforts were for recreation and his own satisfaction, not for others.

While in the trenches, he wrote in pencil on the faintly squared pages of his brown Army Field Service notebook, and continued to use the same book at Luton Hoo. In Juan-les-Pins, with time on his hands, he started to transcribe his war poems, and collected them together in a folder of typescript. The words and scansion could be awkward, but they were affecting. He also added entirely new ones, which seemed partly autobiographical. Arthur had been trained to conceal his emotions and master the stiff upper lip, but the verses showed how he was thinking as he tried to resolve his guilt over his treatment of Masa with his debt to Violet. There were two women in his mind, and one poem was about the difference between kindness and love.

MAYONE

. . . you brought peace
Where had been blank despair.
Your love and care
Made life again seem fair.
You saved me, dear.
Yes, saved a soul slipping
Past all repair.

What did I seek?
A solace to my mind
In you to find?
Oh, God! What faith!
With eyes tight closed, to say
The world is blind.

Soft arms cling close,
Love's tendrils round me grow.
Dear child I know,
Never would you let go.
Unworthy I
Who take your all, and give
But empty show.

Show of love you have. Affection true,
Gratitude too:
All these I give to you;
Could I give love
I would, but this one thing
I cannot do.

One of the features of Arthur and Masa's long relationship had been how well documented it was. The evidence for its strength came in what they had written to each other, week after week, over the years, and the fact that each had kept the other's letters so carefully. Arthur wrote a poem addressed to an old love.

THE BURNING OF THE LETTERS

What does it matter now the years have passed,
That heap of ashes?
E'en though your eyes grow dim
Through downcast lashes.
Read each once more, and in the fire cast,
Attain to freedom as you burn the last.

Fictitious freedom! Were you not as free
Then, as you are now, or can ever be?
It was your own act, dear,
Cut off your life from mine, and you from me.
I knew, and you know now, what pain can be.

Shut tight the door, and lock and lose the key
Of that fair casket
Where your heart should be.
Deny, if any ask it

That you have any heart. . . . They cannot see,
Nor any know it once belonged to me.

"The Burning of the Letters" was the most tantalizing and the most explicit, but still mixed imaginary elements with the autobiographical theme. When Arthur wrote, "It was your own act, dear, / Cut off your life from mine, and you from me. / I knew, and you know now, what pain can be," he seemed to be harking back to his entreaties to Masa to marry and come back with him after his time in Hong Kong. But, unlike in the poem, Masa had not burnt his letters, and had not attained to freedom.

On 1 September 1923, Masa was with Kiyoshi, who was about to start a new term at the Gyosei Middle School and was working hard for the higher-school entrance examinations. A strong wind had been blowing across Tokyo, and the weather was cloudy and hot. Just before noon, they felt a series of faint seismic vibrations. A few minutes later the house in Kashiwagi was jolted by a tremendous shock, the floor buckled and shook, the walls swayed, clouds of dust started to rise from the streets like a white mist, and within seconds an awesome rumble of collapsing buildings was heard. The earthquake was the equivalent of over 8.0 on the scale, the most powerful in living memory, and was followed immediately by ten more major jolts and seventeen hundred lesser tremors over the next three days. Within moments, houses, shops, factories, telephone exchanges, banks, and police stations were tangled heaps of wreckage. Only the most recently built steel-framed buildings survived. In Kojimachi, the Finance Ministry, the Justice Ministry, many other government offices, the French and Italian embassies, and parts of the Imperial Palace collapsed. At the Gyosei School, the main brick building and the elementary school were completely demolished.

With so much of the city still built from wood, overturned char-coal stoves and braziers started fires, which picked up speed and swept through the collapsed areas, burning those who were still alive but trapped in the wreckage and destroying more property than the earthquake itself. By the time the fires had burnt themselves out it was reckoned that 44 percent of Tokyo's buildings had been leveled, and more than 60,000 had lost their lives. In Yokohama, storage tanks burst, sending rivers of oil through the streets, and 90 percent of the city was destroyed in an afternoon, including the Chartered Bank branch that received Masa's money. A tsunami wave up to twelve meters high crashed onto the shore of Tokyo Bay, destroying boats, docks, and warehouses.

Masa and Kiyoshi survived because in Shinjuku, and farther out in Kashiwagi, there was less damage, with fewer fires because the houses were newer and farther apart. That night, crowds on the west-ern spurs of the city looked out on the catastrophe, as great orange-and-scarlet flames rose into the sky towards the dense black smoke. Troops used dynamite in a vain attempt to clear firebreaks, and thud-ding explosions added to the apocalyptic scene. All the progress Tokyo had made in sixty years seemed to have been set back to zero.

For Kiyoshi, now a rather shy adolescent, angry with his father and feeling under pressure because of the crucial exams he was due to take the following spring, the disruption and chaos of the earth-quake came at a bad time. It was weeks before the Gyosei School could return to anything like normal teaching. The First Higher, the school he was aiming for next, was also burnt out and would have to be rebuilt. For Masa, the earthquake destroyed the world she and her family had been brought up in, because the crowded working-class wards on the flatlands on either side of the Sumida River were the worst hit. The house where she had been born in Fukagawa, her father's shop, and the streets and timber yards around it were re-duced to open spaces of blowing cinders. She lost friends and rela-tives, though her brother Seijiro miraculously survived. In Asakusa

Park, where she had walked so many times with Arthur, the kiosks and theaters were incinerated, and the ponds left clogged with corpses. The twelve-story viewing tower was a brick stump in a mountain of its own rubble, though the far older temple dedicated to Kannon, the goddess of mercy, survived. The old house next to the temple at Matsuchiyama was gone, along with most of the places she associated with her first years with Arthur.

Though Arthur was not there to see it, the near-wrecking of Ballymoyer House had come in the summer of the previous year. A column of dark-green Crossley tenders rattled down the drive, past the stone bridge and the deserted chicken runs, and sixty Northern Ireland Police Auxiliaries commandeered the house, despite the steward's protests. The "Specials" cleared aside the Synnot furniture, knocked holes through walls for telephone wires, barricaded the windows with steel gratings and sandbags, uncoiled barbed wire and dug trenches in the garden to make an armed strongpoint for themselves. With no regard for Violet's redecoration, they used the ornate drawing room as a field kitchen and mess hall, emptied the wine cellar, broke the china, and lit fires with whatever wood was available. South Armagh had turned into a war zone since the signing of the Anglo-Irish Treaty, as both the IRA and the loyalists tried to seize control on the ground before the final line of the frontier was set. IRA snipers shot at police patrols from over the border, and from houses and farms they had already taken on the Armagh side, and the government forces felled trees to leave clear fields of fire, knocked down bridges, and blocked roads to create a no-man's-land. Farming became impossible and the rough fields were abandoned. Though the hills and glens were as sublimely beautiful as ever, sudden bursts of machine-gun fire now broke the quiet. IRA squads made frontal attacks on the Specials' fort at Crossmaglen. Protestant farmers living in the wrong place were murdered, and killings were followed by reprisals. In Newry, James Woulfe-Flanagan, brother of Arthur's friend Colonel R. J. Woulfe-Flanagan, who had come back from the Far East with him in 1906, was shot as he left the cathedral after mass. As a magistrate, he had been trying many Sinn Féiners.

Ballymoyer remained a fortified post for many months. By the end, when the windows were broken, the fireplaces and fittings ripped out, banisters and shelves used for firewood, it was uninhabitable. Arthur never returned, though his brother went back on his behalf to list the damage and try to get compensation from the Northern Ireland government. The grim little war in South Armagh marked the end of a chapter in Arthur's family history. He lost pictures and books that went with his mother's Irish past, as well as porcelain and small treasures brought back from Japan. The ransacking convinced Arthur and Violet they were right to stay in the south of France. The Tansleys had already come out to act as manservant and cook, and Arthur looked for a house to buy close to Antibes.

At the end of 1922, they bought a substantial nineteenth-century villa, in heavy Belle Époque style with white stucco and a large garden, that they had passed many times in Juan-les-Pins. The Villa du Golfe had been neglected, but the rooms were a handsome size, with space for furniture that Violet had sent from London. The small resort, with its tired casino, was not as fashionable as its neighbors and had so far escaped the rash of hotel building under way all along the coast. The house was across the road from the sea, and an opening in a low stone wall led to the beach.

With the decision to buy property in France, Arthur accepted the reality of his situation. The combination of the troubles in Ireland, and the effect the damp British climate had on his wounds, meant he could never lead the life he had expected when he married Violet and set out for Ballymoyer. At the same time, his connection with Violet was not the normal one of man and wife. They would not have children, perhaps because of his injuries, and Violet could never occupy the same special place in his imagination that Masa, "the most beautiful woman in the world," had occupied for so long. He might have felt more beleaguered and frustrated if it were not for a part of his old life that came back to him at this time. Notwithstanding his "Burning of the Letters" poem of the previous year, the old correspondence with his former lover was rekindled. At the Villa du Golfe, Arthur once again spent hours of his time writing letters to the woman he had yearned for over so many years, despite the fact that he was now married to someone else.

In 1920 and 1921, when Arthur had been trying to separate himself from Japan, he sent Masa just three letters. In 1922, once Masa had managed to set the exchange going again, and Arthur realized it might be possible to maintain it without upsetting Violet, they began to write to each other once a month. The frequency soon rose to once a fortnight, and since Arthur took several days over each letter, with increasing recourse to the dictionary as his vocabulary slipped away, writing to Masa became one of his major activities. "I like the place where I am living now as it is very quiet. Now that it is getting warmer I am swimming every day. I am writing my letter to you in the garden."[11] For both Arthur and Masa, the letters once again became an essential part of their routine, as they told each other about the minutiae of their very different daily lives, the weather, their health, gardening, and changes in the world outside.

The correspondence began again just as Ireland was degenerating into civil war. "The situation is getting worse and I don't know what will happen. It is such a shame that Ireland is in so bad a way now. If I could find someone to buy the house I would be glad to sell it. I have had enough fighting, especially between my own people."[12] A couple of months later, Arthur wrote, "There is no news about Ballymoyer. It has been turned into a fortress, and all my possessions have been stolen by the soldiers. I am not as upset as before, but I was very angry when it happened."[13] A letter he sent later indicates that Masa must have been telling him to be philosophical. "I feel angry when I think about Ballymoyer. Most of the things we bought in

Japan together were lost, except for the statue of the seven gods and the sake cups. But as you say, I have to learn to accept the situation or it will be bad for my health."[14]

After the news of the Tokyo earthquake Arthur was deeply anxious, and it was almost two months before he heard from Masa. "Oh, I was so happy to receive your letter. I cannot tell you how worried I was about you. . . . I hoped you would be all right as you live a long way from the center, but I could not rest until I heard from you. I am very distressed that so many died. Why does such a terrible thing have to happen? The Japanese are a brave people so I am sure the damage will be repaired and they will be able to rebuild the city soon. I have sent money to the emergency appeal in London. I am so happy to receive your letter. I could not tell you how worried I was while I was waiting."[15] Masa must have relayed to Arthur the popular prejudice that Korean residents of Tokyo were partly to blame, and Arthur accepted this. "It was terrible for the Koreans to start fires during the earthquake. They must be caught immediately and punished. They are not humans but devils." He used the word *oni* (demons) once again.

Though the declarations of passion and everlasting commitment were missing and the farewells less effusive, the old intimacy returned to the correspondence. "You are very sweet to have my photographs in your room and talk to me. I also have two pictures of you in my room. The first one is you at the monastery at Chusonji and the other is you holding a lily on a boat at Matsushima. All the other large ones were lost at Ballymoyer."[16] They remembered anniversaries. In July 1924, Arthur wrote: "Today is your birthday. I woke up at 5 in the morning and thought about you. It is hot here and it must be hot in Tokyo, too. I remember it was sometimes 95 degrees when we lived in Kashiwagi. I am writing under a fig tree in the garden. I will be 54 tomorrow. I went for a swim last night. This is only a short letter but I just wanted to write on your birthday."[17]

Arthur again kept Masa informed about the extended family

that she might, if she had ever come to England, have been part of. His father's brother General Sir Reginald Hart, VC, now lived in Bournemouth and was totally deaf. His own brother Ronald had become bursar of an Oxford college. His married sister was unhappy. "Last night I had a letter from Beatrice and she said Dilly had had a terrible fight with her husband. I detest that man. He is a nasty person. As I haven't heard from her directly I don't know what will happen but I think it will be better if they separate. I don't know if she wants a divorce or not. I will tell you when I find out."[18] Cousin Norman, the only relative Masa had met, was in India, where he had shot a tiger and a panther. Arthur noted the comings and goings and the visitors who passed through Cannes. The matron from the Rouen hospital came to stay again. He met up with officers he had known in his regiment and during the war. General Haldane kept returning. "Haldane is in Cannes now. He was in Manchuria with me during the Russo-Japanese War, and was the commander of my corps when I was injured. He was very worried about me and came to see me in hospital. I have known him now for 29 years. . . . We had lunch. He looks older and all his hair is gray."[19]

Masa must have struggled to master the full cast of characters and the degree of detail provided. "Do you remember Luton Hoo? I stayed there as a patient for three months, before my artificial legs were made. It was owned by Lady Wernher, who was a widow then. After two years she married again but her husband died in October after falling off a horse and breaking his neck. Now she is a widow for the second time. She is on her way to Egypt and came to see me yesterday. She was very kind to me when I was at Luton Hoo. I think I sent you a postcard of the house."[20] With some memories, Arthur was able to combine his two lives. "Recently I have taken up the violin again. Some evenings Violet accompanies my violin on the piano. I enjoy it very much. Do you remember the violin I had in Tokyo? It is the same one."[21]

They exchanged small presents. Arthur sent English illustrated magazines, a five-pound note at the New Year, a statuette of the Virgin Mary he had bought on a visit to Lourdes, and thick winter underwear chosen by Violet. Masa sent fans and Japanese towels, and posted off items that Arthur requested specially, that could only be obtained in Japan. He asked her for a pruning saw for the fruit trees, paper and envelopes, calligraphy brushes, and a replacement handle for his teapot.

Arthur and Violet became part of a social set of minor European aristocrats and retired English that revolved around the Cannes country club at Mougins, with charity fêtes and bridge parties. In the summer they made trips to the Pyrenees and the French Alps, staying by the lake at Annecy. On one journey he returned to the site of the 8th General Hospital. "Now we are in London with Violet's parents. On the way we stopped in Rouen to see the place where I stayed for such a long time after the injury. The big hospital was deserted and the garden and the spot under the tree where I had my bed was overgrown. I visited the nuns who were very kind to me, and they were pleased to see me and had not forgotten me."[22]

Just as the letters of 1917 and 1918 had amounted to a war diary, setting down the horrors of the Western front, Arthur's later letters to Masa became a garden diary, recording the pleasure and satisfaction he was having in the white-walled garden at the Villa du Golfe, with its vines and wisteria and old flower beds. He would lay out a firm cushion on the paved pathway, ease himself down onto it, and plant seeds or cuttings from a sitting position. Other tasks, including hoeing and pruning, had to be done from his wheelchair. "The garden is getting better. I have planted a few fruit trees, including peach, plum, orange, fig, and two persimmons. Everything grows fast here, so there may be fruit next year. I love gardening so I spend the whole day in the garden. . . . The soil is very good. It is different from Hong Kong. Do you remember that red soil? There is a bamboo grove in the garden but it does not grow very tall."[23]

Masa must have found it easier to visualize the flowers and vegetables than she did the expatriate social life, if only because she was directly involved. She posted seeds and bulbs, just as she had for Ballymoyer. "Your parcel arrived on 2 January. The box was broken, the French post is very bad. The lily bulbs were moldy, with a rotten smell. One was completely gone, but I think the other nine are saved. I put each one in its own pot carefully, so I hope they will be all right."[24] She sent seeds not available in Cannes, including the long white radish the Japanese called daikon. "I tried one packet of radish the other day, and I still have two packets left. I will plant them in July. They will be unusual in this country. I will be very pleased if they are successful, coming from so far away. . . . You are very good to give such detailed instructions on how to plant the seeds. I shall sow them just as you tell me."[25]

Arthur sent pressed flowers, and sometimes seeds, in the other direction. "I am gardening as usual. I have three pots of moon-flowers, which you know, and some splendid blue morning glories. I enclose a morning glory for you. It has been very dry, but it rained last night. The sweet peas will germinate five or six days after sowing."[26] "As it is cooler this year we have only a few strawberries so far. Normally we have them in May but the slugs have eaten almost half of them. Horrible creatures. The daikon radishes did very well. I ate them in soup."[27] Arthur and Tansley picked the grapes from the vines to make his own wine, and shook the trees to bring down the olives. "The other day we made oil. We take the olives to a press at an old water mill, and make them into oil. It was enjoyable. We can use the oil for cooking."[28]

Though the Mediterranean climate was far better for him, there were still times when Arthur was in acute discomfort, uncontrollable spasms jangling the nerves in his stumps. "When I received your letter I was going to write straightaway, but I had trouble with my legs and was in pain for five or six days, but I am much better now. I also had trouble in my right ear. I am well, but sometimes the wounds are painful, and it cannot be helped."[29] He still told her about his walking. With new lightweight artificial legs fitted during his visit back to London in 1925, made from metal rather than wood, he could manage with only one stick rather than two, on level ground. He sent her an illustration showing the new design.

The change that made the greatest difference to him came in 1928, when an engineer friend adapted the controls of a car, so that the accelerator, brake, and gearshift could be operated by his hands, and the clutch engaged by leaning forward with his chest. "I can drive the car well. It is amazing. I can do everything and I like it very much. If I can get a driving license I will buy a small car, but I don't know whether a person without legs can get a license or not."[30] Three months later, he had mastered all the problems and wrote triumphantly, "I took the driving test and passed. In England the test is easy but it is difficult in this country. I am really good at driving now. I think I am the only person to have passed without legs. I will be very careful, as you told me."[31] The general could now take his visitors spinning along the Corniche, or up to Grasse.

He stopped mentioning Ireland, and seemed to put Ballymoyer behind him. He had an expatriate's interest in local prices, and exchange rates. "Prices are going up in France. The other day postage went up, so I shall stop using the registered mail. Let's try regular mail. If it is no good I will go back to registering. The French economy is in a mess. The government and the country are all suffering."[32] He still followed events in Japan as closely as he could, and wrote to Masa about the death of the Taisho Emperor. He did not like what she told him about changing fashions. "In your letter you said that Japanese women and children were wearing Western clothes now. What a pity. I think the old way was a hundred times better. It is the same everywhere. I don't like the way things are going."[33] He ruminated about the state of the world in general. "According to you the Japanese people have forgotten about the earthquake. It is the same in the West, people have forgotten all about the Great War. There are conflicts everywhere. The Americans don't like Japanese immigrants, and they want a fight with the Japanese."[34]

Arthur was worried by what was happening in China. Since his time in Manchuria, and in Hong Kong just before the deposing of the Chinese Emperor in 1911, he had despaired of the chaotic anarchy into which the country was falling, compared with the self-discipline he admired in Japan. When the revolutionary Cantonese nationalists, the Kuomintang, launched a military expedition against the Northern warlords with Soviet arms and support, he was convinced this would bring communism. "I am very concerned about what is going on in China. I would like to be there if I had legs. How do you say 'Bolshevik,' for the Russian Revolutionaries, in Japanese? It is a new word and I do not know."[35] "I read that in China everything is in chaos. It is all the fault of the Russians. They have done such a lot of damage to the world."[36] Whereas the Americans, and most Western governments, were putting pressure on the Japanese to keep out of China's internal affairs, Arthur was for intervention to restore order. When Japan's prime minister Giichi Tanaka said his country "would not remain indifferent to the spread of communism"[37] and would be ready to act alongside the other powers if necessary, he wrote to Masa approvingly, "I am glad the Japanese government is taking a tough position on China."[38] "China is a nuisance. I hope she will not start a war with Japan."[39] Arthur was a natural conservative, with a simple, military man's view of politics. His fear of Bolshevism and socialism was shared by the generation of young Japanese officers he had known in Manchuria. The difference was that, while he was on the retired list, they were now the colonels and generals running the Japanese Army, and exercising a growing influence over the country as a whole. Many of them were still stationed in North China, in Manchuria, though this was for the moment still under the political control of a Chinese warlord. Manchuria had a long common frontier with the Soviet Union, and a fear of the ideological germs that might cross this border, as well as communist sedition in the rest of China, shaped their thinking.

As Arthur and Masa went on writing to each other, it was memories of the past that increasingly took over. Before the breakup, their letters had always looked forward, to the blissful moment sometime in the indefinite future, when Arthur would be out of the army, or the war would be over, or he would have conquered his injuries, and their life could really start. Now the letters had a calm, almost wistful character, as they looked back to the years between 1905 and 1913, and saw that this had been the idyll, even if they had not known it at the time. "You wrote about many of those journeys we made, to Lake Kawaguchi, Lake Nishi, to Funatsu, the Kinkakuji Temple in Kyoto, and those beautiful lilies. I remember them all very well. I still have many of the pictures. Yes, I do remember the stone steps at Tamagawa, and the shrine, and the wonderful peaches. I have never had peaches like that here."[40] There had always been an inequality between them. Arthur had already seen much of the world when he met Masa, and had taken her out of Tokyo to places she had never seen before. Twenty years later, the inequity continued. Arthur was living in one of the most beautiful parts of France, with servants and the income to live well. Masa was confined to a small wooden house on the edge of a growing urban sprawl, depending on Arthur's remittances, and so the memories were even more exotic for her than they were for him. Her time with Arthur had been her one experience of travel, not just in Japan but abroad. "Our house in Hong Kong was in a beautiful position, wasn't it? I wonder what Konwa is doing now. You say you sometimes look at the pictures from Hong Kong. Those were good days, weren't they?"[41]

In their letters to each other, they recalled inns they had visited, characters they had met, beaches they had swum from, and walks in the mountains. "I certainly remember the fireflies in Nakano very well. They went inside your kimono sleeves, didn't they? And one night I swam in that small stream. I remember it all so well. We had such fun together."[42] The high points of the seven summers they had been together, when they had gone out on long train journeys, taken rickshaws down country roads through thatched villages, or rented houses, were systematically revisited by Masa. "You talk about so many places we went to. You were very happy then, we were happy together then. Do you remember buying the goldfish, and the Naka-ya inn at Funatsu? And the roast beef? There were so many fleas, though it was a wonderful place."[43]

They wrote about meals they had eaten, and fishing trips together. "You said a lot about fish. I remember the trout from Tamagawa. I always liked saury. Your favorite fish was sea bream. You used to go fishing in Ayukawa. I also remember a goby fish in Matsuyama. It wouldn't be possible to buy a bucket of fish for 10 sen now."[44] "When you write about fish I always smile. There are so many fish stories. I liked that old country saying, 'A sea bream is sea bream even if it is rotten.' I often think about our memories, and you must do the same. We were happy when we were together."

Arthur let Masa know how thinking about her could move him. "I was pleased to read you have bought a Western-style umbrella. While I was reading it, though I was smiling, tears came to my eyes. Why was this?"[45]

It was always the two of them together, rather than the times with the children, that they remembered. They had taken their longest journeys before Kiyoshi and Hideo were born, and even after that they had often managed to leave the children with her mother. In their correspondence there was little mention of Kiyoshi, though Arthur was dutiful and responded to Masa's practical requests. He had already sent Kiyoshi his old shoes, and size 12 socks were equally hard to find in Japan. "I am writing this under the large fig tree. It is quite hot here, about 80 degrees, but it is cooler in the shade and there is some breeze. I am glad to hear Kiyoshi's socks have arrived. I don't understand why they took so long. I will order another half-dozen again so that they get there before he needs them this time."[46] The socks became a frequent concern. When Masa asked for black ones, Arthur could only find white. "I have sent the parcel to Kiyoshi. I put in a jacket and socks. Unfortunately the socks are white. You could send them to be dyed black. They are strong socks."[47] With Kiyoshi growing to nearly the same size as Arthur, Masa made more requests. "You asked me to send Kiyoshi some white trousers. I don't have any now. I used to have a lot of them as I wore them in India, but they were all stolen from Ballymoyer. I sent a suit for him the other day. The parcel was insured so it should arrive safely."[48]

At the beginning of 1931, more than seventeen years after they had last seen one another, Arthur was still keeping up the tradition. "How are you? On New Year's Day, when I woke up I spoke to the photograph which was taken at Chusonji and sent you the first letter of the year as I always do."[49] That summer he spoke Japanese again for the first time in many years. Due to come back to

London on one of his visits, he decided to go the long way round by sea from Marseilles, rather than travel north by train. He found a passage on a Japanese ship steaming through from Yokohama to London via Suez, the route he had taken many times and had hoped to take with Masa in 1911. The *Haruna Maru* was a modern ship three times the size of the *Wakasa Maru,* on which he had started out in 1904. For seven days he was able to experience a little outpost of Japan, talk with the captain and tell his stories of the Russo-Japanese War, and enjoy the constant green tea in his stateroom. It was a declaratory gesture, if a very minor one, at a time when Japan was under growing international criticism. As he was sailing back from London, the Japanese Army, obsessed with the threat from the neighboring Soviet Union, and the danger Bolshevism posed to the emperor system, took another step to control North China. After contriving an incident, they began the military occupation of all of Manchuria and took control in Mukden, the city where Arthur had eaten roasted salmon with the victorious troops of the army he so admired in 1905.

Through the 1930s, while Japan was becoming a pariah state in many Western eyes, the Chartered Bank continued to transfer payments to Masa, and Arthur and Masa continued to write to each other, though his later letters to her did not survive. We do not know what he said to her about Japan's creation of the puppet state of Manchukuo in 1932, Japan's departure from the League of Nations, the widening of the conflict in China into a full-scale war with Chiang Kai-shek in 1937, the rape of the Chinese capital Nanking, or the anti-Soviet pact that Japan signed with Germany. Arthur remained a supporter of Japan long after others had ceased to defend her, and made the sea journey from Marseilles to London by the NYK several more times. He continued to keep much of his capital in the shares of Japanese companies, and the small dividend from Tokyo Electric helped fund the Villa du Golfe.

Ballymoyer was never lived in again, and attempts to sell or rent the dilapidated house failed. In 1937, Arthur gave the land to the Northern Ireland National Trust, and shortly afterwards the remains of the building were pulled down, and the park, and the place where the Japanese garden had been, were planted over with pine trees. By 1938, twenty years after his injury, some old wounds had healed. Arthur, Masa, and the accommodating and tolerant Violet had found a way of existing together. It was only Arthur's connection with his son that was tense and awkward, and Kiyoshi was now a student in France.

FOURTEEN

KIYOSHI

You lead a sheltered life and know nothing about the
way of the world, so you make things harder than
they are. They are pointless worries. You must
trust me and leave things to me.

· Kiyoshi Suzuki, 1939[1] ·

I n the early years at the Villa du Golfe, Arthur would wrap up
parcels for Kiyoshi with brown paper and string, secure the
knots with hot wax sealed with his family crest showing a
stag with rampant antlers, and send them off from the Juan-les-Pins
post office just as he had from White Cross. He dispatched socks,
bathing trunks, his own old trousers and jackets, and new suits for
which he had guessed his son's measurements. His assiduous attention to Kiyoshi's physical needs, prompted by Masa, was the easiest
part of his role as father, and the limit of it. He had last seen the boy
when he was six, and knew little about Kiyoshi as a character, or his
worries or ambitions. Real empathy between father and son would
have been hard enough to achieve given the distance between them
in years and miles. It was even harder because all through Kiyoshi's
childhood Arthur had seen him as an appendage to Masa rather
than as a person in his own right, and because after the break in

1919 Kiyoshi was aggrieved and resentful towards his father. As he grew up and could make more adult judgments about the way the English officer had treated Masa, he became more critical of him. As the single child of a single parent, he was extremely close to his mother and naturally protective. A brooding anger at the war hero he had once looked up to, and insecurity about his Japaneseness, were added to the normal worries of a young man of his age. They were compounded by the fierce competition for entrance to the best higher schools, according to which whole careers were decided when students were eighteen years old.

In Kiyoshi's last year at the Gyosei Middle School, in the months after the earthquake, his teachers judged he was not going to get into the First Higher School, the route to Tokyo Imperial University. Paradoxically, they judged that the English grammar and comprehension of this half-English boy were insufficiently good because of his concentration on French. He was redirected to try for the Third Higher School, which in turn fed the next-ranked imperial university, at Kyoto. Early in 1924, Kiyoshi made the eight-hour journey to Kyoto to sit the exam alongside two thousand others seeking a few hundred places. When he heard that he had failed, he was deeply disappointed, and his confidence suffered. He could not stay on at the Gyosei School after his eighteenth birthday and was left in an educational limbo. Like many others in the same situation, he would have to study at home and go to coaching until he could take the entry exam in 1925. Arthur told Masa how sorry he was when he learnt Kiyoshi had failed, but made no attempt to engage with him or write to him directly. When Arthur was eighteen, life had been more straightforward, as Hart sons moved smoothly into the British Army along familiar routes, with a confident sense of purpose and their own value.

One year later, Kiyoshi sat the entrance tests for the Third Higher School in Kyoto again, and passed successfully. He now had to say goodbye to Masa and leave home for the first time to go and live more than two hundred miles away. With the need to stay in a school hostel, his living costs would be higher, and he had clothes and books to buy. Masa wrote to Arthur, and he responded quickly. He may not have understood the academic pressure Kiyoshi had been under, but he was concerned on behalf of Masa. "I am so happy to hear Kiyoshi has passed his exam. *Banzai, Banzai!* I am also sorry that you will miss him and are concerned about the money. I cannot bear to think of you worrying about this. As I am so far away I cannot be there to help you. So I have written to the bank and they will send you 200 yen straightaway, and 350 yen from June on. I would like to go on helping until Kiyoshi gets a job."[2]

For a few weeks Kiyoshi was depressed and exhausted after the exams. His fragile state was not improved when Masa handed him a copy of the family registration certificate to satisfy the Third Higher School's admission procedure, and he saw for the first time the little conspiracy that had been entered into just after he was born. He was upset to discover that his father's name did not appear in the official birth record and that he was technically the son of his Aunt Rei and his deceased Uncle Yokichi, who had passed him to Masa for adoption. But once he was settled at the Third Higher School—an educational forcing house with wood-planked classrooms, bare echoing corridors, and a draped picture of the Emperor in an honored position—Kiyoshi's self-esteem was helped by his Hart-Synnot genes in an unexpected way.

With Arthur's build, Kiyoshi quickly emerged as the school's leading athlete and an unbeatable short- and middle-distance runner. Boys who wanted to do athletics joined the White Silver Shield Club, coached by Ishibashi-san, and the mixed-race boy with a long stride and large lungs helped the club win a series of matches against other higher schools. Kiyoshi's successes at distances up to 5,000 meters on the packed-earth games field that was also used for daily assemblies and physical exercises gave him kudos in the school, and he became the captain of the club. He achieved a brief moment of national fame when he beat the Japanese record for the 800 meters with the first time under two minutes. Masa proudly sent Arthur a newspaper cutting, and his father wrote back to say that he, too, had been a runner at school, and gave some of his times for the 100 yards and the 440 yards for comparison.

Masa had to read about Kiyoshi's first successes from a distance, and since he was the focus of her life and she was missing him desperately, she decided to follow him and move to the place where she had spent such happy times with Arthur. Kyoto now had a population of 800,000, but it was still the cultural heart of the country and retained far more of the atmosphere of old Japan than Tokyo or Osaka. Masa and Kiyoshi looked for somewhere to live in the northeastern district, where the straight, grid-pattern streets turned into country lanes as they ran up to the wooded hills that encircled the city. They rented a one-story house a little way up the hillside, with a fine view across the roofs and towers, pagodas and palaces of the ancient imperial capital. Kiyoshi had a short journey to school, and Masa found the neighbors friendlier and more tolerant than in Kashiwagi. In these peaceful surroundings, quiet except for the clanging of old bells, where foxes came down into the gardens at night, Masa planted vegetables again and walked to temples she had last visited with Arthur when they had stayed at the Matsunoya inn. Arthur wrote back after she told him how happy she was about the shift. "When you wrote that you were thinking of moving I did not say anything. I wasn't sure you would be happy as you are so familiar with Tokyo but do not know Kyoto well. But I am very happy you like it, and it must be wonderful to have a house in the countryside."[3]

Kyoto was indissolubly linked with the religion, history, and identity of the Japanese race, and in November 1928 a new emperor traveled from Tokyo for his official enthronement. Groups of boys from the Third Higher School squatted on the pavements among the silent and respectful crowds to watch parts of the Shinto ceremonies that symbolized Hirohito's divine status as a descendant of the sun goddess, 124th in a direct line of succession that went back twenty-seven hundred years. The complex rituals took ten days to complete, advancing in stages from the "Grand Etiquette" to the "Grand Thanksgiving" and finally to the "Mystic Purification," conducted in the middle of the night. At the climax, the Emperor moved by candlelight towards a storehouse of sacred rice, along a strip of matting that attendants slowly unrolled before him and rolled up behind him as he walked. He communed with his ancestors in an inner room and emerged wearing an outfit described as the "Robe of Heaven's Feathers," just as the rising sun, the emblem of the nation, was appearing over the eastern Kyoto hills. An American journalist described the lengthy proceedings as "a sacred pantomime,"[4] and it was a production with a clear national message, like other imperial spectaculars before it. The enthronement was brought to the whole country for the first time over the radio, with hours of solemn coverage linking family and nation with a mythological past and stressing loyalty, service, and duty.

The most demanding duty Kiyoshi owed his emperor was the two years of military service for which all young men were liable when they reached the age of twenty. In 1927 he was summoned for a medical examination by an artillery regiment and classified as "A" class, or "completely fit," but was able to defer the call-up until he had finished his education. When he was twenty-two, he moved from the school to the Kyoto Imperial University close by, and was accepted into the Faculty of Law. He gave up athletics and worked conscientiously. Though he studied law because the department was regarded as the elite stream, and Masa believed it would open the best jobs, Kiyoshi would have preferred to do moral philosophy and ethics. He was turning out to be a serious and sensitive soul, fascinated by intellectual arguments about the role of reason as against religion, different concepts of society, and the meaning of life. Like all thoughtful students of his time, he had to ask himself a private question: whether it was really possible to reconcile an industrially modern nation, dependent on technology and science, with the way the government was promoting a state philosophy based on ancestor worship and the esoteric national cult of Shintoism. Only half Japanese by blood, Kiyoshi was having to judge for himself if Japan was a unique and superior society, as the nationalists claimed, or whether he was at heart a universalist, placing more stress on the similarities between nations and peoples in a wider brotherhood of man.

It was not a time for challenge or open debate. The brief period of "Taisho Democracy" that had blossomed after 1918 was over. The authorities were intent on rooting out Bolshevism wherever it showed its head, and the Japanese Communist Party was banned. Under the Maintenance of Public Order Act, passed in 1925, anyone trying to change the imperial status quo, or advocate the elimination of private property, faced arrest. Hundreds of labor activists were rounded up and imprisoned. Even in the higher schools, boys were expelled for ideological unsoundness, and once at university, students suspected to be radical were watched carefully. Many were arrested, though the Tokko—the Special Higher Police, who were known as the Thought Police—would often call them in for a chat over a bowl of noodles with a fatherly officer before resorting to tougher measures. The object was to get them to abandon their leftist beliefs and achieve *tenko,* an ideological conversion to the new way of thinking. A mood of nationalist fervor was starting to build up. One of the new superpatriots, Professor Minoda, wrote, "When we serve our Emperor as a living God and defend our home country, we serve humanity."[5]

During the four years in which Kiyoshi was a student in Kyoto, Japan was abandoning the Meiji modernizers' aim to become part of the community of great powers and moving in a new, increasingly insular direction. As Kiyoshi went to classes each day, crossing the courtyard in front of the new university clock tower with his books wrapped in a *furoshiki,* a traditional square of dark-blue cloth, and talking with other students as they ate rice and grilled fish, it was impossible not to be aware of what was happening to the empire. The world depression was hitting Japan with a vengeance, and the market for raw silk, still the country's greatest export, had plummeted. With the price of rice also falling, farmers driven into debt, and mill and factory workers unemployed, disillusion with party politics was growing. The ultranationalists offered simpler and more aggressive solutions. Secret organizations of captains and colonels deplored Japan's wrangling politicians and "weak" foreign policy and plotted to throw out the civilian government.

In 1931, a group of middle-level Japanese Army officers in China took matters into their own hands and occupied all of the province of Manchuria, an area as big as France and Spain, in defiance of their political masters in Tokyo. The official reason given was to protect coal, iron, and minerals essential to Japan's security. The takeover was so popular with the public, who also saw space for emigration and a secure bulwark against the Soviet Union, that the government had to go along with it. When Kiyoshi started at Kyoto University in 1929, political parties still competed for power, and acknowledged a need to cooperate with other countries over disarmament and the League of Nations. By the time he graduated, another prime minister had been assassinated, once again at Tokyo Station, and army officers and right-wingers were even more vocal in their demands for a stronger and assertive Japan. Civilian politicians and the press were joining the jingoism to keep up.

The Japanese military would probably have approved of Arthur's favorite uncle, and the great-uncle Kiyoshi had never met, the warlike General Sir Reginald Hart, VC, who died in 1931. Shortly after the Russo-Japanese War, Sir Reginald had written an article under the title "A Vindication of War" in which he put his case. "History proves up to the hilt that nations languish and perish under peace conditions, and it has only been by war that a people has continued to thrive and exist. . . . To be prosperous peace and war must alternate. Peace for a nation is like sleep for an individual, it gives time for rest and recuperation. But we must not sleep too long. . . . Peace is a disintegrating force, whereas war consolidates people."[6] Despite his Hart genes, Kiyoshi had no interest in military matters, and his disillusion with his own father had added to his suspicion of the military class and military solutions. After his graduation, he and his mother moved back to Tokyo, now rebuilt after the earthquake. Though others in his Kyoto class went into the army or looked for jobs, Kiyoshi enrolled in a graduate course at Tokyo University to do philosophy, the subject he had always wanted to study, and was able to postpone his call-up once again. To Masa's concern, he was showing signs of becoming a perpetual student. Though the Tokyo department was centered on the German school of philosophy, he wanted to study the French philosophers of the eighteenth and nineteenth centuries, and he tried to improve his French with a course at the French Institute in Tokyo so he could read their work in the original.

Kiyoshi's intellectual interest in the most fundamental questions about man's place in the universe grew up alongside his own personal insecurities. Though he had had a privileged education and his school and university friends would work for ministries and take academic posts, he had often been made to feel an outsider by his fellow Japanese. As a fully grown adult, he still felt disconnected from his fellow countrymen in many situations. He was increasingly at odds with his mother, a working-class woman who had devoted years of her life to helping her son into the Japanese ruling class and now feared he would fritter away the chance she had given him. He was alienated from his father and unable to forgive him for the way he had treated his mother, even though she had long since come to her own accommodation, and though he could only carry on studying because of Arthur's continuing financial support. In Tokyo, two things happened to improve Kiyoshi's situation, though there was a conflict between them. He met a girl he liked, and a few months later he saw a chance of getting out of Japan.

One day at the French Institute, a girl called to Kiyoshi from across a hallway, having recognized his blue eyes and half-European appearance though she had not seen him for seventeen years. Tetsuko Katsuda had been at the same Tokyo elementary school with him in 1915, at the time when he was being bullied by other children as not a real Japanese, and just before Masa transferred him to private school. She was one of the few children to befriend him, and they had played together. Her parents, liberals with a strong belief in women's education, sent her on to an English-language high school in Tokyo and then to four years of university in the United States. She had just returned to Japan and was teaching English in the Seika Gakuen private school her father ran in Tokyo. Her interests coincided with Kiyoshi's, and they must have talked about what she had learnt abroad and her time in Wisconsin. She was pretty, and they spent an increasing amount of time together in Hongo, where Kiyoshi was going to classes. Then, in early 1935, Kiyoshi saw an advertisement for a French government scheme to allow Japanese to study at French universities.

Tetsuko encouraged him to apply to do philosophy at the Sorbonne in Paris, and he took an examination and was awarded a scholarship. The good news was tempered by the fact that Kiyoshi would now have to leave his mother and be away from her for four years. He hoped to take Tetsuko with him, but she had to stay to look after her own parents. Masa was horrified at losing Kiyoshi for so long, but was finally brought round to the idea. Kiyoshi applied for a passport—which recorded him as "1.78 meters," or five feet, nine inches tall, with blue eyes—and prepared to leave.

In early October 1935, an NYK liner stopped in Marseilles on the journey from Yokohama to London, with a small group of Japanese students among the second-class passengers. It would have been easy for Kiyoshi to stop and visit his father, who was just along the coast and probably gardening, but he caught a train straight to Paris. For the previous sixteen years there had been almost no direct contact between father and son. Arthur showed no sign of being in the least distressed by this, and was content to get occasional news of Kiyoshi via Masa. Kiyoshi was determined to make his own independent way in France and did not want to see him, though Arthur would have been able to help him in his early weeks. Nevertheless, the culture shock for Kiyoshi arriving in Europe was far less than Arthur had faced when he first arrived in Japan. He was already a fluent French speaker, having started to learn the language from the priests at the Gyosei School when he was ten, and having immersed himself in French culture and literature. As he explored the wonders of Paris that autumn, he was constantly reminded of historical associations and characters he knew, from the names of the streets and metro stations to the tombs of Voltaire and Rousseau in the Pantheon.

Kiyoshi moved into a dormitory for Japanese students in the new Cité Universitaire, on the southern outskirts of Paris, near the Montsouris Park. A number of countries had been induced to set up hostels for their own nationals around a lavish building for foreign students donated by the American millionaire John D. Rockefeller, which offered a theater, a library, gymnasia, and the largest swimming pool in Paris. The Japanese House was itself a showpiece, with uptilting Oriental eaves and wide windows, competing with the nearby Swiss House, designed by Le Corbusier, and the Italian and Spanish hostels nearby. To attend his lectures, Kiyoshi took the short train ride to the Gare de Luxembourg and walked through the old streets of the Latin Quarter to the main building of the University of Paris at the Sorbonne. He enrolled in the faculty of philosophy, in the city of the Enlightenment, where scientific thought and reasoning had been wielded as weapons against religious superstition and absolutism two hundred years earlier.

In the intellectual hotbed of the Sorbonne, a growing number of philosophy students were discovering existentialism, and the study

of being that originated from the work of Kierkegaard and Nietz-
sche. Existentialists emphasized the voidness of human reality, the
lack of meaning and purpose in life, and the solitude of human existence. To the lanky, bespectacled Japanese student in Paris, wearing his father's patched old jackets, the idea that the human being is
condemned to be free and must live with the responsibility and guilt
of his actions seemed to ring true and suit the times. It could not
have been further from the spiritual idealism of state Shintoism. At
the same time, Kiyoshi became a keen reader and admirer of the
French thinker and essayist Émile-Auguste Chartier, who wrote under the name Alain. Chartier was teaching in Paris and had a wide
following through his books and newspaper columns. A pacifist, he
had nevertheless served in the French Army as a private in the Great
War and published a book, *Mars, or The Truth About War,* which he
had written in an artillery dugout. A set of essays, with titles that
included "On Violence," "Rhetoric," "The Corpse," "The Spirit of
War," "Right and Might," and many others, Alain's book was received as a powerful antiwar message. In one essay he wrote, "We
should never listen to nor allow ourselves to believe the statement
that war can ever be compatible, in any sense whatsoever, with justice and humanity."[7] Kiyoshi was so struck by Alain that he started
to translate some of his pieces into Japanese.

The intellectual atmosphere of Paris was challenging, open, and
livelier than the inhibited mood of Tokyo, but the sense of ominous
political shifts in the world outside was the same. Hitler was openly
rearming Germany, which had left the League of Nations like Japan,
and in the streets of Paris demonstrators were soon marching in support of the Republican side in the Spanish Civil War. Over crackling
propaganda radio and at floodlit rallies, the mass ideologies of Soviet
communism and fascism denounced each other ever more stridently,
and students were acutely aware of the implications of all this for
themselves. By 1937 many of the young people Kiyoshi met in the
cafeterias of the International Center, built to foster entente between

nations, believed that another war in Europe was inevitable and that their generation would have to fight it.

Kiyoshi was older than most of the Europeans he was studying with. With the help of letters from Tetsuko and the scant reports in the newspapers, he was following a different slide, far away in Asia. On a snowy morning in February 1936, young officers attempted another coup d'état in Tokyo, when truckloads of troops occupied the War Ministry, the Diet, and the police headquarters, killed three government ministers, and attempted to assassinate the prime minister. The rising was put down and the rebels were executed, but the civilian leadership agreed to more of the army's demands for increased defense spending, and Japan went further down the militarist road. In 1937, the fighting in China was extended into a full-scale war, and the capture of the Chinese capital of Nanking was hailed as a magnificent victory but condemned by the rest of the world as a racist massacre.

On the packed-earth playing fields of schools all over Japan, military instructors barked out drill commands to columns of marching children. All middle schools, higher schools, and universities were now required to include army training as part of their curriculum. In 1938, a former minister of war, General Sadao Araki, was made minister of education. He revised and further fanaticized the teaching in schools, and tried to stamp out any remaining traces of "dangerous thought" in the universities. Kiyoshi was sitting all this out, but would soon be required to rejoin the Japanese national family and fulfill his obligations to the Son of Heaven.

All this time Masa was writing regular but quite separate letters to two addresses in France, to the Villa du Golfe in Juan-les-Pins, and to the Japanese student hostel in the Cité Universitaire in Paris. A few of the letters and cards Kiyoshi sent back to her survive, and though they say nothing about what he was actually doing

in Paris, because Masa knew nothing about the existentialists, they
show him concerned about his mother. "How are you? I am anxious
to know how your hands are. It has been raining here all the time.
Please do not worry about me as I am well and keeping myself
busy. . . . You must be missing me very much, and waiting for me to
return. Please wait a little longer. Japan must have changed so much
since I left, I find it hard to think about."[8]

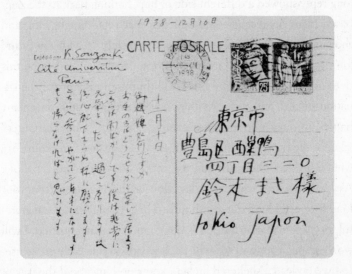

At the end of 1938, Kiyoshi wrote thanking Masa for money she
had posted by registered mail, and indicating that he had started to
consider his future. "Paris has been extremely cold for the last week.
It has been –15 centigrade for two or three days. I hear it may even
go down to –20. This is the coldest I have known in my life, but there
is nothing to worry about as my room is kept very warm. You must
not worry too much about me. You must stay calm, because it is not
good for you to be overanxious. Luckily I have not caught a cold
even once this year. I hear Tetsuko came to see you. Tetsuko and I are
friends from childhood and I admire her very much. I would like to
do my best for her as long as she trusts me. The trouble is that in the
three years in France I have not been able to achieve what I hoped.

Don't you think Tetsuko is a gentle and kind person? The time here has certainly been very valuable to me. I have been able to do many things that would have been impossible in Japan, and have been stimulated. Please take care and greetings to everyone. To my mother, from Kiyoshi. P.S. Thank you very much for what you sent me."[9]

Masa fretted about how Kiyoshi was going to find a job and urged him to make use of personal introductions and contacts. His long reply showed a different side of him, harking back to the Zen-based focus his teachers and athletics coach had taught him, and showing some irritation at all Masa's worrying. "As for my future job, I am not interested in asking favors from people. I hope this does not sound ungrateful but I will think seriously about the situation once I am back. As they say, in order to sink an enemy battleship, a real samurai must 'compose himself,' 'judge the target,' 'choose the time,' and 'fire the bullet.' Courage and composure are what is needed. One must not fuss, that is for small-minded people. As you know well, whatever I have done in the past, apart from your kind support, I have done without any help from others. I am grateful for all your concern but it is not good. If you are worried, I will worry about you, and we will be worrying about each other uselessly. You lead a sheltered life and know nothing about the way of the world, so you make things harder than they are. They are pointless worries. You must trust me and leave things to me. . . . I must get ready to leave soon."[10]

As he prepared to leave Europe and go back to Japan, he made a few more references to the world situation in both Asia and Europe. In Tokyo, the taciturn extreme nationalist Baron Kiichiro Hiranuma became prime minister pledging to create an even more authoritarian government. The new government was taking further mobilization measures. "The other day I had a letter from my old friends from the Third Higher School. It was from Ishibashi, Ichikawa, Umetani, and Suzuki. I was surprised to hear how many members of the athletics club are serving in the army on active service. Europe is calm for the time being. France is building up her defenses and is in a tense state, but it will be all right for a while."[11]

Though she did not agree with it, Masa had long ago had to accept the adult Kiyoshi's stubbornly harsh attitude to his father. His view was that in continuing to send money Arthur was not being generous, or particularly kind, but simply doing the minimum that he was bound to do. Nevertheless, she had pressed Kiyoshi at least to get in contact with him, and he and his father had exchanged letters. As the time for Kiyoshi's return approached, Masa urged her son to go and visit Arthur, if only on her behalf. She was very happy when she heard from Kiyoshi in early 1939. "I am hoping to go and see my father before I leave. Please do not worry about the details. I will deal with it calmly and in the right way. Please be relaxed about this."[12] Kiyoshi's line had finally softened, and it seemed he was prepared to do what he had steadfastly refused to do for three years, because he knew it would please his mother so much.

When Masa heard the visit was going to take place, she started to worry that Kiyoshi might spoil things by being offensive. She told him he had to behave properly, and he wrote back rather irritably. "I am not a person who does not understand manners. I may ignore a person when he behaves in a way that lacks principle and manners, but I will not be rude without good reason. Please don't misjudge me. I am the son of a remarkable mother and have been well educated despite a difficult situation. I will not act unreasonably, I realize a man has to do his duty. Please do not worry."[13] His letter was clearly written with a degree of indignation, with crucial sections underlined.

At the end of May 1939, Kiyoshi packed up his luggage, including the many books he had bought in France, his notes on Alain, and the presents for relatives that all returning travelers were expected to bring, and left from the Gare de Lyon. For nearly four years he had been on the edge of things, sitting out Japan's militarist takeover, not having to earn a living, able to put off decisions until his scholarship was up. He could not have stayed in Paris even if he had wanted to, because that summer the Ministry of Education was recalling all its students from overseas. There were many uncertainties ahead. He did not know how he would find his mother, who would be sixty-one when he got back, or the effect her time alone had had on her. He did not know if he could get married to the woman he hoped was still waiting for him, or whether he would be able to find a job that would use his now totally fluent French, or would be called up for the army. Before any of this, he had to make his peace with the British general he had blamed for so much that had been difficult in his life.

In Juan-les-Pins, the temperature was seventy, and it was raining. He found the Villa du Golfe easily, a few minutes' walk from the station, directly beside the sea, and now one of the older and more solid villas in a town that had been heavily rebuilt and developed in the previous fifteen years. A gate opened through the wall to a short gravel drive, surrounded by vines and figs, leading up to the front door. Kiyoshi had not seen his father for twenty-five years, and his childhood memories were of the large and strong man he had played with on the beach on the Boso Peninsula in the summer of 1913. Arthur greeted him from his wheelchair, looking rather small and fragile, and Kiyoshi had to lean down to embrace him.

He was introduced to Violet, who had sent him so many pairs of socks, and they showed him the garden and the Japanese plants. They questioned him about his time in Paris, and about changes in Tokyo and about Masa. He stayed with the Hart-Synnots for two nights, in a house that was comfortable in a European bourgeois way, with polished floors, gilt furniture, heavy pictures and ornaments, and reminders of Ballymoyer, India, and Japan. During that time, Arthur talked about the years before 1914 and about how he had met Masa under the peach tree, but much was left unsaid. Kiyoshi told Tetsuko later that he had been most moved when Arthur took him into his study and he saw the photographs of his mother as a young woman, a cabinet with small mementoes that she had sent him, the piles of her letters tied with ribbon, and on his desk the supplies of *makigami* paper, the inkstone, and the tattered dictionaries that had helped to keep the bond going over the years.

Kiyoshi wrote a letter to Masa before he left, on Villa du Golfe–headed paper. It was short, because he might be back before she received it, and he would give a full account when he saw her. It just said: "When I arrived here, your letter of 26 April was waiting for me. Father is fine but looks very tired. He received me calmly. I was overwhelmed when I saw him. I thanked him for all the things he had done. I forgot all my old grievances, once I saw how kind a person he is. I will leave here tomorrow evening and spend the night in Marseilles and board the ship the day after tomorrow. I was relieved to hear from you as it has been some time. Please keep well. I can hear frogs outside. To my mother, from Kiyoshi."[14]

EPILOGUE

*We should never listen to nor allow ourselves to believe the
statement that war can ever be compatible, in any sense
whatsoever, with justice and humanity.*

· Alain, 1927[1] ·

Arthur went on sending money through his bank to Masa
until November 1941. Then, forty years after the glory
days of the alliance, when the British had admired "the
sturdy Jap" and a Japanese had said, "The basic ideals and the aspirations of the two are identically the same,"[2] the "everlasting friendship" was broken. The two island peoples were at war with one
another, each denouncing the other with mounting vehemence. Soon
British cartoonists were depicting the Japanese in crude racial terms
as apes and buck-toothed monkeys, while the Japanese called the
British *oni,* demons or ogres, the word Arthur had used about the
Germans in the First World War. After Pearl Harbor, the long correspondence between Arthur and Masa was extinguished, and just
as the First World War had torn them apart, a new world war added
a final coda to the story that had begun under a peach tree in Tokyo
in 1904.

. . .

Arthur Hart-Synnot was immediately affected by the outbreak of the war in Europe when he and Violet were left homeless. They had been back in London for Arthur to have a leg fitting in the summer of 1939, and when the war began in September, they were unable to return to Juan-les-Pins. The Villa du Golfe was left abandoned, along with all their furniture and possessions, including the bundles of Masa's letters and the mementoes and photographs of Japan. Arthur's brother Ronald, bursar at an Oxford college, took in the two refugees and gave them temporary rooms at St. John's. They were still in Oxford two years later, when Japan went to war with the United States and Britain.

The general must have followed the reports of the early Japanese victories, the surrender of Hong Kong, the sinking of the battleship *Prince of Wales,* and the fall of Singapore with a mix of personal horror and a wider anguish. The successors of the Japanese troops Arthur had once called "this wonderful army" still showed the same bravery and devotion to the Emperor, but there was one change. Nearly forty years earlier, the observers had admired the way the Japanese treated their Russian prisoners and Chinese civilians, and their punctilious respect for what had up to then been thought of as uniquely "Western" codes of behavior in war. This time, the Japanese ignored those restraints, and officers' discipline over ordinary soldiers was less tight. From the very first days, there were reports of atrocities and barbarity towards local populations and prisoners.

To men like Arthur, who respected Japan and had tried to understand it, the previous twenty years seemed a catalogue of misunderstandings, mishandlings, misconceptions, and delusions that had ended in Japan's extraordinary gamble. That winter the grass quadrangles and lecture theaters of the university were quieter and emptier, with so many young men away in the forces, and sections of the colleges taken over for other purposes. Violet Hart-Synnot worried about her twenty-seven-year-old nephew, William Drower, who had studied at Oxford, and had come to stay with them at Juan-les-Pins the year before Kiyoshi's visit. With Arthur's encouragement, he had been learning Japanese. He had gone into the army and been taken prisoner in Singapore along with 60,000 British and empire troops, and was now in a Japanese camp. Meanwhile Arthur knew he was the only British general with a son in the Japanese Army, though from now on there was no way he could get news of either Kiyoshi or Masa.

For Masa Suzuki, the war in China had been going on for four years before Pearl Harbor, and any philosophical sense of detachment was hard to maintain in the shrill atmosphere of Tokyo. Huge posters and billboards sounded the call for national mobilization, *Ichioku isshin*—"One hundred million hearts beating as one." Flags with the red disk of the *hinomaru* hung from the fronts of government ministries, as they had when Arthur first arrived in 1904, but the genuine patriotism that had been so universal and heartfelt forty years before, when little Japan took on the might of the Russian Empire, was hard to replicate. Many Japanese had mixed feelings about their government's war, even if they kept them private. This time the patriotic fervor was being manipulated and directed from the top, rather than springing from the grass roots. The war had begun in 1937 when the Japanese Army launched a full-scale attack on the rest of China, beyond already occupied Manchuria. The Chinese resisted more stubbornly than ever expected, and the fighting dragged on. In 1939 alone, 27,000 Japanese soldiers were killed in China. While the Japanese watched their own dead come back in white caskets, and the radio played emotional dirges about patriotic mothers, the rest of the world condemned them for atrocities against the Chinese and demanded they withdraw.

While Kiyoshi was in France, Masa saved money by moving to a smaller house in Sugamo. She was already living as thriftily as she could, but this had now become a national duty as well. With the country desperately short of rubber, petrol, steel, and the raw materials needed to pursue the war, the army required civilians to make sacrifices. All the Japanese capacity for attention to fine detail and planning, once so admired by foreigners, was applied to ever more complex controls. Domestic lightbulbs were to be no stronger than thirty watts. Matches were to be shortened by .029 inch to save wood, and households were not to use more than four a day. The list of banned "luxuries" that could not be made or sold at all included men's suits, fountain pens, and gold-rimmed spectacles. Soap, dried milk, and everyday necessities were disappearing from the shops. The public was told, "Extravagance is the enemy!," and austerity was becoming a grim cult of its own. Ersatz substitutes replaced imports. A version of coffee could be made with dried sweet potatoes. With no cotton or wool, women tried to make clothes from "Patriotic Fibre," an all-Japanese synthetic concocted from coal and wood pulp that fell apart after a few months' wear. With the army taking all supplies of leather, shoes were made from whale hide.

A stream of propaganda told the public that their country was surrounded by enemies—China, the Soviet Union in the north, Britain and America in the Pacific—denying her the resources and the freedom to defend herself to which she was entitled. As part of the "Anti-Foreign Campaign," the army warned against Western spies. "The first stage of British policy consists of efforts to implant British ideas which form a hotbed of espionage. There has never been a need for greater care in accepting foreign ideas."[3] Several British businessmen were arrested and tried. It was not a good time for Masa to be receiving letters from a British general, even a friend of Japan such as Arthur. At some point she may have cautiously hidden or disposed of the letters she had accumulated since 1931 and only kept the older ones. She still heard from him occasionally, but the letters took longer to get through.

In December 1941, when Imperial Headquarters announced the attack on the U.S. Navy at Pearl Harbor, the bombing of Singapore and Hong Kong, and the simultaneous landing of troops in the Philippines and Malaya, the news was met with a mix of shock, admiration for the sheer boldness, and fear for the long-term future. For Masa there was an additional dimension of private tragedy she could hardly discuss with her neighbors. Arthur and she were now on different sides, with the possibility that the Anglo-Japanese Kiyoshi might soon be fighting the army his father and so many of his forebears had dedicated their lives to.

K iyoshi Suzuki had no way of knowing how the war in China would interfere with his personal plans. When he returned to Tokyo in the late summer of 1939, he told Masa about the reconciliation with his father and his stay at the Villa du Golfe, saw his fiancée, Tetsuko, again, and talked about getting married. First he had to finish his studies and find a job. Though he knew he was liable for military service, he was still on the register of Tokyo University as a postgraduate student, and it was possible the fighting would be over by the time his number came up.

Kiyoshi came from the comforts and sophistication of Paris, where food was still in abundant supply, whale-hide shoes were unknown, and the French were nervously enjoying what they suspected could be the last summer of peacetime, to the shortages and dimmed lights of wartime Japan. After the freedoms and fierce debate of Paris, it was harder to make the mental readjustment to the mood of a country in which almost all open criticism and debate had been eliminated. The Thought Police watched out for dissent or grumbling in workplaces, in railway carriages, or at the public baths. The entire nation was being led, or browbeaten, into support for Japan's "holy war" and the claims that lay behind it.

The basis for Japan's special brand of authoritarianism was state

Shinto. Language once used about the Emperor rhetorically was now treated seriously as firm fact, and the national myth was to be taken literally. The Japanese were reminded that the Yamato race was uniquely blessed, the only country to have an emperor who was descended from the gods, which now needed to expand militarily to have greater control of its destiny. A textbook on public morality from the Ministry of Education said the Japanese were "intrinsically quite different from the so-called citizens of Occidental countries."[4] In March 1940, a senior Japanese officer, General Akira Muto, told the Diet, "Liberalism based on individuality must be eliminated. . . . We are convinced that even in peacetime the people should aid in the promotion of the State rather than their own welfare."[5]

Kiyoshi was not a dissident, but he knew his own mind and had studied the radical and liberal French philosophers who wrote about the defense of the individual and of liberty. The modern French writer whose work he had discovered in Paris, Alain, was a humanist in the same tradition, setting up what he called "the individual against the powers" in contrast to doctrines of authority and social control. Alain was suspicious of all political power and hated fascism and dictatorial capitalism as much as socialism and communism.

With a perspective that had inevitably been affected by his four years in Europe, and with the campaign of national indoctrination continuing in the background, Kiyoshi returned to the philosophy department of Tokyo University to complete his course. In the now dowdy Meiji-era buildings in Hongo, academic life continued, but in a cowed form. Students were forbidden to wear long hair and did daily military drill under army officers, and the university was obliged to give courses in "the history of the Japanese spirit." More professors and teachers had been detained for "dangerous thought." A few mildly critical small-circulation magazines continued to appear, and books were still published, though leftist authors were banned. Kiyoshi managed to get a commission from a publisher to translate one of Alain's books, *Esquisses de l'homme*[6] (Sketches of Man), and worked on this at Masa's small house in Sugamo, which was close to the prison where communists and thought criminals were detained.

At the end of 1940, Kiyoshi at last found a permanent job that used his perfect French, when he joined the overseas service of the government radio organization, NHK. With a secure salary, Kiyoshi and Tetsuko finally married in April 1941, with a ceremony at the Sanno Shrine in Akasaka, on a small hill that looked across to the government center of Tokyo and the heavily guarded prime minister's office. Austerity rules meant the celebrations had to be kept to a minimum. Kiyoshi, Tetsuko, and Masa moved out to a house in Kunitachi, a middle-class university suburb fifteen miles west of Shinjuku Station on the electric railway. Masa was now performing the role her own mother had played for her when she was first living with Arthur, helping to cook and keep the house.

In his daily work as an announcer in the short-wave French service, Kiyoshi had to relay the official line, telling listeners in the colonies of Southeast Asia about Japan's divine mission to liberate them from the shackles of Western capitalism. His real interest was still elsewhere, and he was an intellectual, not a natural propagandist. His translation of Alain's book finally appeared with the Japanese title *Ningenron* (Human Theory) in the summer of 1941. If the militarists had understood Alain's record of Great War pacifism, they would have disapproved. Luckily his ideas were so imprecisely stated and compressed that it was hard to tell what he really meant, but in his translator's foreword Kiyoshi revealed a little of how he felt himself. He explained that Alain made the reader look at reality, rather than "conceptual constructions. . . . What he endeavors is to awaken and inspire the indefatigable, energetic human spirit. . . . Alain preaches that you must open your eyes and contemplate the world around you."[7] The essays, written in the 1920s, were oblique, but some of their titles promised a certain frisson in the Japan of 1941. They included "Racism," "Technology Against Spirit," and "The Military Man." In an essay titled "Fanaticism," Alain wrote, "Voltaire was right: it is fanaticism that is the sickness of humanity, and it is nothing more than the intellect thinking convulsively, with too ready an ambition. Fanaticism has in no way retreated, it has changed its objectives or, rather, simply changed the words."[8] Alain's essays were too broad to be "dangerous thought," but a statement of different values nevertheless. For a brief period, when socialist and Marxist books were prohibited, the gentle French pedant became a cult figure in certain circles.

Kiyoshi knew he was living on borrowed time. He could no longer claim his student exemption from army service and might receive his call-up papers at any moment. A settlement with China looked no nearer, and the army had moved into northern Indochina. Japan stood more exposed than ever. The United States had already blocked the export of aviation fuel along with vital metals and believed it could cripple the Japanese war machine by more sanctions. The Japanese government was having to choose between a military strike south to seize the rubber and oil of Malaya and the Dutch East Indies, or giving up the gains they had made in China, including Manchuria, as the Americans were asking. At the same time, there was intermittent fighting on the Soviet border.

In July 1941, with a showdown approaching, Kiyoshi was ordered to report to the 10th Heavy Field Artillery Regiment at Ichikawa, to the west of Tokyo, where he had taken his army medical more than fourteen years earlier. The night before he left, Tetsuko and Masa gave him a *senninbari,* a "thousand-stitch belt," the strip of cloth with sewing stitches collected from friends and neighbors that families gave departing soldiers as a traditional talisman. The British general's son enlisted as a private. As a graduate of one of Japan's most esteemed universities, he was officer material, and conscripted privates could transfer to officer-training school after eight months if they passed an examination, but he had no interest in doing this. Before he left, he told Tetsuko that he did not want to give orders to others, and hoped to return alive. He was against the war, but as critical of the Americans as he was of Japan's militarists.

At the age of thirty-four Kiyoshi was inducted into the rigmaroles and rituals of military life his father had grown up with from the time he was a cadet at Sandhurst. He was given his uniform, a rifle stamped with the imperial chrysanthemum crest, and a bunk in a barracks room that housed a squad of sixteen men. He learnt to salute correctly both indoors and out, the indoor variant requiring a forward bend at precisely fifteen degrees and touching the cap lightly with the right hand. At morning and evening roll calls, he and the rest of his squad chanted Meiji's five principles for soldiers, stressing loyalty, propriety, bravery, righteousness, and simplicity. Moral and spiritual training was based on the Field Service Code that every soldier carried, which enshrined the *bushido* fighting spirit and the idea of self-sacrifice for the state. "In defense, always retain the spirit of attack. . . . Never give up a position but rather die."[9] The artillery regiments had a high status in the Imperial Army, along with the engineers. Because they had to operate complex machinery and signal systems, they were given the first pick of the conscripts. Kiyoshi found his fellow recruits came from educated backgrounds, and his corporal, Keiichiro Kondo, was a German-language graduate who later became a professor. In the infantry regiments, new entrants were harshly treated and physically abused in their first few months as a matter of course, but this was not part of his regiment's way. Since they also had to do heavy physical work manhandling guns that weighed four or five tons and carrying shells, they were given a better food ration. Within weeks of Kiyoshi's joining, the battalion was told to get ready to leave for China.

Kiyoshi made the same journey Arthur had taken in 1904, through the Inland Sea and across to the port of Dalny, now renamed Dairen, where additional divisions and thousands of guns and tanks were arriving as part of a Japanese buildup in Manchuria.

With their 150-millimeter howitzers, heavy tractors, ammunition carriers, and observation vehicles loaded onto flatbed railway wagons, the regiment moved north across the maize fields and past neat stations and new settlements, on the rich plains where the Japanese had beaten the Russians almost forty years before. They made their first stop in Mukden. The muddy Manchu capital Arthur had stayed in was now a booming city, the most industrialized center of China after Shanghai, the horizon gray with the smoke from new Japanese-owned plants making arms and aircraft, electrical machinery and railway engines.

Between the time they left Tokyo and arrived in China, the Asian crisis had ratcheted up another turn. When the Japanese Army moved farther south, into the rest of Indochina, the United States and Britain retaliated by stopping all oil sales to Japan. Since 90 percent of Japan's oil had to be imported, the embargo made a military solution, and a further strike south to the oil fields of Sumatra, almost inevitable, unless some compromise could be achieved in last-minute negotiations in Washington. This seemed less likely after October, when General Hideki Tojo became prime minister. An uncompromising militarist, he believed Japan would have to fight in order to break "the encirclement ring," and pronounced that the "whole nation should move as one cannon ball of fiery resolution."[10] The 10th Heavy Field Artillery were at Kairyu, a small town in southern Manchuria, not far from Mukden, when the news came that Japan had widened the war and was now taking on the United States and the British Empire, as well as China.

From the point of view of Kiyoshi's chances of survival, he was in one of the safer places for a Japanese soldier to be. It now seemed less likely that the troops in Manchuria would be called on to attack the Soviet Union, as many had believed they were being sent to do. For the moment the war was firmly in the south, and it was the Japanese divisions in the Yangtze Valley, the jungles of Burma, and the Philippines who were doing the fighting. Kiyoshi's battalion moved up to Muling, only 150 miles from the Russian Pacific port of Vladivostok, set up their gun positions, ranged the howitzers—which could hit targets seven miles away—and looked across the snow-covered mountains towards the Soviet border. A call went out for suitable candidates to train as Russian interpreters, and Private Suzuki was nominated. Kiyoshi was sent to the army's own language school in Harbin, the Manchuria city in which most Russian was spoken. In 1943, when the war was turning against Japan and whole garrisons were being annihilated in the fierce fighting on the South Pacific islands, Kiyoshi was a student again, going to classes. On his days off he could walk by the river and see the onion-domed churches and white wooden houses, or sit and talk with his comrades in the smoky tearooms of the old Russian settlement. If he had not inherited his father's military instincts, he had Arthur's gift for languages, and when he graduated, Private Suzuki could speak French, English, and Russian. After a year, in early 1944, he rejoined his battalion up in the hills on what was still the quietest front. His father's war had been far grimmer and more prolonged, but as a staff officer and commander he had always known the tactical context and the greater picture. Kiyoshi was completely isolated, caught in circumstances over which he had no control, in the lowest rank in the Japanese Army, knowing less about the war, or what was happening in Japan or Europe, with each month that passed.

In Tokyo, Masa heard only occasionally from Kiyoshi, who was allowed two of the army's letter forms a month, and could hear nothing from Arthur. Meanwhile, the campaign to denigrate the country she had heard so much about, and that Arthur had wanted to take her back to, gathered pace. The British and Americans were portrayed as decadent, arrogant, and racist. One cartoon showed a student speaking English into a waste bin, ugly foreign words spewing from his lips, and his mother standing by with salt at the ready to clean his mouth out afterwards. Another showed a woman, though not Yamatohime, energetically combing through her hair to bring out the detritus of Anglo-American ideas. Flakes of dandruff labeled extravagance, selfishness, liberalism, materialism, and worship of money fell to the ground.[11] Popular newspapers subtly changed the Japanese characters used for the enemy to make them more dismissive, so the British were now represented by the three ideographs "An-gu-ro" (Anglo), which could read as "Dark-stupid-foolish." As the war began to go badly for Japan, after the naval defeat at Midway, the portrayal of the enemy became more vicious, with more stress on the need to wipe out the "Allied devils." The vocabulary of extermination was not limited to the Japanese side. In the United States, where the Japanese were often referred to as yellow vermin, civilians were now being advised, "Every war bond kills a Jap."

The daily hardships affecting Masa and Tetsuko increased. With coastal shipping easy prey for American submarines, food was no longer being imported from the Japanese Empire overseas, and rations were cut further. Buses wheezed through the streets billowing black smoke from the charcoal burners bolted onto engines for which there was no petrol. Once the Americans reached Saipan and the Mariana Islands, they were within flying distance of Japan, and the populations of the Japanese cities knew what was in store for them. Schoolchildren were evacuated, firebreaks were bulldozed through whole districts, neighborhood associations organized fire drills and labor service to dig shelters and evacuation trenches, and households were told they could leave a small suitcase of personal papers at the local ward offices to be taken to the countryside for safe keeping. The air attacks started in late November 1944, and culminated in the raid on the night of 10 March 1945, when three hundred B-29s flew low over Tokyo, raining down clusters of incendiary bombs that burst on the closely packed wooden buildings, starting fires and spraying a highly inflammable petroleum jelly. A gusty wind helped turn the flames into an inferno, and in a

few hours the city that Arthur and Masa had known together was
reduced to ashes a second time. The fiery cannonball was striking in
the other direction. More than 100,000 were killed, roasted in the
streets, drowned in rivers and canals, or suffocated in the air-raid
shelters as the huge firestorm sucked all available oxygen out of the
air. More died than in the earthquake and fires of 1923, or in either
of the atom-bomb raids on Hiroshima and Nagasaki that were still
to come. Again it was the Shitamachi and the flat areas of eastern
Tokyo, where Masa had grown up, that suffered most. One of Masa's
sisters and many other relatives died in Fukagawa. Once again Masa
was saved, indirectly, by her link with Arthur Hart-Synnot. It was
Arthur's allowance that had allowed her to move to the higher land
on the western edges of Tokyo and survive the 1923 fires, and she
was now in the relative safety of Kunitachi, fifteen miles farther
west.

By the summer of 1945, the Japanese knew the war was lost. The
streets of Kunitachi were full of evacuees, and sirens sounded daily
as American planes flew overhead unchallenged to attack airfields
and military installations west of Tokyo. Though children were taken
out of high school to work in the defense plants, and old men were
being trained to resist Americans with bamboo spears, the Japanese spirit, *Yamato-damashii,* had not been enough. When the atomic
bomb was dropped, Japanese feared the awesome new weapon
would now be used against other cities, but it was the second piece
of news, coming two days after Hiroshima, that caused most dread
to Masa and Tetsuko. The Soviet Union finally came into the war
against Japan, and the radio reported that the Russian invasion of
Manchuria had begun. Three separate Soviet armies with tanks were
said to be crashing across the borders, with an outnumbered Japanese Army making gallant efforts to resist them. For months now,
Manchuria had been effectively cut off, there had been no news of
Kiyoshi, and Tetsuko and Masa had no idea where he was.

. . .

Four months earlier, in April 1945, Kiyoshi's artillery regiment was ordered to pull back from the Russian border and return to take part in the final fight to the death in the main Japanese islands. Kiyoshi stayed behind because the Russian interpreters were not allowed to leave. The thirty-eight-year-old philosophy graduate was sent to a run-of-the-mill railway regiment, whose task was to guard the lines against sabotage by Chinese guerrillas and keep the troop trains running. Once the Russian invasion began, they were ordered to destroy as much of Manchuria's railway system as possible, and for a few days in August they dynamited bridges and tunnels, and burnt stations and workshops in a scorched-earth policy that failed to have any effect on the speed of the enemy advance. On 15 August, Emperor Hirohito made his surrender broadcast from Tokyo, conceding that "despite the best that has been done by everyone— the gallant fighting of the military and naval forces, the diligence and assiduity of our servants of the state, and the devoted service of our hundred million people—the war situation has developed not necessarily to Japan's advantage." Over the next few days, with order breaking down in Manchuria and with more than a million Japanese civilians fearing for their lives and fleeing south towards the ports of Dairen and Fusan, Japanese Army units gave themselves up. Kiyoshi survived the brief burst of fighting, and the 19th Railway Regiment were among more than 600,000 troops who surrendered, in an orderly Japanese fashion. For a few weeks they were kept under Russian guard in former military camps and holding pens, and then put into railway wagons and taken north. As they crossed the Soviet border, they did not know if they were on their way to the port of Vladivostok for repatriation to Japan, or going into captivity. The trains turned east, heading back into Siberia.

Kiyoshi and the remnants of his regiment were taken on a halting

journey to a station in a forested river basin eight hundred miles from
Vladivostok. To the Russians, the Japanese prisoners were war booty,
like the industrial plant they were stripping from Manchuria's cities, a
pool of educated labor to put to work in the mines, factories, and
forests, and the Russians had only had to fight for six days to acquire
them. Arriving in the coal-mining town of Raychikhinsk, Kiyoshi's
little group of five hundred prisoners were locked into cattle sheds
with earth floors, and their first task was to build the camp that would
house them, one of two thousand similar camps sprouting up in the
new Gulag for Japanese prisoners. They were still in their summer
uniforms, with the temperature dropping fast, and were fed a ration
of thin millet porridge twice a day.

I n the autumn of 1945, with soldiers and civilians straggling back to
Japan from the ruins of an empire, millions of families were desperate to find news of missing sons and husbands. Masa listened to
the special *Missing Persons' Hour* radio programs and read the lists of
names in the papers. She had still heard nothing of Kiyoshi, but in
November she had news of his father. Once the international post
was operating again, a letter arrived from England, with a brief note
from Arthur's sister Beatrice. She apologized for not having been able
to contact her sooner and told her that Arthur was dead. The general
had been struck by a heart attack three years earlier, in 1942, and she
enclosed a newspaper obituary which noted his marriage to Violet
Drower and his military record in India, South Africa, and France.
The only mention of Japan came at the end of the list of his decorations, which recorded that he had received the Order of the Sacred
Treasure, Fourth Class, from the Mikado. He was seventy-two when
he died. Beatrice asked Masa if there was anything she wanted from
his possessions to remember him by. Since Masa still kept a canteen
of silver teaspoons, nail scissors, some carved Irish bogwood, and a
stereoscopic viewer that Arthur once thought might entice her with

scenes of the world outside Japan, she declined the offer. There was no contact with Violet, who sold the Villa du Golfe, which had been stripped of its contents, including the Japanese letters, by the time she went back to reclaim it after the war. She lived on comfortably in a house in Sussex on her widow's pension from Arthur.

Masa lived through the period of the American occupation still hearing nothing from Kiyoshi, still telling herself he was alive. She kept his clothes aired, including the suits and jackets sent by Arthur in the 1920s, and still had his English children's books and toys, but was increasingly quiet and withdrawn. She became more religious and prayed daily. She had been able to save money over the years, and Tetsuko took responsibility for her as a conscientious daughter-in-law. After the war they bought a house together. Masa had the flat upstairs, and Tetsuko, who continued as a teacher and eventually became principal of her school, lived below.

Tetsuko looked after Masa as Kiyoshi would have wanted, but was keeping a secret from her. In 1947, a letter arrived addressed to her at the Seika Gakuen school from a Japanese soldier who was in one of the first batches of prisoners to be released from the Soviet camps and shipped back to Japan, who wanted to come and see her. Tojo Yamanaka had been with Kiyoshi at Raychikhinsk in the Soviet Far East in the winter of 1945, and when he met Tetsuko he told her what had happened.

Among the batch of five hundred Japanese who arrived in the Siberian town in September 1945, Kiyoshi had stood out as different, not just because of his appearance but because of his education and his experience. He was thirty-eight when most of the captured men were in their early twenties. The others relied on him totally in the first weeks, when the Russians were ordering them to cut timber and level the ground for a camp, and he was the only Russian speaker. As the weather grew colder, and they were driving posts into hard-frozen ground, men started to go down from malnutrition, dysentery, and exhaustion, until several were dying every day. Kiyoshi collapsed with a fever and was taken away, and the other prisoners assumed he had died. A few days later, Yamanaka caught pneumonia and was driven through the snow to a military hospital at Zavitinsk. He found forty Japanese in one badly lit room without proper drugs or medical care, and Kiyoshi, though desperately ill himself, translating between the Soviet Army doctor and the prisoners. By December, Kiyoshi was much weaker, his hair was falling out, he was emaciated, and he could not eat. Kiyoshi had called Yamanaka to his bedside on 24 December 1945, whispered that he was sure the younger man would get back to Japan eventually, and asked him to take a message to his wife, Tetsuko. He wanted to send her his love and wish her good luck, and to thank Masa for all she had done for him, though he did not know if the two women had survived the bombing of Tokyo. He died later that night. He had just passed his thirty-ninth birthday.

Tetsuko never told Masa, because she thought she would not be able to bear the double loss, of the Englishman she had believed would come back to her, and then the son who had become the substitute for him, and who might have had the married happiness she never had herself. Masa's wait for Kiyoshi was longer than her wait for Arthur, and the woman who might have become Mrs. Hart-Synnot lived on into the 1960s, with her photograph albums and letters and old jackets with leather patches. By that time, Tokyo had been reconstructed again and was as different from the smoldering ruins of 1945 as the city of 1941 was different from the Tokyo in which she had first met Arthur, in the blossom-filled garden of the Kaikosha. She died in 1965, almost exactly sixty years after Arthur returned from Manchuria across the Straits of Tsushima to keep his promise.

NOTES

Notes have been limited to citations for quotations taken from published sources and archival collections. The bulk of the references, however, are to Arthur Hart-Synnot's own letters in Japanese, which are still with Masa Suzuki's papers in Tokyo. The translations are by the authors. The dates come from the post office franking on the envelopes. Any numbers that appear in addition to these dates are Arthur's own, and need some explanation: In the winter of 1904–1905 he started to number his letters and cards from Manchuria sequentially, but soon stopped. After May 1906, he started numbering from 1 again, and the numbers climb until he next returned to Japan and saw Masa. Subsequently he started a new sequence, from 1, each time they parted. Numbering stopped at the end of 1919. By 1923 he was numbering his letters again, beginning from 1 at the start of each year.

One. Return to Ballymoyer

1. Harold C. Hart, *The Hart Family of Netherbury, Dorset* (privately printed, 1930), p. 63. In the Dorset History Centre, Dorchester.
2. Ibid., p. 98.
3. Sir Reginald Clare Hart, *Reflections on the Art of War* (London: W. Clowes, 1894).
4. Harold C. Hart, *The Hart Family*.
5. Arthur Conan Doyle, *The Great Boer War* (London: Thomas Nelson, 1908), p. 245.
6. *Daily Telegraph*, 8 Aug. 1902, quoted in Hugh Cortazzi and Gordon Daniels, eds., *Britain and Japan* (London: Routledge, 1991), p. 15.
7. *The Playgoer*, Feb. 1904, p. 69.
8. Ibid.
9. *Transactions of the Japan Society,* London, 1904, p. 314.
10. Everard Calthrop, letter, 7 Feb. 1904, Royal Artillery Historical Trust, James Clavell Library, Royal Artillery Museum, Woolwich, MD/1119.

11. J. N. Westwood, *Russia Against Japan,* (London: Macmillan, 1986), p. 40.

12. Everard Calthrop, letter, 16 Feb. 1904.

Two. Dai Nippon

1. Elizabeth Bisland, *Life and Letters of Lafcadio Hearn* (London: Constable, 1906), p. 35.

2. Elizabeth Bisland, *Flying Trip Around the World* (London: Osgood and McIlvaine, 1891).

3. Baron K. Suyematsu, *The Risen Sun* (London: Constable, 1905), p. 261.

4. Augusta Campbell-Davidson, *Present Day Japan* (London: Fisher Unwin, 1907), p. 261.

5. Everard Calthrop, letter, 20 June 1904, Royal Artillery Historical Trust, James Clavell Library, Royal Artillery Museum, Woolwich, MD/1119.

6. Henry T. Finck, *Lotos-Time in Japan* (New York: Scribner, 1895).

7. *New York Times,* 9 June 1895.

8. Douglas Sladen, *The Japs at Home* (London: Hutchinson, 1892), p. 150.

9. Sir Edwin Arnold, in *Scribner's Magazine,* vol. 9 (1891), p. 65.

10. Sladen, *Japs at Home,* p. 152.

11. General Sir Ian Hamilton, *A Staff Officer's Scrapbook,* vol. 1 (London: Edward Arnold, 1905), p. 17.

12. Ibid., p. 18.

13. Baron Kikuchi, "Female Education in Japan," *Transactions of the Japan Society,* 1907, p. 422.

14. F. S. Piggott, writing as "James Weymouth," "The Language Officer in Japan," *United Services Magazine,* Sept. 1914, p. 647.

15. General Sir Ian Hamilton, *A Staff Officer's Scrapbook,* vol. 2 (London: Edward Arnold, 1907), p. 63.

16. Ibid., p. 64.

17. Erwin Baez, *Awakening Japan* (New York: Viking, 1932), p. 288.

18. Pierre Loti, *Madame Chrysanthème,* trans. Laura Ensor (New York: Frederick Stokes, 1920).

19. Arthur Hart-Synnot, postcard no. 1, 14 Dec. 1904. All subsequent letters and postcards cited are from him unless stated otherwise.

20. Postcard no. 2, 14 Dec. 1904.

21. Postcard no. 3, 16 Dec. 1904.

Three. The Promise

1. Letter, 25 Dec. 1904.

2. General Sir Ian Hamilton, *A Staff Officer's Scrapbook,* vol. 1 (London: Edward Arnold, 1905), p. 46.

3. Letter, 25 Dec. 1904.

4. Postcard, 12 Jan. 1905.

5. Letter, 13 Jan. 1905.

6. Ibid.

7. Tetsuya Ohama, ed., *Letters of Russo-Japanese War Officers* (Tokyo: Doseisha, 2001), p. 449.

8. Shintaro Amano, ed., *Diary of General Nogi* (Yokohama, 1936).

9. Letter, 11 Feb. 1905.

10. Letter, 20 Feb. 1905.

11. Letter, 27 Feb. 1905.

12. *The Russo-Japanese War: Reports from British Officers Attached to the Japanese Forces in the Field,* vol. 2 (London: HMSO, 1907), p. 151.

13. Ibid., p. 152.

14. Ibid., p. 153.

15. Ibid., p. 156.

16. Ibid., p. 162.

17. Ibid., p. 163.

18. Ibid., p. 173.

19. Major General F. S. Piggott, *Broken Thread* (Aldershot, UK: Gale and Polden, 1950), p. 26.

20. *The Russo-Japanese War: Reports from British Officers Attached to the Japanese Forces in the Field,* vol. 2 (London: HMSO, 1907), p. 179.

21. Everard Calthrop, letter, 19 March 1905, Royal Artillery Historical Trust, James Clavell Library, Royal Artillery Museum, Woolwich, MD/1119.

22. Diary of Roundell Toke, 28 May 1905, collection of Jean S. and Frederic A. Sharf, Chestnut Hill, Mass.

Four. Together in Shinjuku

1. Letter no. 24, 21 June 1906.

2. Diary of Roundell Toke, 9 Dec. 1905, collection of Jean S. and Frederic A. Sharf, Chestnut Hill, Mass.

3. Quoted in *Japan Weekly Mail,* 14 Oct. 1905.

4. Count Okuma, quoted in *Japan Weekly Mail,* 21 Oct. 1905.

5. Hugh Cortazzi, *Mitford's Japan* (London: Athlone Press, 1985), p. 206.

6. General Sir Aylmer Haldane, *A Soldier's Saga* (London: William Blackwood, 1948), p. 233.

7. Letter no. 6, 19 May 1906.

8. Letter no. 7, 20 May 1906.

9. Letter no. 14, 3 June 1906.

10. Letter no. 24, 21 June 1906.

11. Letter no. 23, 12 June 1906.

12. Letter no. 11, 26 May 1906.

13. Letter no. 42, 13 July 1906.

14. Letter no. 44, 26 July 1906.

15. Letter no. 46, 11 Aug. 1906.

16. Letter no. 52, 19 Sept. 1906.

17. Letter no. 47, 17 Aug. 1906.

18. Letter no. 44, 26 July 1906.

19. Letter no. 50, 7 Sept. 1906.

20. Letter no. 46, 11 Aug. 1906.

21. Letter no. 51, 16 Sept. 1906.

22. *The Geisha—A Story of a Teahouse.* Book by Owen Hall, lyrics by Harry Greenbank, music by Sydney Jones (London: Hopwood and Crew, 1897).

23. Letter no. 54, 2 Oct. 1906.

Five. *"Close to Japan"*

1. Letter no. 7, 26 May 1907.

2. Letter no. 73, 1 Jan. 1907.

3. Letter no. 74, 6 Jan. 1907.

4. Letter no. 75, 13 Jan. 1907.

5. Letter no. 74, 6 Jan. 1907.

6. Letter no. 76, 23 Jan. 1907.

7. Letter no. 78, 27 Jan. 1907.

8. Letter no. 86, 9 March 1907.

9. Ibid.

10. Letter no. 6, 19 May 1907.

11. George Feaver, ed., *The Webbs in Asia: The 1911 Travel Diary of Sidney and Beatrice Webb* (London: Macmillan, 1992), p. 165.

12. *Military Report and General Information Concerning Hong Kong* (General Staff, 1907), in National Archives, WO33/543, p. 138.

13. Ibid.

14. Letter no. 7, 26 May 1907.

15. Letter no. 26, 6 Aug. 1907.

16. Letter no. 72, 25 Dec. 1906.

17. Letter no. 14, 26 June 1907.

18. Letter no. 57, 31 May 1908.

19. Advertisement in *Fujokai,* Tokyo, 1907.

20. Letter no. 7, 27 Oct. 1907.

21. *Hong Kong Daily Press,* 30 June 1910, p. 5.

22. *Hong Kong Daily Press,* 6 July 1910, p. 3.

23. Letter no. 15, 1 Dec. 1907.

24. Letter no. 10, 3 Nov. 1907.

25. Letter no. 58, 7 June 1908.

26. Letter no. 29, 26 Jan. 1908.

27. Ibid.

28. Letter no. 38, 22 March 1908.

29. Letter no. 42, 5 April 1908.

30. Ibid.

31. Letter no. 46, 12 April 1908.

32. Letter no. 49, 26 April 1908.

33. Letter no. 63, 28 June 1908.

34. Letter no. 47, 19 April 1908.

35. Ibid.

36. Letter no. 52, 10 May 1908.

37. Letter no. 56, 24 May 1908.

38. Letter no. 63, 28 June 1908.

39. Letter no. 5, 15 Sept. 1908.

40. Letter no. 4, 13 Sept. 1908.

41. Letter no. 6, 20 Sept. 1908.

42. *Report and Information Concerning Hong Kong,* p. 37.

43. Letter no. 1, 10 June 1909.

44. Letter no. 7, 24 June 1909.

45. Letter no. 1, 4 June 1910.

46. Letter no. 11, 6 Aug. 1910.

47. Letter, 14 July 1910.

48. Letter no. 17, 20 July 1910.

49. Letter no. 9, 1 July 1910.

50. Letter no. 16, 18 July 1910.

51. Letter no. 19, 24 July 1910.

52. Ibid.

53. Letter no. 32, 29 Jan. 1911.

54. Ibid.

55. Letter no. 35, 7 Feb. 1911.

56. Ibid.

57. Letter no. 39, 23 Feb. 1911.

58. Letter no. 40, 24 Feb. 1911.

59. Ibid.

Six. Up the Irrawaddy

1. Letter no. 72, 7 July 1912.

2. Letter no. 40, 24 Feb. 1911.

3. *New York Times,* 22 June 1911, p. 10.

4. Ayako Hotta-Lister, *The Japan-British Exhibition of 1910* (London: Japan Library, 1999), p. 178.

5. *Times* (London), 29 July 1911, p. 11.

6. Ibid.

7. Letter no. 15, 6 Aug. 1911.

8. Letter no. 8, 25 June 1911.

9. Letter no. 10, 2 July 1911.

10. Letter no. 18, 27 Aug. 1911.

11. Letter no. 13, 23 July 1911.

12. Letter no. 14, 30 July 1911.

13. Letter no. 15, 6 Aug. 1911.

14. Letter no. 14, 30 July 1911.

15. Ibid.

16. Letter no. 23, 1 Oct. 1911.

17. Letter no. 12, 16 July 1911.

18. Letter no. 19, 3 Sept. 1911.

19. Letter no. 13, 23 July 1911.

20. Letter no. 12, 16 July 1911.

21. Letter no. 27, 22 Oct. 1911.

22. Letter no. 28, 29 Oct. 1911.

23. Letter no. 29, 5 Nov. 1911.

24. Letter no. 36, 17 Dec. 1911.

25. Letter no. 18, 27 Aug. 1911.

26. Letter no. 43, 17 Jan. 1912.

27. Letter no. 45, 29 Jan. 1912.

28. Letter no. 57, 7 April 1912.

29. Letter no. 48, 18 Feb. 1912.

30. Letter no. 49, 22 Feb. 1912.

31. Kenneth Ballhatchet, *Race, Sex and Class Under the Raj* (London: Weidenfeld & Nicolson, 1980), p. 153.

32. Ronald Hyam, *Journal of Imperial and Commonwealth History,* vol. 14 (May 1986), p. 170.

33. Letter no. 65, 19 May 1912.

34. Violet Hart-Synnot, letter, 2 May 1912, Masa Suzuki papers.

35. Ibid.

36. Letter no. 71, 30 June 1912.

37. Letter no. 72, 7 July 1912.

38. F. Hadland Davis, *Japan from the Age of the Gods to the Fall of Tsingtau* (London: T. C. Jack, 1916), p. 286.

39. Letter no. 12, 20 Oct. 1912.

40. Letter no. 11, 14 Oct. 1912.
41. Letter no. 17, 24 Nov. 1912.
42. Ibid.
43. Letter no. 18, 1 Dec. 1912.
44. Letter no. 26, 14 Jan. 1913.
45. Letter no. 20, 15 Dec. 1912.
46. Letter no. 24, 5 Jan. 1913.
47. Letter no. 31, 4 Feb. 1913.
48. Ronald Hart-Synnot, letter, 3 March 1913, Masa Suzuki papers.
49. Letter no. 45, 27 April 1913.
50. Letter no. 36, 2 March 1913.
51. Letter no. 44, 20 April 1913.
52. Letter no. 45, 27 April 1913.
53. Letter no. 46, 4 May 1913.
54. Letter no. 47, 11 May 1913.

Seven. Dog or Lion?

1. Letter no. 214, 14 March 1917.
2. Letter no. 175, 8 July 1916.
3. Letter no. 150, 30 Jan. 1916.
4. Letter no. 110, 15 May 1915.
5. Letter no. 113, 5 June 1915.
6. Letter no. 109, 7 May 1915.
7. Letter no. 111, 21 May 1915.
8. Letter no. 77, 24 Oct. 1914.
9. Letter no. 111, 21 May 1915.
10. Letter no. 74, 9 Oct. 1914.
11. Letter no. 169, 2 June 1916.
12. Letter no. 175, 8 July 1916.
13. Violet Hart-Synnot, letter, 12 July 1915, Masa Suzuki papers.
14. Letter no. 136, 29 Oct. 1915.
15. Letter no. 108, 1 May 1915.
16. Letter no. 120, 18 July 1915.
17. Letter no. 123, 9 Aug. 1915.
18. Letter no. 150, 30 Jan. 1916.
19. Letter no. 151, 5 Feb. 1916.
20. Letter no. 167, 20 May 1916.
21. Letter no. 176, 15 July 1916.
22. Letter no. 196, 17 Nov. 1916.
23. Letter no. 198, 4 Dec. 1916.

24. Letter no. 199, 10 Dec. 1916.

25. Ibid.

26. Letter no. 200, 15 Dec. 1916.

Eight. Forget-Me-Not from Arras

1. Letter no. 214, 14 March 1917.

2. Letter no. 204, 5 Jan. 1917.

3. Letter no. 205, 12 Jan. 1917.

4. Letter no. 206, 20 Jan. 1917.

5. Letter no. 204, 5 Jan. 1917.

6. Letter no. 205, 12 Jan. 1917.

7. Letter no. 209, 8 Feb. 1917.

8. Letter no. 211, 22 Feb. 1917.

9. Letter no. 210, 15 Feb. 1917.

10. Letter no. 215, 22 March 1917.

11. Letter no. 216, 28 March 1917.

12. Letter no. 214, 14 March 1917.

13. Ibid.

14. Ibid.

15. Letter no. 227, 13 June 1917.

16. Letter no. 231, 10 July 1917.

17. Letter no. 226, 6 June 1917.

18. Letter no. 227, 13 June 1917.

19. Letter no. 210, 15 Feb. 1917.

20. Letter no. 224, 25 May 1917.

21. Letter no. 240, 7 Sept. 1917.

22. Letter no. 248, 21 Oct. 1917.

23. Letter no. 216, 28 March 1917.

24. Letter no. 224, 25 May 1917.

25. Letter no. 227, 13 June 1917.

26. Letter no. 228, 20 June 1917.

27. Letter no. 229, 27 June 1917.

28. Ibid.

29. Letter no. 231, 10 July 1917.

30. Ibid.

31. Letter no. 235, 7 Aug. 1917.

32. Letter no. 242, 18 Sept. 1917.

33. Letter no. 243, 20 Sept. 1917.

34. Letter no. 246, 6 Oct. 1917.

35. Ibid.

36. War Diary of 1st Battalion Lancashire Fusiliers, 1917, in United Kingdom National Archives, Kew, WO95/2300.

37. Major General J. C. Latter, *History of the Lancashire Fusiliers 1914–18,* vol. 2 (Aldershot: Gale and Polden, 1949), p. 242.

38. Letter no. 247, 14 Oct. 1917.

39. Violet Hart-Synnot, letter, 21 Oct. 1917, Masa Suzuki papers.

40. Letter no. 197, 21 Nov. 1916.

41. "Kit and Kat," in Arthur Hart-Synnot, "Broken Sword," typescript collection of poems, 1921.

42. Letter no. 253, 27 Nov. 1917.

43. Letter no. 255, 10 Dec. 1917.

44. Letter no. 262, 28 Jan. 1918.

45. Letter no. 265, 17 Feb. 1918.

46. Letter no. 252, 16 Nov. 1917.

47. Letter no. 251, 11 Nov. 1917.

48. Letter no. 268, 18 March 1918.

Nine. Broken Sword

1. Included in Arthur Hart-Synnot, "Broken Sword," typescript collection of poems, 1921.

2. Letter no. 275, 23 April 1918.

3. Letter no. 276, 5 May 1918.

4. Ibid.

5. Letter no. 278, 11 May 1918.

6. Japanese press comment, *Japan Advertiser,* 3 May 1916.

7. Baron Kato, quoted in *What Japan Says About the Anglo-Japanese Alliance* (Tokyo: Japan Times Publishing Company, 1916).

8. Captain Malcolm D. Kennedy, *The Estrangement of Great Britain and Japan, 1917–1935* (Manchester University Press, 1969).

9. Nagahisa Uyeshima, quoted in *What Japan Says About the Alliance.*

10. *Asahi,* 26 March 1918.

11. Aylmer Haldane, diary entry, 12 May 1918. 1918 Diary, Papers of General Sir J. Aylmer Haldane, National Library of Scotland, MS 20250.

12. Letter no. 279, 20 May 1918.

13. Letter no. 280, 27 May 1918.

14. Letter no. 282, 9 June 1918.

15. Letter no. 286, 7 July 1918.

16. Letter no. 287, 14 July 1918.

17. Included in Arthur Hart-Synnot, "Broken Sword."

18. Letter no. 287, 14 July 1918.

19. Ibid.

20. Norman Hart, letter, July 1918, Masa Suzuki papers.

21. Letter no. 288, 21 July 1918.

22. Letter no. 289, 28 July 1918.

23. Letter no. 292, 19 Aug. 1918.

24. Letter no. 293, 25 Aug. 1918.

25. Letter no. 294, 1 Sept. 1918.

26. Letter no. 293, 25 Aug. 1918.

27. Letter no. 298, 29 Sept. 1918.

28. Letter no. 297, 22 Sept. 1918.

29. Letter no. 296, 15 Sept. 1918.

30. Letter no. 300, 13 Oct. 1918.

31. Letter no. 291, 11 Aug. 1918.

32. Letter no. 300, 13 Oct. 1918.

33. Arthur Hart-Synnot, "Rouen, September 1918," poem in notebook.

34. Letter no. 301, 20 Oct. 1918.

35. Letter no. 303, 3 Nov. 1918.

36. Letter no. 305, 17 Nov. 1918.

37. Ibid.

Ten. Falling on the Hill

1. Letter no. 306, 24 Nov. 1918.

2. J.O.P. Bland, *China, Japan and Korea* (London: William Heineman, 1921), p. 222.

3. Timothy D. Saxon, "Anglo-Japanese Naval Co-operation 1914–1918," *Naval War College Review* (Newport, R.I.), vol. 53 (Winter 2000).

4. *New York Times,* 10 Dec. 1918, p. 12.

5. Calculated as 395 at Tsingtao and 68 sailors lost on the Japanese ship *Sakaki,* June 1917.

6. Ian Nish, *Alliance in Decline: A Study in Anglo-Japanese Relations* (London: Athlone Press, 1972), p. 255.

7. Sir Conyngham Greene to Sir Edward Grey, 5 Dec. 1914, in United Kingdom National Archives, Kew, FO800/68.

8. Letter no. 318, 9 Feb. 1919.

9. Letter no. 306, 24 Nov. 1918.

10. Letter no. 309, 15 Dec. 1918.

11. Arthur Hart-Synnot, "Dai Nippon," in "Broken Sword," typescript collection of poems, 1921.

12. Arthur Hart-Synnot, "Voices of the Sea," in "Broken Sword."

13. Letter no. 301, 20 Oct. 1918.

14. Letter no. 306, 24 Nov. 1918.

15. Ibid.

16. Letter no. 309, 15 Dec. 1918.

17. Letter no. 314, 12 Jan. 1919.

18. Letter no. 315, 19 Jan. 1919.

19. Letter no. 316, 26 Jan. 1919.

20. Letter no. 319, 16 Feb. 1919.

21. Letter no. 318, 9 Feb. 1919.

22. Letter no. 319, 16 Feb. 1919.

23. Letter no. 322, 9 March 1919.

24. Letter no. 324, 23 March 1919.

25. Hugh Cortazzi and George Webb, *Kipling's Japan* (London: Athlone Press, 1988), p. 54.

26. Letter no. 321, 5 March 1919.

27. Letter no. 322, 9 March 1919.

28. Letter no. 330, 29 April 1919.

29. Letter no. 323, 16 March 1919.

30. Letter no. 322, 9 March 1919.

31. Letter no. 325, 30 March 1919.

32. Letter no. 328, 21 April 1919.

33. Letter no. 330, 29 April 1919.

34. Letter no. 322, 9 March 1919.

35. Letter no. 333, 26 May 1919.

36. Letter no. 326, 6 April 1919.

37. Letter no. 330, 6 May 1919.

38. Letter no. 332, 20 May 1919.

39. Letter no. 334, 8 June 1919.

40. Ibid.

41. Ibid.

Eleven. On the Croisette

1. Letter no. 321, 5 March 1919.

2. Letter no. 335, 19 June 1919.

3. Letter no. 48, 19 Aug. 1906.

4. Letter no. 322, 9 March 1919.

5. Aylmer Haldane, diary entry, 12 April 1919. 1919 Diary, Papers of General Sir J. Aylmer Haldane, National Library of Scotland, MS 20250.

6. VAD Phyllis Goodliff, letters in Imperial War Museum, London, 88/51/1.

7. Ibid.

8. Letter no. 326, 6 April 1919.

9. Letter no. 333, 26 May 1919.

10. Letter no. 35, 7 Feb. 1911.

11. Letter no. 336, 16 July 1919.

12. Ibid.

Twelve. A Fury Roused

1. Letter no. 337, 17 Aug. 1919.

2. Letter no. 35, 7 Feb. 1911.

3. Letter no. 14, 30 July 1911.

4. Letter no. 337, 17 Aug. 1919.

5. Ibid.

6. *Times,* 28 Oct. 1919, p. 15.

7. Letter no. 338, 19 Sept. 1919.

8. Letter no. 335, 19 June 1919.

9. Letter no. 339, 29 Sept. 1919.

Thirteen. Passions Remembered

1. Arthur Hart-Synnot, "The Burning of the Letters," in "Broken Sword," type-script collection of poems, 1921.

2. Letter no. 312, 1 Jan. 1919.

3. Letter no. 16, 26 Oct. 1913.

4. Letter, 4 Jan. 1920.

5. Letter, 30 May 1920.

6. Ibid.

7. Violet Hart-Synnot, letter, 29 May 1920, Masa Suzuki papers.

8. Lord Curzon to Sir Charles Eliot, 17 Feb. 1922, in United Kingdom National Archives, Kew, FO371/8042 (F654/1/23).

9. Viscount Kikujiro Ishii, *Diplomatic Commentaries* (Baltimore: Johns Hopkins University Press, 1936), p. 59.

10. Letter no. 15, 6 Aug. 1911.

11. Letter, 25 May 1922.

12. Letter, 11 June 1922.

13. Letter, 22 Oct. 1922.

14. Letter no. 7, 23 April 1924.

15. Letter no. 14, 23 Oct. 1923.

16. Letter no. 9, 6 May 1923.

17. Letter no. 13, 18 July 1924.

18. Letter, 22 Oct. 1922.

19. Letter no. 5, 13 March 1926.

20. Letter no. 4, 14 Jan. 1923.

21. Letter no. 16, 18 Nov. 1925.
22. Letter no. 12, 15 July 1923.
23. Letter no. 5, 12 Feb. 1923.
24. Letter no. 2, 12 Jan. 1926.
25. Letter no. 8, 26 April 1926.
26. Letter no. 14, 23 Oct. 1923.
27. Letter no. 11, 7 July 1926.
28. Letter no. 19, 27 Dec. 1926.
29. Letter no. 7, 23 April 1924.
30. Letter no. 2, 27 Jan. 1928.
31. Letter no. 7, 29 April 1928.
32. Letter no. 3, 5 Feb. 1926.
33. Letter no. 8, 5 April 1923.
34. Letter no. 9, 19 May 1924.
35. Letter no. 3, 4 Feb. 1927.
36. Letter no. 5, 19 March 1927.
37. *New York Times,* 23 April 1927.
38. Letter no. 7, 27 April 1927.
39. Letter no. 9, 24 June 1928.
40. Letter, 25 May 1922.
41. Letter no. 10, 27 May 1930.
42. Letter no. 13, 19 Aug. 1926.
43. Letter no. 18, 8 Nov. 1928.
44. Letter no. 21, 12 Dec. 1924.
45. Letter no. 9, 16 May 1930.
46. Letter no. 13, 19 Aug. 1926.
47. Letter, 25 May 1922.
48. Letter no. 18, 28 Nov. 1926.
49. Letter no. 2, 13 Jan. 1931.

Fourteen. Kiyoshi

1. Kiyoshi Suzuki, letter, 23 Feb. 1939, Masa Suzuki papers.
2. Letter no. 7, 13 May 1925.
3. Letter no. 11, 7 July 1926.
4. "Japan Enthrones a New Son of Heaven," *New York Times,* 4 Nov. 1928, p. 84.
5. Shunsuke Tsurumi, *An Intellectual History of Wartime Japan* (London: KPI Ltd, 1986), p. 29.
6. Major General Sir Reginald Hart, "A Vindication of War," *19th Century,* vol. 19, no. 414 (Aug. 1911), p. 226.
7. Alain [Émile-Auguste Chartier], *Mars, or The Truth About War,* trans. Doris Mudie and Elizabeth Hill (London: Jonathan Cape, 1930), p. 56.

8. Kiyoshi Suzuki, letter, 10 Dec. 1938.

9. Kiyoshi Suzuki, letter, 25 Dec. 1938.

10. Kiyoshi Suzuki, letter, 23 Feb. 1939.

11. Kiyoshi Suzuki, letter, 15 Feb. 1939.

12. Kiyoshi Suzuki, letter, 2 Feb. 1939.

13. Kiyoshi Suzuki, letter, 23 Feb. 1939.

14. Kiyoshi Suzuki, letter, 24 May 1939.

Epilogue

1. Alain [Émile-Auguste Chartier], *Mars, or The Truth About War,* trans. Doris Mudie and Elizabeth Hill (London: Jonathan Cape, 1930), p. 56.

2. Nagahisa Uyeshima, in *What Japan Says About the Anglo-Japanese Alliance* (Japan Times Publishing Company, 1916).

3. *New York Times,* 3 Aug. 1940, p. 10.

4. "Cardinal Principles of the National Polity" ("Kokutai no Hongi"), quoted in John Dower, *War Without Mercy* (New York: Pantheon, 1986), p. 221.

5. *New York Times,* 21 March 1940, p. 12.

6. Alain [Émile-Auguste Chartier], *Esquisses de l'homme* (Paris: Éditions Gallimard, 1927).

7. Alain [Émile-Auguste Chartier], *Ningenron,* trans. Kiyoshi Suzuki (Tokyo, 1941), p. 4.

8. Alain, *Esquisses de l'homme.*

9. Quoted in Dower, *War Without Mercy,* p. 26.

10. *New York Times,* 18 Oct. 1941, p. 5.

11. *Manga,* May 1942, quoted in Dower, *War Without Mercy,* p. 229.

ACKNOWLEDGMENTS

Many people have helped us in both Japan and Britain. We should first thank the present-day relatives of Arthur Hart-Synnot, Masa Suzuki, and Violet Drower. Neither Arthur, his brother Ronald, nor his two sisters have any direct descendants, so there are no surviving Hart-Synnots, and it is the family of Arthur's gallant uncle, Major General Sir Reginald Hart, VC, who continue the line. Alison Bennett has on her wall an engraving of her great-great-grandfather Sir Reginald winning his Victoria Cross in 1879, and an old suitcase full of nineteenth- and early-twentieth-century family and military photographs that came to her through her father. We owe her special thanks for the interest she has taken in this book and for allowing us to reproduce photographs and the small watercolor of Ballymoyer. Sadly, most of Arthur's correspondence and diaries were lost either in Ireland in 1922, or in France during the Second World War, but Peggy Hackforth-Jones, née Drower, has Arthur's wartime Army Field Service notebook, the typescript collection of poems he put together under the title "Broken Sword," and an album of pictures from the Villa du Golfe. Peggy was a small bridesmaid at St. Paul's Knightsbridge, in 1919, and was the principal heir of Violet Hart-Synnot by her aunt's will. William Drower, Peggy's brother, remembers staying at Juan-les-Pins in 1938 and has a fine portrait of Violet as a girl painted by Philip Streatfield. Peggy's older brother, Denys, recalls the Hart-Synnot visits to their grandparents' house in Streatham in the 1930s. Though they knew of Arthur's time in Japan, the Drower family did not know the full extent of his involvement there until we went to see them. But they were helpful and encouraging, undisturbed by this rewriting of the family history by others, and fascinated by the new perspective on the general that the Japanese letters had revealed.

In Tokyo, members of the Suzuki family are still living in the Shitamachi wards. The haircutting tradition has continued, and Yokichi's great-grandson keeps a barbershop in Nakano, in the west of the city. We are grateful for the help we received from several descendants of Masa's brothers and sisters, including Harue Suzuki, Teruko Shimura, Akiko Koyama, and Kazuko Kasai. Teruko recalled seeing Kiyoshi at his mother's when she was a child, just as he was going into the army. Akiko remembered Masa as a rather formidable aunt in the years after the war, and the old English suits and jackets she hung out to air. They knew nothing of Arthur's family in Britain and were intrigued to learn more about Kiyoshi's father and his landed background.

Among many others who helped us in Japan, we are especially grateful to Katsumasa Hasegawa, Akiko Hiramatsu-Fish, Yukiko Shimahara, Miho Kometani, Setsu Yoshizumi, and Mayumi Shimizu, who answered many questions and sometimes found themselves swept into arcane areas of research. Masato Kubota brought along his wind-up gramophone to play a ninety-year-old 78-rpm record of the Tokuko Takagi troupe from Asakusa singing numbers from *The Women's Army Is Off to the Front.* Akira Takizawa, Shinsuke Daito, and Hiroshi Shiraishi supplied information on the movements and equipment of Imperial Army units during the Pacific War. Sadao Oba contributed a detailed account of the military call-up, based on his own experience, and other aspects of wartime Japan. Yoshio Fujiwara has been acknowledged separately in the preface, but members of his staff at Fujiwara Shoten, including Yuko Yamazaki and Masatoshi Goma, kindly shared the burden of handling and copying the Hart-Synnot letters. Though their records were lost in the 1923 earthquake, the staff at Kiyoshi's old school, the Gyosei Gakuen, provided what help they could. In Kyoto we were assisted by the Jinkan-Sojin Library of Kyoto University. We are indebted to the library at International House, the National Diet Library, the Tokyo Municipal Library, the Shinjuku Historical Museum, the Yasukuni Kaiko Library, the Yokohama Archives of History, and the Kumamoto Gakuen University Library. We also thank those who helped find the sites of the houses where Arthur and Masa lived in Tokyo, using land records and pre-1914 maps. The couple spent their longest time together in 1905 and 1906 west of Shinjuku, next to the Juniso Kumano Shrine. The Shinto shrine still exists, but while in those days it was surrounded by groves of trees, a lake, and open fields, it is now in a small city park, hemmed in by traffic on all four sides, and the lake has long since been built over. Towering directly above the shrine is the forty-eight-story Tokyo Metropolitan City Hall, for a time the tallest building in Japan and a strident symbol of the country's new wealth; the green copper roof of the shrine can be seen from City Hall's observation gallery. Arthur and Masa's rented house must have been just at the foot of where this skyscraper now stands. Masa's stone grave is in Honbutsuji Cemetery, in Suginami-ku, Tokyo.

In Ireland, the foundations of Ballymoyer House are now covered by scrub and undergrowth, in a clearing in what is now a National Trust woodland planted with conifers. Part of the stable block remains, and the small church of St. Luke's is still there, with its stained glass given by the Hart-Synnots. We are grateful to Trevor Geary, William King, James McIlvaine, and Canon C. F. Moore for helping us in Armagh and showing us the few remaining landmarks that can be linked to the estate. Edith Watson remembered seeing Arthur and Violet when they took up residence in 1919. In London, the New War Office building, where Arthur's postings were decided, still stands on Whitehall but is now referred to as the "Old War Office," superseded by the labyrinthine Ministry of Defence Main Building. Arthur's club is still on the same site, at the corner of Pall Mall and St. James's Square but in less grand quarters. There is a small plaque in memory of Arthur and Violet Hart-Synnot at the Oxford Crematorium in Headington.

We are grateful to Sebastian Dobson for all his advice and special knowledge of the Russo-Japanese War military observers, and to Fred Sharf, who showed us Roundell Toke's diaries. We thank Sarah Wallis, Kishi Yamamoto, and Lisa Hynes for translations and other help, and John Underwood for his insights into the writing of "Alain" (Émile-Auguste Chartier). We thank the Japan Society in London for the use of its library, and the British Red Cross for searching its archives. In Vienna, Jakob Coudenhove-Kalergi produced information on the marriage of his grandmother Mitsuko Aoyama. For the Hong Kong years we were helped by Brian Hook, and Sir David Akers-Jones confirmed the likely position of Arthur's house at North Point. Hirokazu Fukumitsu of the Nippon Club provided background on the Japanese community in the former colony. In Belgium, David Martin helped locate the ground Arthur fought over at Ypres. Fifty miles to the south, the French village of Blairville is still surrounded by open farmland, and it is possible to walk down the section of sunken road where Arthur was hit.

We owe special thanks to William Horsley, Carol Holland, Louise Panton, Keiko Itoh, and Zoe Pagnamenta, who read the manuscript and picked up many points, and to the historians who helped put this story into its wider context. Professor Ian Nish, emeritus professor of international history at the London School of Economics, and the greatest authority on the Anglo-Japanese Alliance, was immensely helpful at the start and in his comments on the completed chapters. Professor Chiharu Inaba, Professor Ben-Ami Shillony, and Professor Rotem Kowner gave guidance on the Russo-Japanese War period. Dr. John Bourne, Dr. John Breen, Dr. Andrew Godley, Professor Andrew Gordon, Dr. Ann Waswo, and Dr. Richard Daehler were equally generous with their time and expertise.

We thank Gill Coleridge for her sharp insights and tremendous encouragement, as well as Lucy Luck at Rogers, Coleridge and White, and Melanie Jackson in New York. We are grateful to our publisher, Ann Godoff at The Penguin Press, for her enthusiasm and skilled editing, and to Liza Darnton for easing the production process. And we owe final thanks to Sybil Pagnamenta and Michael Williams, who provided an ever-changing mix of editorial and moral support, and had to put up with endless talk of Meiji Tokyo and Ballymoyer when they might have wanted to hear about somewhere else.

We are grateful to the following for permission to use passages from letters and diaries: the Documents Collection at the Imperial War Museum in London, for the extract from the letters of Miss P. E. Goodliff; the Trustees of the National

Library of Scotland, Edinburgh, for extracts from the letters and diary of Major General Sir Aylmer Haldane; the Royal Artillery Historic Trust and the James Clavell Library at the Royal Artillery Museum, Woolwich, for permission to quote from the letters of Colonel Everard Calthrop; the Collection of Jean S. and Frederic A. Sharf, Chestnut Hill, Massachusetts, for extracts from the diary of Major Roundell Toke.

PHOTOGRAPH CREDITS

Alison Bennett: insert one, page 1 (top), page 2 (all), page 4 (top and middle); insert two, page 2 (all), page 5 (bottom).

Keisho Ishiguro: insert one, page 1 (bottom), page 3 (middle and bottom), page 4 (bottom), page 5 (top), page 6 (all).

Takako Inoue: insert one, page 3 (top left and right), page 7 (top), page 8; insert two, page 1 (bottom), page 3 (top left and right, bottom left), page 4 (top right), page 5 (top and middle left), page 6 (top right), page 7 (bottom left and right), page 8 (middle and bottom); page 219.

Sotheby's Picture Library, London: insert one, page 5 (bottom left and right).

Momoko Williams: insert one, page 7 (middle and bottom).

Hong Kong Museum of History: insert two, page 1 (top).

Royal Geographical Society: insert two, page 3 (bottom right).

Margaret Hackforth-Jones: insert two, page 4 (top left), page 5 (middle right), page 6 (top left), page 7 (top and middle), page 8 (top).

Trustees of the Imperial War Museum, London: insert two, page 4 (bottom).

Getty Images: insert two, page 6 (bottom).

INDEX

FOR THE BEST IN PAPERBACKS, LOOK FOR THE

In every corner of the world, on every subject under the sun, Penguin represents quality and variety—the very best in publishing today.

For complete information about books available from Penguin—including Penguin Classics and Puffins—and how to order them, write to us at the appropriate address below. Please note that for copyright reasons the selection of books varies from country to country.

In the United States: Please write to *Penguin Group (USA), P.O. Box 12289 Dept. B, Newark, New Jersey 07101-5289* or call 1-800-788-6262.

In the United Kingdom: Please write to *Dept. EP, Penguin Books Ltd, Bath Road, Harmondsworth, West Drayton, Middlesex UB7 0DA.*

In Canada: Please write to *Penguin Books Canada Ltd, 90 Eglinton Avenue East, Suite 700, Toronto, Ontario M4P 2Y3.*

In Australia: Please write to *Penguin Books Australia Ltd, P.O. Box 257, Ringwood, Victoria 3134.*

In New Zealand: Please write to *Penguin Books (NZ) Ltd, Private Bag 102902, North Shore Mail Centre, Auckland 10.*

In India: Please write to *Penguin Books India Pvt Ltd, 11 Panchsheel Shopping Centre, Panchsheel Park, New Delhi 110 017.*

In the Netherlands: Please write to *Penguin Books Netherlands bv, Postbus 3507, NL-1001 AH Amsterdam.*

In Germany: Please write to *Penguin Books Deutschland GmbH, Metzlerstrasse 26, 60594 Frankfurt am Main.*

In Spain: Please write to *Penguin Books S. A., Bravo Murillo 19, 1° B, 28015 Madrid.*

In Italy: Please write to *Penguin Italia s.r.l., Via Benedetto Croce 2, 20094 Corsico, Milano.*

In France: Please write to *Penguin France, Le Carré Wilson, 62 rue Benjamin Baillaud, 31500 Toulouse.*

In Japan: Please write to *Penguin Books Japan Ltd, Kaneko Building, 2-3-25 Koraku, Bunkyo-Ku, Tokyo 112.*

In South Africa: Please write to *Penguin Books South Africa (Pty) Ltd, Private Bag X14, Parkview, 2122 Johannesburg.*